The Loire Valley

The Loire Valley

A Phaidon Cultural Guide

with over 250 color illustrations
and 6 pages of maps

PRENTICE HALL PRESS
NEW YORK

Editor: Dr Marianne Mehling

Contributors: Gerda Kurz, Dr Dieter Maier, Dr Manfred Saar, Siglinde Summerer

Photographs: Ernst Höhne, Werner Grabinger

Maps: Huber & Oberländer, Munich

Ground-plans: Herstellung + Grafik, Lidl

Library of Congress Cataloging in Publication Data

Knaurs Kulturführer in Farbe. Tal der Loire. English.
   The Loire Valley.

   Translation of: Knaurs Kulturführer in Farbe.
Tal der Loire.
   Includes index.
   1. Loire River Valley (France)—Description and
travel—Guide-books. 2. Art—France—Loire River
Valley—Guide-books. 3. Architecture—France—Loire
River Valley—Guide-books. I. Mehling, Marianne.
II. Title.
DC611.L81K6213 1986   914.4'504838   85-25770
ISBN 0-13-540121-6

This edition published in the United States and Canada in 1986 by Prentice Hall Press
A division of Simon and Schuster, Inc.
Simon and Schuster Building
Rockefeller Center
1230 Avenue of the Americas
New York, New York 10020

PRENTICE HALL PRESS is a trademark of Simon & Schuster, Inc.

Originally published as *Knaurs Kulturführer in Farbe, Tal der Loire*
© Droemersche Verlagsanstalt Th. Knaur Nachf. Munich 1983
Translation © Phaidon Press Limited, Oxford, 1986

ISBN 0-13-540121-6

Translated and edited by Babel Translations, London
Typeset by Hourds Typographica, Stafford
Printed in West Germany by Druckerei Appl, Wemding

Cover illustration: Azay-le-Rideau, château

Preface

This highly illustrated and informative guide is a survey of the rich cultural heritage of the Loire Valley. Some 400 places are described, together with their castles, churches, châteaux, town halls, museums and works of art, and the text is illustrated by over 250 colour photographs, maps and ground-plans. This enables the readers to form in advance an accurate impression of the places and objects of interest they would like to see during a visit to the region.

With its favourable climate and fertile soil, the Loire Valley is known as 'the garden of France', and it has attracted people throughout history. The area has been inhabited since prehistoric times, and there was a flint mine at Le Grand-Pressigny during the Stone Age. But the Loire as we know it today has largely been shaped by two forces: aristocracy and Christianity. The old towns and villages are dominated by churches, monasteries and over 300 châteaux. Anyone interested in castles and fortifications will find abundant examples here – ranging from the simple keep to the solid fortress, or the *cité* encircled by a massive wall, such as those at Chinon, Loches and Angers. Then there are the medieval châteaux of Chaumont, Saumur and Ussé, also fortified but more habitable, and the Renaissance country palaces of Amboise, Chambord, Azay-le-Rideau and Chenonceaux. This last kind prevails in the Loire, for it was here that the Renaissance first made itself felt in France, and where it also found its finest expression.

The Loire Valley also has some notable religious buildings, for instance those of Saint-Benoît-sur-Loire, Cunault, Fontevraud and Candes. Of particular interest is the Plantagenet style, which developed in Anjou during the period of Angevin rule (1154–1399) and spread as far as Westphalia.

Something should be said of the selection of towns in this guide book, which mainly confines itself to the four areas of

Orléanais, Blésois, Touraine and Anjou. Each of these areas has played a special part in French history: Orléans was the capital of the territory of the Western Franks, Anjou was the home territory of the English royal house of Plantagenet, and Touraine and Blésois were the favourite provinces of the Valois kings in the sixteenth century.

As with the other guides in this series, the text is arranged in alphabetical order of place names. This gives the book the clarity of a work of reference and avoids the need for lengthy searching. The link between places which are geographically close, but which are separated by the alphabet, is provided by the maps on pages 134–9. This section shows all the places mentioned which are within a short distance from any given destination and which, therefore, it might be possible to include in a tour.

The heading to each entry gives the name of the town, and, below, the name and number of its geographical region (*département*) and a reference to the map section, giving page number and grid reference. Within each entry the particular sites of interest are printed in bold type, while less significant objects of interest appear under the heading **Also worth seeing** and places in the immediate vicinity under **Environs.**

The appendices consist of a glossary of technical terms and an index of all the towns and places of interest mentioned in the text.

The publishers would be grateful for notification of any errors or omissions.

Amboise

37 Indre-et-Loire p.138☐L 4

Today Amboise is a quiet but aspiring town with a population growing by almost 10 per cent annually. However, this charming little town on the Loire with its homely old houses and avenues of plane trees has in the past frequently witnessed disputes and fighting. Because the area around Amboise has good communications, it was settled and fortified at an early date. A rocky projection rising above the left bank of the Loire was ideally suited for defending the river crossing and the first fortifications here were built in the Gallo-Roman period. Amboise was the scene of a brilliant and peaceful pageant in 496, when Alaric II king of the Visigoths, and Clovis king of the Franks, met on the island of Saint-Jean in the Loire to conclude a treaty of friendship. However, this was only a brief interlude, for the Frank soon broke his word, and the disputes continued. In the Middle Ages, Amboise had three castles whose lords were constantly feuding with one another, leading to much unrest until Hugues I of Amboise succeeded in defeating his two rivals in 1080. This paved the way for an improvement in the town's fortunes and, when a bridge was built across the Loire, things looked up for

Amboise, old château, detail

Amboise, partly because there were only seven bridges between Gien and Angers in the Middle Ages.

The struggle for this territory continued unrelentingly in the high Middle Ages, when Amboise played an important part in the dispute for the Torraine territory between the Counts of Blois and the Counts of Anjou. Initially the Counts of Blois built a wooden tower and after the impetuous Foulques Nerra succeeded in capturing the fortress, the Counts of Anjou erected a tall stone watch-tower. It was not until the Hundred Years War (1339–1453) that the French kings became interested in Amboise. During that war, the man who was later to become King Charles VII (1422–61) took refuge in Amboise and Chinon. In 1431, Louis d'Amboise was accused of conspiring against Charles VII and Amboise was confiscated. From this time on the

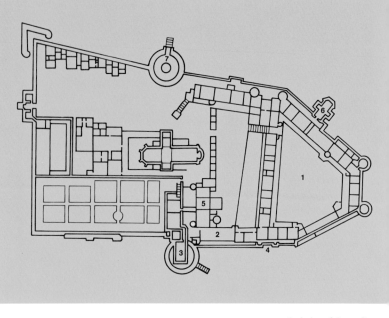

Amboise, château ▷

Amboise, château (from an engraving by the French architect and engraver Jacques Androuet, known as Du Cerceau, published 1607) **1** courtyard **2** Charles VIII wing **3** Tour des Minimes **4** keep **5** Louis XIII wing **6** chapel of St-Hubert **7** Hurtault tower

kings regularly came to the Loire to hold court and the town enjoyed an unprecedented heyday, which came to an end when the Valois family died out in 1589. The château of Amboise became a favoured residence under Charles' son Louis XI (1461–83), although Louis himself liked to withdraw to the little château of Plessis-lès-Tours.

A period of feverish building activity began under Louis XI's son Charles VIII (1483–98), who was born in Amboise and felt at home here. Both day and night, winter and summer, work was pursued by torchlight with the aid of large fires. In 1494 Charles VIII returned from his Neapolitan campaign (militarily unsuccessful)

and, being a man with a taste for beautiful and splendid things, brought in his train vast quantities of furniture, objets d'art, books and tapestries, as well as many artists, architects and garden designers. In short, Charles VIII brought the Renaissance to France and from Amboise it spread over the whole country. The Loire's heritage from the Renaissance is, however, especially fine. In Amboise itself, the château, which had developed from a plain rectangular watchtower, took on a habitable and elegant appearance and this fortified tower became a country seat. Charles VIII himself—who cracked his skull against a low doorpost and died a few hours later—did not live to enjoy this transformation. Building work which had been started before the Italian campaign was completed in Gothic style. The royal household also changed radi-

Amboise, château courtyard

cally during his reign. During the reign of Charlotte of Savoy, Charles' mother, Amboise had 15 maids of honour, 12 ladies-in-waiting, and 100 officers and court officials. Under Charles VIII the château was transformed into a place of pageantry, especially internally; it boasted 60 chests, 60 tables, marble statues, countless wall hangings from Flanders and Paris, and 220 tapestries from the Orient. Such expenditure had previously been undertaken only in connection with divine worship.

However, it was not until the time of Francis I (1515–47) that Amboise became a Renaissance court in any real sense. Francis grew up here with his sister Margaret of Navarre, the author of 'Heptameron'. She also made a name for herself as a promoter of the Renaissance and as a protector of persecuted Huguenots. Francis surrounded himself with artists, poets and learned men and made the royal court the centre of cultural life. He summoned the great Leonardo da Vinci to Amboise and also brought to the court aristocratic ladies who had formerly wasted away their joyless lives in fortified towers. It was in this way that Francis founded the brilliant and typically French royal household, the gallant court, which was to reach its zenith under Louis XIV. Francis I organized sumptuous festivals—tournaments, balls, masquerades, animal fights—and once even ordered the construction of an artificial wooden town in the open fields. He then arranged for it to be attacked with heavy artillery, which resulted in a number of dead and wounded.

Amboise was abandoned by the kings shortly after this. During the Wars of Religion, in *c.* 1560, the so-called Amboise conspiracy occurred. Huguenots attempted to kidnap the

Amboise, chapel of St-Hubert

young King Francis II (1559–60) to bring him under their influence. But they were captured, and some killed on the spot, while others were arrested. These were later sewn up in sacks and either thrown into the Loire or hanged from the château balcony and battlements in full view of Catherine de Medici, Francis II and his young wife Mary Queen of Scots. The edict of Amboise, granting limited religious freedom to the Huguenots, was signed in the château in 1563. After this the building was no longer occupied by kings except occasionally when a hunt was in progress. In the 17C it was reduced to the role of a State prison. In the 18C it was transferred to the Duke of Choiseul along with the barony of Amboise. But the Duke preferred the nearby country seat of Chanteloup. The château was expropriated in the 19C during the revolution. Under Napoleon, Senator Roger Duco used it as his summer residence and ordered large sections to be pulled down. During the Third Republic it returned to the Orléans family by order of the National Assembly. They restored those buildings which still survived. In the 20C it was a centre of the Resistance and suffered severe bomb damage. It has since been rebuilt and is once again owned by the State.

Château: Only a fragment survives of what was formerly a cité, that is to say a complex comprising not merely the nobles' residence, but also a church, residential buildings for officers and servants, as well as buildings functioning as law courts and barracks.

Steps lead up to a large terrace or courtyard from which the view extends as far as Tours. Formerly surrounded by buildings on all sides,

Amboise, St-Denis

Amboise, chapel of St-Hubert, portal

the courtyard was the scene of brilliant festivals held by Francis I when it was decorated with hundreds of tapestries and covered over with a sky-blue tarpaulin adorned with sun, moon and stars.

Of the former buildings two wings of the *Logis du Roi* are still standing. The *Charles VIII wing*, with the massive round Tour des Minimes and an older rectangular section (the keep or donjon, which looks imperiously down over the Loire) has round arches, tall windows in the upper storey and luxuriously decorated gables with dormer windows. The other surviving part, the *Louis XII wing*, adjoins the Charles VIII wing at right angles and is flanked by two small asymmetrical round towers. The upper storey and dormer windows with their chandelier-like decorations clearly mark the transition to the Renaissance.

The following also survive: The *Chapelle St-Hubert* from the time of Charles VIII which was formerly part of the Queen's section of the château. Today the Queen's section no longer survives and the chapel has been moved—for no particularly good reason—to a projection extending from the wall where it is somewhat unrelated to its surroundings. The *Tour Hurtault* also dates back to the time of Charles VIII, although it was not completed until later. With a diameter of 260 ft. and walls almost 13 ft. thick it is sturdier than the *Tour des Minimes*; like the latter it has a spiral ramp inside on which horses and coaches could ascend to the terrace.

Interior: The main room of interest is the *Salle des États* in the Charles VIII wing. During the 19C this was converted into a suite of rooms for the famous prisoner Emir Abd-el-Kader but its original form was restored in 1908. A double-aisled hall, it occupies the entire upper storey and has a fine Gothic rib vault supported by slender, elegant central columns whose capitals and shafts are decorated with reliefs. The hall's windows open on to a balcony (on which the conspirators of 1560 were hanged) whose wrought-iron balustrade of simple design is a 15C masterpiece. Other rooms have wall hangings and furniture in late Gothic and Renaissance styles which bring to mind the great days of the Loire châteaux.

The gem of the château is the small Gothic *Chapelle Saint-Hubert*, formerly the queen's chapel, which has Gothic filigree roof decorations and a ridge turret, both of which were rebuilt in the 19C.

The little town spreads out at the foot of the château; some fine old houses and two churches deserve a visit.

St-Denis: A Romanesque basilica with three bays, a transept, crossing tower and choir; rebuilding and extensions date from the 15&16C. The first bay of the nave has Romanesque capitals with strange people with animals' heads. The Angevin vault, raised so as to resemble a dome, is in the Plantagenet style (the name given to a style transitional between Romanesque and Gothic which developed in the Loire Valley). The right aisle has an Entombment and a 16C recumbent figure of St.Mary Magdalene; the left aisle has a marble sculpture of a drowned woman, for which one of King Francis I's mistresses is said to have served as a model.

St-Florentin (known as Notre-Dame-de-Grève before the chapel in the château was torn down): Built in the 2nd half of the 15C by order of Louis XI, who had banned the citizens of the town from visiting the chapel in the château.

Museums: *Musée de la Vieille Poste* (in the Hôtel Joyeuse, a distinguished 16C residence). This museum documents the development of postal

Amboise, Chanteloup

services. Exhibits include uniforms, signs, models of mail coaches, handles from State coach doors, etc.

Musée de l'Hôtel de Ville (in the town hall, which was built by Morin, France's treasurer in the early 16C.) Exhibits include tapestries from Chanteloup, a 14C Madonna as well as autographs of French kings.

Also worth seeing: The *Porte de l'Amasse*, a remnant of the old town fortifications including the clock tower (1495–1500), which is one of the most charming spots in Amboise. The lovely *Promenade du Mail* extends downstream along the Loire and includes the playful fountain by Max Ernst (1966–8). The *Rue de la Concorde*, in the old Quartier du Petit-Fort, between the château and the Loire, with *No. 20*, Hôtel Louis XIII, and *No. 42*, a 16C residence. At the very end are the *Greniers de César*,

Angers, St-Maurice cathedral

Angers, Petit-Château

caves said to have been hewn from the rock by the Romans. *Cave dwellings* at the edge of the valley have wooden ceilings and floors, piped water and electricity.

Environs: Clos-Lucé: This country seat just outside the town was built under Louis XI in the late 15C (the N. wing was added in the 19C). Leonardo da Vinci died here in 1519 after Francis I had induced him to spend the last years of his life in France. His remains were buried in the château chapel of St-Florentin, which was burned down in the 19C; today they are said to be in the Chapelle St-Hubert.
Pagoda of Chanteloup (2.5 km. S.): Some 144 ft. high, built by Le Camus in 1775–8 in the Chinese style according with the taste of the time, today it is all that remains of one of the most splendid 18C French châteaux. It

formerly stood at the centre of the château, which was designed on the model of the château at Versailles.
Pocé-sur-Cisse (4 km. NNE): 15C *château.*
Saint-Ouen-les-Vignes (3 km. N. of Pocé): 17C *château.*

Angers
49 Maine-et-Loire   p.136☐F 3

Angers, an old town whose influence was extensive even in early times, is today the main town of the department of Maine-et-Loire. In the pre-Christian period it was the seat of the Gallic Andegavi, as the town's present name recalls. From the early Middle Ages onwards it was the main town of the counts of Anjou, and of the dukes of Anjou from 1360 onwards. During this time there were

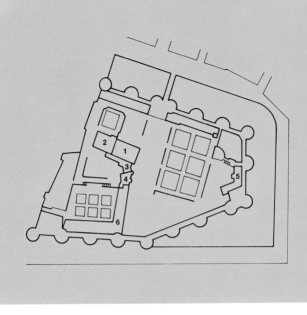

many different rulers. The Romans were here in the first few centuries AD, and they were followed in 471 by the Franks under Childerich in 471 and then by the Normans in the 9C (though this was for less than ten years). Angers fell to the English throne in 1154 and in 1204 came into the possession of France for good. Traces of the different rulers have survived through the ages. Under the Romans the town was called *Juliomagus* and like all the more important Roman camps it was provided with fortifications; thermal baths and an amphitheatre were also built. The Middle Ages saw the building of churches and monasteries, especially during the rule of the notorious Foulques Nerra of the Foulques family who were the counts of Anjou in the 10–13C. Foulques Nerra the warrior is in particular wreathed in legend, for whenever he considered his misdeeds

Angers, château (a medieval 'cité' with residence for the prince and buildings for the officers, the servants and the prince's court of justice) **1** chapel **2** King's lodging **3** N. gallery **4** Petit-Château **5** governor's building **6** exhibition building

were excessive he tended to do penance and found monasteries. Building of this sort continued until the 2nd half of the 12C, at which time Angers was tantamount to being the second capital of England (for a period of about 50 years). The Foulques were distinguished not merely by their military abilities, but also by their great skill in diplomacy and, in 1154, as a result of a shrewd policy of marriage, they occupied the English throne in the person of the Plantagenet family (1154–1399). The name Plantagenet derives from Geoffrey V of Anjou, who was in the habit of wearing a sprig of broom, plante genêt, in his helmet. The vast territory ruled by the Angevins spread from the N. of England across the English Channel through the W. of France and as far as the Pyrenees. During the first 50 years of their rule they liked to hold court in their former capital. Building activity flourished, an influential school of architecture grew up, and the foundations of the *style angevin* or Plantagenet style were developed. However, the tide turned in 1204 when as a result of quarrels among themselves, the Plantagenets were obliged to yield Angers to the French throne. Angers then came into the possession of direct successors of the Capetians, and subsequently to nobles of the house of Valois. Good King René (1409–80), prominent among these kings, was very popular with the people owing to his love of peace and his amiability and today he lives on in folklore. An art lover and a poet himself, he promoted the arts and sciences in Angers and this fact, together with the presence of the university which had existed from as early as 1364, gained the city the repuation of being the Athens of the West. When Angers finally passed to the French throne, it was no longer the centre of a royal court and became a provincial town. Angers was later often the scene of much fighting, e.g. during the Wars of Religion (1562–98) and the Vendée war during the French Revolution. However the town became increasingly aware of its position at the intersection of numerous trade routes, both land and water, and it developed into a 'town of flowers' becoming a very important market for vegetables, fruit and wine, and also hemp, linen and slate. Further it became a popular centre of education for the whole region, having many schools some of which were artisti-

Angers, château wall with tower

Angers, tapestry, Apocalypse

cally and others agriculturally oriented.

Château: Occupying a steep cliff overlooking the Maine valley which had been the site of a Roman fortress, the *château* is one of the most imposing fortifications in France. The defensive wall, 2,165 ft. long and taking the form of an irregular pentagon, is flanked by 17 round towers 130–200 ft. high; the whole is surrounded by a moat 100 ft. wide and 36 ft. deep, which was hewn out of the rock. Except for the moat, which is 15C, the whole structure took only 10 years to build (1228–38). The towers are now not as high as originally since some were pulled down in 1585 on the orders of Henry III, who ordered the entire fortification be razed to prevent it falling into the hands of the Protestants. However, the governor delayed this and the king was murdered in 1589. From the 17C onwards the château was used alternately as a prison and a garrison. In World War 2 the Germans set up an ammunition dump here.

The buildings inside the walls are later: the *chapel of Ste-Geneviève* and the adjoining *royal logis* were built by order of Yolande d'Aragon in the early 15C; the *N. gallery* and the *small château* with its round corner towers were built by her son, Good King René, who also ordered splendid gardens and enclosures for animals to be laid out. The *governor's building* in the SE corner was given its present form in the 18C. Today's plantations are based on 16C gardens. The exhibition building, an idea by Bernard Vitry, is a 20C addition; over 320 ft. long, it integrates well into the surroundings. The famous cycle of Apocalypse tapestries is on display here.

Angers, tapestry, Apocalypse

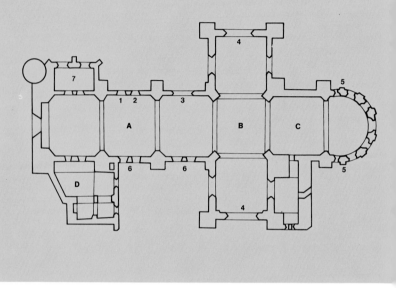

Angers, St-Maurice cathedral **A** nave **B** transept **C** choir **D** chapel of Notre-Dame de Pitié **1** St.Catherine of Alexandria **2** Death and Assumption of Mary **3** Martyrdom of St.Vincent of Spain **4** transept rose window (15C): l. Man of Sorrows, r. Christ Enthroned **5** choir window (16C): l. St.Christopher, r. St.Peter **6** modern windows **7** church treasure

The *Apocalypse Tapestries* form the oldest surviving work of its kind, as well as possibly being the largest. After almost seven years, the series was completed in 1380 in the workshop of Nicolas Bataille, the famous Parisian weaver, and was based on cartoons by Hennequin de Bruges, Charles V's court artist. The Dukes of Anjou regarded the tapestries as a precious possession which they used as a decoration at festivals, e.g. Louis II's wedding festivities; and which was listed as a separate item in their will. When Good King René ceded Anjou to the French throne, he bequeathed the tapestry cycle to the cathedral of Angers by way of a parting gift, where it was on public display on high holy days. However, attitudes towards it changed radically in the baroque period, when it was considered primitive. The tapestry was offered for sale in 1782 and during the French Revolution it was cut into pieces which were then used as canopies or bed covers. In 1843 the Bishop of Angers bought back all the parts he was able to find, but between a quarter and a third was lost for ever—a matter of great regret to experts, who hold the work in the highest regard.

The cycle was originally 550 ft. long and 16 ft. tall and consisted of seven tapestries which were themselves divided into two sets of seven, one set illustrating the rule of Antichrist with

Angers, cathedral, tympanum

all its horrors and sufferings, and the other the triumph and glory of the power of God (John, the author of the Apocalypse, uses the number seven to mean perfection). At the edge of each tapestry a large figure which may represent John appears seven times; the bodily attitude and facial expression varies greatly on each occasion and the figure faces towards the next series of pictures which are ranged in two rows one above the other. Each row has seven panels with a short explanatory caption. These pictures are framed, like a chessboard, by an alternately red and blue background; above there is a starry or clouded sky peopled with angels, while below there is a meadow studded with flowers, the earth. In the depiction of Christ with the sword in his mouth, it is the very plainness of the originally monochromatic background that makes such an overwhelming

impression. The background of the later tapestries, in order to avoid monotony, was made more varied by the use of flowers and butterflies.

More *tapestries* are to be seen in the royal apartments and these include the captivatingly colourful late-15C *Passion wall hanging*; there are also some in the governor's apartments.

Cathedral of St-Maurice (2nd half of 12C, and 13C): Built above two previous buildings (an 11C church and a Gallo-Roman basilica) consecrated by St.Martin of Tours in the 4C, this is an impressive Gothic building; the *portal* in the twin-towered façade is among the best of French Gothic portals. The door case is particularly beautiful with its severe, dignified, elegantly draped Old Testament figures. These are followed by angels and four Apostles; the archivolts have the Elders of the

Apocalypse and more angels. The pointed typanum has Christ Enthroned, surrounded by symbols of the four Evangelists. The remaining eight Apostles were removed in the 18C, along with the central column and lintel, to make room for processions.

Inside: The nave is *c.* 54 ft. wide, which makes it the widest of all French cathedrals, the width usually being some 30–39 ft. The vault, which is raised in dome-like manner, was one of the first of the Angevin vaults, as those built in Anjou in the mid-12C are called. In the other Gothic vaults, the keystone of the pointed arches is on the same level as the conclusions of the arched ribs and wall arches, but in Angevin vaults it is some 10 ft. above that level. The Angevin vault in the transept and choir, with its numerous graceful ribs, is of later date and shows the further development of this architectural form.

Former Benedictine abbey of St-Aubin: (12C) All that survives of this structure is the tower which was the monastery's bell tower and keep. The associated church disappeared in *c.* 1800; the prefecture is housed in the former 17C residential building. Remains of 13C *frescos* are to be seen in the former cloister.

Toussaint abbey (*c.* 1235): Only ruins survive of the church which collapsed in 1815.

St-Martin (Rue St-Martin): Collapsed in 1828; the only parts to have survived are the transept with its cut-off crossing tower (11C), choir (11C & late-12C), and the angel chapel (early-13C) with its fine Angevin vault.

St-Serge: Early-13C. The *choir,* a splendid example of Plantagenet

Angers, cathedral, rose window

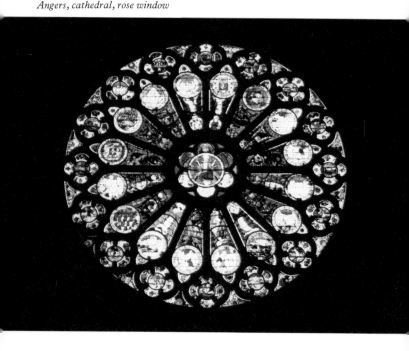

style, consists of a large hall with four bays, three aisles and 13 vault panels whose concluding stones and rib brackets are decorated with sculptures and images making up a cycle of the Last Judgement. The vault cycle of St.Sergius is among the most compact and extensive in French early-Gothic architecture (cycles such as this only occur in the Plantagenet style). In three of the choir windows, the grisaille windows, unstained glass is used—something which the Cistercians often did in the 12&13C.

Église da la Trinité: 12C; 16C bell tower. The crypt has a painted 15C Pietà.

Secular buildings: Opposite the cathedral stands the richly decorated *Maison d'Adam*, a 15C half-timbered building of 4 storeys. *Rue St-Laud 21:* Late-15C house with statues of Adam and Eve on the façade. *Rue Plantagenet 73:* Formerly Angers town hall (1484–1529). *Rue de l'Oisellerie*, Maison diocésaine des Oeuvres: The former bishop's palace, it has been restored many times and extended in Romanesque style; some parts are early 12C. The Counts of Anjou, who owned it originally, donated it to Bishop Odon in 851. Opposite, *No. 5* is 16C and has strange wooden figures. *No. 7* is a late-15C house. In *Rue David d'Angers 38* P.J. David d'Angers (1788–1856) was born.

Museums: *Musée Turpin de Crissé* (in the Logis Pincé, Rue de l'Enepveu, a former Renaissance palace, which the then mayor of Angers ordered to be built for himself in 1523–35): Ancient vessels, medieval ivory and enamel work, printed designs, Japanese and Chinese art (including works by Utamaro). *Musée des Beaux Arts* (in the Logis Barrault, Rue du Musée, a former late Renaissance palace from the 15C): medieval panels, 18C French paintings (Watteau, Boucher, Fragonard, etc.) and works by the sculptor P.J. David d'Angers.

La Doutre: The quarter on the far side (French: d'outre) of the river already existed in the Middle Ages; it was also fortified and the *Tour des Anglais* on the Haute-Chaîne bridge is a remnant of the old town wall. From the 16C onwards it was the winter quarters of the Angevin provincial aristocracy and accordingly lost its importance along with the fall of that social class in the French Revolution.

Former Hôpital St-Jean: Founded in 1153, it consists of a hall with three aisles, eight bays and an Angevin vault which makes the place feel light and airy. Sick people were tended not so much medically as spiritually in this hall by the canons. Beds were set up in such a way that all could see the

Angers, cathedral

Angers, Tour St-Aubin

Angers, Eglise de la Trinité

altar in the main aisle. Today this hall is used to exhibit wall hangings, including the 'Song of the World' by J.Lurçat (1892–1966). The chapel, which is accessible from the cloister at the back of the hospital, dates from the late 12C.

Special events: During the last two weeks of January every year a *wine market* is held in Angers, and indeed it could be said that the town lives mainly by the wine trade.

Environs: Bouchemaine (9 km. SW): 12C Romanesque *church*.
Champ des Martyrs (3 km. NW): *Memorial* to 2,000 dead who were shot here in 1794. Nearby are the ruins of the *Priory of la Haie aus-Bons-Hommes*, founded in 1178. Its Prior, Pierre Roger de Beaufort, later became Pope Gregory XI.
Pignerolle (5 km. E.): The *château*

was built by the Angevin architect B.de la Bigottière in the late 18C on the model of the Petit Trianon of Versailles (1766). The Polish government-in-exile used it as a residence at the beginning of World War 2 and during the German occupation Admiral Dönitz made it his command headquarters. The Germans added underground defences. The interior decorations were badly damaged; today the château is owned by the town of Angers which is planning to restore the building.
Plessis-Macé, Le (13 km. NW): The village has a 15C church and an 11C *castle*. The 12C surrounding wall has survived with a parapet walk, four round towers, a fosse and impressive ruins of the keep which was rebuilt in c. 1450 when it was separated from the rest of the château by a moat and wall. The chapel is Flamboyant (1460) with a wooden gallery in the

Aubigny-sur-Nère, St-Martin, inscription

Aubigny-sur-Nère, St-Martin, window

same style. The two balconies, which are supported partly by an arcade and partly by tall brackets and the projecting roof, are an original feature of the residential and domestic buildings.

Abbey of St-Nicolas (1.5 km. W.): One of the many monasteries founded by Foulques Nerra (11C). Today, all that survives from the Middle Ages is a side apse of the church (rebuilt *c.* 1180), a 13C hall and parts of the 13C cloister.

Savennières (15.5 km. SW): One of the oldest churches in Anjou; the façade may even date back to the 9C or 10C. The apse and bell tower are 12C. A bridge links the town to the *Ile Béhuard,* an old pilgrimage site, where boatmen were said to have made their vows in order to survive unscathed the dangers of the river, which was at this point difficult to navigate. The *church,* a strange build-ing whose single aisle is partly hewn from the rock, was built in the 15C and enlarged at the end of the same year through the generosity of Louis XI.

Trélazé (6 km. SE): A large slate quarry has been here since the 12C. Today it employs 4,000 workers and supplies 100,000 tonnes of slate every year (75 per cent of French production).

Lion-d'Angers, Le (22 km. NW): A pretty little town on the right bank of the Oudon. *St-Martin* dates back to the early 11C (nave, transept and bell tower) and has traces of 15C wall paintings.

Aubigny-sur-Nère

18 Cher   p.138□P 3

Today this 'town of the Stuarts' is a

small town of medieval half-timbered houses with splendid old tiled roofs and it is hard to imagine the struggle for power which the town once witnessed. In 1423, Charles VII transferred the town to John Stuart, a Scot who had allied himself with the king in order to fight the English. Robert Stuart, one of John's descendants who later became marshal of Aubigny, went to war for Francis I against Italy. Their descendants continued manufacturing the white Sologne wool and practising the clothier's trade up into the 19C. Most of the old half-timbered houses date from the 16C; one house in the Rue du Pont-aux-Foulons is early 15C.

St-Martin: The church in its present form dates from the 16C and contains some interesting decorations. The choir has a 16C stained-glass window showing scenes from the life of St.Martin. Towards the back of the nave there are two 17C Evangelists and at the entrance to the choir are two painted statues, also 17C. The first of these depicts the Madonna and Child; the other shows Christ as Man of Sorrows. The third side chapel on the right contains a fine 17C Pietà.

Environs: Château de la Verrerie (11 km. SE): Built at the edge of the Forest of Ivoy by order of John Stuart, it has a picturesque location on a lake formed by the Nère. The building has a Renaissance gallery and a chapel in which 16C frescos survive.

Sainte-Montaine (9 km. W.): A 16C *church* dedicated to the patron saint of the Sologne who—so tradition has it—was a daughter of Pippin the Short. There are pilgrimages every Whit Monday.

Azay-le-Rideau, St-Symphorien

Azay-le-Rideau
37 Indre-et-Loire   p.136□I 4

Azay-le-Rideau is one of the finest châteaux in the Loire and it is also possibly stylistically the most unified. Mainly of interest for its architecture, it was not however totally bypassed by history. Founded by the Romans, the town was completely burned down in 1418 because Charles VII was jeered at by the garrison whilst travelling through. The château we see today was built by Gilles Berthelot in 1518–28, apart from some later alterations. Berthelot, Treasurer under Francis I and mayor of Tours, had to flee before the building was completed in order to avoid becoming involved in a scandal concerning the embezzlement of public money. He died shortly after and as a result only two of the four sections originally planned were actually built.

Château: This is one of the finest

Azay-le-Rideau, château ▷

Azay-le-Rideau, château

buildings from the transitional period between medieval fortress and country seat. Significantly, it was not built on a strategically favourable hill or rocky projection, as was the practice before, but in the river. The building has Renaissance features, for the Renaissance was flourishing in France at the time. Hence the façade does not present a defiant, defensive aspect, but rather it looks inviting and comfortable. The defensive features have become decorative elements, e.g. the fortified towers have become elegant corner towers built out over the river. The projecting parapet walk with its machicolations and richly decorated dormer windows has also become a decorative addition.

Many of the individual stylistic elements date from earlier times. Thus the tall slate roofs, the enormous fireplaces, the uniform windows and the stonework of the dormer windows are clearly Gothic relics, while the horizontal articulation and a delight in symmetry and decoration have also influenced the character of the building. Only a genius could achieve such a perfectly harmonious merging of regional traditions and new ideas imported from Italy, however, his name is not known. We only know that the building was probably influenced by Blois and that Philippe Lesbahy, Berthelot's wife, evidently supervised building operations and fetched Étienne Rousseau, master mason, from Tours.

The four-storeyed *stairwell*, with its round-arched double portal, niches, small columns, angular pilasters, and friezes decorated with arabesques, is in another rhythm but fits most harmoniously into the three-storeyed façade. It ends in a monumental gable reaching as far as the roof ridge. The strongest architectural element in this stairwell is, not surprisingly, the staircase, which is not a spiral, but runs straight up with landings where the direction reverses—a new feature in the 16C. The coffered vault, whose medallions show profiles of the French kings and queens from Louis XI to Henry IV, should be seen. The *park* has none of the spirit of the château. It is not designed in the manner of the Renaissance gardens in which nature is subjugated to the order of art and geometry. Rather, the park extends freely around the 'polished diamond framed by the Indre', as Balzac described the château built on piles into the river. In the park there are 17C domestic buildings and a small chapel dating from 1603.

St-Symphorien: Parts of the gabled façade of this church—built in the 11C and enlarged in the

12&16C—derive from the previous Merovingian building (5&6C), e.g. two panels with archaic figures. The large chapel on the right dates from the time of the restoration of the monarchy.

Environs: Cheillé (5.5 km. W.): *Church* with a fine 15C wooden Christ and a Renaissance *manor house.*
Château d'Islette (2.5 km. NW): Built at about the same time as Azay-le-Rideau (1526–31), it has a similarly plain style and was much influenced by the latter building, see horizontal articulation, round corner towers, parapet walk with battlements and brackets, tall roof. Tradition has it that the building, which was also enclosed by the arms of the Indre, was built by the very same workers as those involved in Azay-le-Rideau.
Villaines-les-Rochers (6.5 km. SE): Old basket-weavers' village.

Baugé
49 Maine-et-Loire   p.136☐G 3

The once proverbial poverty of Baugé (to the French, to use one's Baugé income means to make empty promises) has diminished since asparagus and fruit growing and dairy farming have been introduced into the economy. However, Baugeois (30

inhabitants per sq.km.) is still one of the most sparsely populated parts of the Anjou.

Château: This castle-like structure was rebuilt in 1430 by Yolande d'Aragon, mother of Good King René. Today it houses the town hall and a small *museum* with faience, old coins and weapons. The stairwell with its fine vault is interesting. On the landing there is a statue of Guérin des Fontaines, who won a famous victory against the English in the Hundred Years War.

Spital (founded in 1643): Today a *pharmacie* with fine wood panelling. As in the 17C, it has pans for herbs, earthenware pots and glass and pewter vessels. In the chapel adjoining the large sick bay there is a gilded wooden chest.

Chapelle des Incurables (Rue de la Girouadière): Houses a precious 13C *relic* from Constantinople, a cross

Baugé, château

with two transverse arms, said to be made of wood from the True Cross; in the 14C it had two crucified figures in gold and precious stones. First owned by the house of Anjou, in the 16C the cross became part of the heraldic emblem of the dukes of Lorraine, and since then it has been known as the Cross of Lorraine.

Also worth seeing: *Town houses* from the 16,17&18C, and the former *Capuchin monastery*, which is privately owned today. The Altrée flows underground for 980 ft. before flowing into the Couasnon.

Environs: L'Auberdière (5 km. SE): Late 15C *château*.
Pontigné (5 km. E.): *Church* from the 12C (aisle and transept) and 13C (choir). The choir vault, which at one time threatened to cave in, is supported with the assistance of the

monumental marble and stone altarpiece which dates from 1708. Different styles are apparent in the capitals in the transept; the wall paintings and especially those in the two side chapels of the transept, some of which are 13C, should be seen.
Le Vieil-Baugé (1.5 km. SW): Old *church* whose tower has a twisted helm roof of strange helical design. 11C stylistic features (nave and N. transept) are united with elements from the late 12/early 13C (choir with surrounding chapels) and the Renaissance (S. transept with coffered vault).

Beaufort-en-Vallée
49 Maine-et-Loire   p.136☐G 3

Only the polygonal tower rebuilt under Good King René in 1455 and

Baugé, detail of portal

Beaufort-en-Vallée, Renaissance house

the ruins of the château rebuilt in 1346 by the Count of Beaufort (father of Pope Gregory XI), bear witness to the defensive character of the town, which is today a peaceful centre of flower and seed growing in the fertile, picturesque Vallée d'Anjou.

Château: Two square towers still survive. Each has a hall with a pointed vault; between the towers is the sally port.

Church: An interesting 15&16C building, partly renovated in the 19C. The enormous bell tower, which rises 155 ft. above the left transept, was built in 1542 by Jean de l'Espine the famous Angevin architect.

Museum (in the square outside the church): Houses exhibits from Greek, Roman and Egyptian antiquity and also items relating to the town's

history (ceramics, paintings, seals, etc.).

Also worth seeing: Some historic *houses* from the time of Louis XIII (29–31 Rue de l'Hôtel-de-Ville), from the Renaissance (on the Chardavoine crossing), and from the 17C (hospital), as well as a fine *half-timbered building* (3 Rue du Bourguillaume).

Environs: Avrillé (1.5 km. SW): Remains of a *priory* from the 13&17C. The Romanesque *St-Léobin chapel* is today used as a residence.
Brion (4.5 km. E.): Very fine Romanesque *church* from the second half of the 12C, which was fortified in the Hundred Years' War and used for defence.
Fontaine-Guérin (6 km. NE): The *church* partly dates back to the 11C; panelling with 15C paintings. *Dolmen*.

Beaugency

45 Loiret   p.138 □ N 2

This small town makes a somewhat fairy-tale impression, and brings the Middle Ages alive at every step, even though many features have not survived the centuries. Strategically important because it provided the only Loire crossing between Orléans and Blois, Beaugency was hotly contested throughout history, up to and including modern times.

The first of two ecclesiastical councils was held here in 1104. At this council Philip I stood accused because he had cast out his wife and abducted and married Bertrade, wife of the Count of Anjou. The king was excommunicated for this act, but was buried in St-Benoît because he reconciled himself with the church before his death. Royal marital life was also the subject of the second council held in 1152. 40 bishops, headed by the Archbishop of Bordeaux, annulled the marriage of Louis VII and Eleanor of Aquitaine. The king's allegation that his wife had had immoral relations was held to be less serious than the queen's statement that she was related to her husband by blood. In the same year, Eleanor married Henry Plantagenet, heir of Anjou, Maine, Touraine and Normandy. In marrying Henry, she brought him the old Aquitaine possessions of Poitou, Périgord, Limousin, Angoumois, Saintonge and Gascony. When Henry became Henry II of England two years later, nearly all the SW of France came under English rule, and thus the foundations for the Hundred Years' War were laid. Beaugency fell into the hands of the English four times during this war alone, before being liberated by Joan of Arc in 1429. The

Beaufort-en-Vallée, church

Beaugency, Town Hall

town experienced the full ravages of war once again during the Wars of Religion (1562–1609), falling alternately into the hands of the Protestants and the Catholic League. Huguenots set Beaugency on fire in 1567 and, more recently, German bombs caused severe damage in 1944. However, a number of old houses and the picturesque bridge with its 22 arches (six of them from the 16C) have survived.

The *Place du Martroi* in the town centre has a plain 11C church and a 15C wooden house. The *Maison des Templiers* (Templars' house) in the Rue du Puits-de-l'Ange has a fine 12C Romanesque façade decorated with round arches in the upper storey. A *Renaissance house*, restored in the 19C, has been added to the town hall built by Charles Viart in 1526. The coats-of-arms of Francis I (the Salamander), and also of the town of Beaugency and the Longueville family, are to be seen underneath the windows of the first storey. Eight valuable embroidered wall hangings from the 17C are on display in the main room of the *town hall*. They formerly hung in the abbey of Notre-Dame, which is now in ruins.

Church of Notre-Dame: The former abbey church dates back to the 12C. Its fine Romanesque vaults were destroyed in 1567 in the fire raised by the Huguenots. The church was restored in the 17C, when Gothic-style wooden vaults were installed (*c.* 1660).

Fortified tower: An impressive 11C structure practically identical to that of Loches. The magnificent rectangular tower supported by buttresses was built by order of the barons of Landry. It was much damaged in the

Beaugency, Notre-Dame

Beaugency, keep

Beauregard, château

Wars of Religion, when the roof was destroyed. The vaulted ceilings of the five storeys collapsed in 1840, and all that survives today are the surrounding walls articulated by pilaster strips.

Château: Built in the 15C by order of Count Dunois, it was originally joined to the tower by a covered passage. This undecorated three-storey building is today the *regional museum*. The polygonal staircase tower was erected at a later date by order of Jean II de Longueville.

Environs: Meung-sur-Loire (6 km. NE): Formerly called *Magdunum*. It was the residence of the bishops of Orléans up to the 17C and a large hall and a 13C cellar, as well as several medieval towers, survive from the bishops' residence (built 1206–21). The fine early-13C church of *St-Liphard* has semicircular apses at each end of the transept. The Romanesque tower above the façade is 11C, while the tower's helm roof and the bell turret are late 12C. To the left of the church tower are the ruins of an old 12C keep, where François Villon, one of France's most famous poets (1431–63), served one of his many prison sentences. In the Mail, the town authorities commissioned Bouret to build a monument to another poet, Jean de Meung (b. *c.* 1240, d. *c.* 1305), a famous son of the town who, in *c.* 1280/90, completed the 'Romance of the Rose' ('Roman de la Rose'), the work by Guillaume de Lorris which was extremely popular in the Middle Ages.

Saint-Laurent-Nouan (10 km. SW): The church dates from the 11C; 17C altarpiece, pulpit and wooden statues.

sections, and also the private chapel with its splendid frescos by N. dell'Abbate, have disappeared. Monsieur De Gaucourt, owner at the time, was responsible for this 'modernization'. Today the château is composed of a central section which corresponds largely to the etching by Androuet du Cerceau. The ground floor of this has an arcaded gallery with five arches. The three large windows on the first floor accord with the original, as do the three dormer windows, although these were given more lavish treatment in the 19C. On either side of the central section there are two narrow, intermediate parts to which the asymmetrical wings are joined. Italian artists who were employed at the court of Henry II worked on the *interior* of the château. The *Cabinet aux Grelots* near the library (17C furniture) is of particular interest. The finely carved oak panelling decorated with gold is the work of F.Scibec. However, the château is above all famous for its *portrait gallery* which occupies the upper storey of the central section. This is based on the collection of Paul Ardier, a state councellor who died in 1638. Today it contains no less than 363 historical portraits of important personalities framed by wooden panelling. Portraits range from Philip de Valois to Louis XIII and all 15 kings who ruled during that time are portrayed. Numerous individual portraits have been copied for Versailles. Underneath the series of portraits on the wall, a panel painted by J.Mosnier from Blois shows the emblems and devices of various French kings. The massive timber ceiling is decorated with painted scenes, also by J.Mosnier. The floor consists entirely of Dutch tiles and is unique in France. Painted blue on a white background, they depict an entire army of infantry and cavalry in uniforms from the time of Louis XIII. The teeming military throngs are depicted in every detail, including the flags. A second gallery, which had a collection of portraits of

Beauregard

41 Loir-et-Cher   p.138□M 3

Château: In the mid 16C this hunting lodge in the valley of the Beuvron at the edge of the forest of Russy belonged to the humanist Jean du Thier, Secretary of State to Henry II. The structure as a whole is strikingly irregular in design. The arrangement of the buildings themselves, and also of the individual farmyards, looks to be accidental rather than planned. Only the orchards and vineyards are more regularly laid out.

All that survives of the château and farm, which date from the time of Jean du Thier, is the two-storeyed core of the old château, and even this is only in the form which resulted from the 19C reconstructions. Most of the formerly extensive side famous people surrounding of Louis XIV, fell victim to the alterations of the 19C. However, the kitchen from the time of Jean du Thier survives, along with a splendid collection of copper kitchen implements.

Bellegarde
45 Loiret   p.138□P 1

Originally called 'Choisy-aux-Loges', it was the seat of a marquisate. The present name derives from Roger de Saint-Lary, Duke of Bellegarde-Seurre, who moved his main residence from Burgundy to this area in 1646.

Château: The oldest part is the 14C keep, a massive structure flanked by four small turrets with an extensive moat on the E. side. Various brick annexes dating from the early 18C were built by order of the Duke of Antin, who also had the symmetrically arranged entrance pavilions built. The pavilion on the right is known as the *Pavillon de la Salamandre*, because of a fine 16C sculpture of a salamander on the inner façade. Today this building houses the local government offices and a small *museum* devoted to the works of C.Desvergnes, the sculptor.

Church: The fine mid-12C Romanesque façade has an arch decorated with human figures and grotesque faces, along with animal and plant ornaments. The central tower is also entirely Romanesque and dates from the closing years of the 12C. The simple Romanesque aisle contains several interesting paintings from the 17C French school, including the Blessed Virgin and Child with St.Genoveva, the Holy Family, and St.Sebastian.

Environs: Lorris (14 km. SE):

Bellegarde, Romanesque church portal ▷

There was a royal residence here in the Middle Ages, and St.Louis signed a treaty with the Count of Toulouse here in 1243. During the first half of the 13C, this little town was the home of the troubadour Guillaume de Lorris who began his 'Roman de la Rose' here. The *church* has a nave and two aisles, with square pillars which give a somewhat severe appearance. Most of the building is 12C; the rectangular ambulatory and the last bay of the choir are 13C. The façade still has the Romanesque portal, but its upper section and the square tower, were rebuilt in brick in the 15C. Inside the church, the choir has a triforium, and the 15C choir stalls have fine carvings. **Boiscommun** (7 km. NW): The village *church*, conspicuously pure in style, dates from the 13C. Its central tower was restored in 1713, but most of it dates from the 13C. The façade

was partly rebuilt in the 15C but the 12C Romanesque portal survived. The most interesting detail inside the church is a 12C stained-glass window depicting the Madonna and Child in the chapel in the S. aisle.

Blois
41 Loir-et-Cher   p.138☐M 3

This royal town on the Loire is of importance both historically and artistically and was the birthplace of Louis XII (1462), Denis Papin (1647), and Augustin Thierry (1795). First mentioned in 584 by Gregory of Tours, who called it *Blisenses*, the town developed as the seat of a powerful count in the Middle Ages and in the 11&12C controlled parts of Touraine and also parts of Champagne. Count Thibaut I ordered a fortified

Bellegarde, Pavillon de la Salamandre, detail

keep to be built and this was completed sometime before 978. Count Stephen of Blois became King of England in 1135. Duke Louis d'Orléans acquired the powerful county in 1391 and when he was murdered by John the Fearless in 1407, the Duke of Burgundy (his eldest son Charles) inherited the possession, but was captured by the English at the Battle of Agincourt and held prisoner for 25 years. During this period the château and the count's possessions were looked after by Count Dunois, the 'Bastard of Orléans' and companion-in-arms of Joan of Arc. After returning from English captivity Charles, then 50 years old, married the 14-year-old Mary of Cleves and ordered large parts of the old château to be torn down and replaced by buildings which were more comfortable to live in. In 1462, when he was 72 years old, he had a son who in 1498 became Louis XII of France. During the reign of Louis XII, the château of Blois played the part later assumed by Versailles, Louis XII preferring life in Blois to that in Paris. Louis XII was also a great builder adding another wing to the château and laying out extensive terraced gardens which occupied the entire area between the château and the site of today's railway station. However, the château's greatest builder was Francis I, who succeeded Louis XII in 1515 and to whom large parts of the present château can be attributed.

Turbulent times began during the Reformation under Henry III. The States General were convened in Blois on two occasions. In 1576 the Catholic League called for the Protestant doctrine to be repudiated. In 1588 Duke Henry of Guise, the

Bellegarde, château

Bellegarde, church, painting of the French school

Blois, Jeanne d'Arc

Blois, château, dome

head of the League, compelled the King to convene the States General once again, hoping to be able to depose the King with the aid of the 500 deputies, the vast majority of whom were loyal to the Duke. However, on 23 December 1588 the King retaliated by having the Duke murdered in the château in his very presence. The Duke's brother, the Cardinal of Lorraine, was taken prisoner at the same time and he was murdered the next day. Both bodies were burned and the ashes strewn into the Loire. Just eight months after ordering these murders, the King himself was assassinated. Henry II's successors were not too keen to live in Blois. In 1617 Louis XIII ordered his mother, Marie de Medici, to go into exile at Blois, a place he disliked and in 1626 he presented the count's lands to his brother Duke Gaston d'Orléans in order to remove from Paris his rival to the throne. Because Louis XIII initially had no children, Duke Gaston continued to have hopes of gaining the throne and, with the aid of F.Mansart, proceeded with great zeal to expand the château of Blois into a future royal residence. It must have been a correspondingly great disappointment to the Duke when Louis XIII did beget a son and successor to the throne and Duke Gaston's prospects of gaining the throne were finally blighted. Richelieu went a step further and blocked the flow of funds to the King's brother, thus compelling him to abandon further architectural plans. Duke Gaston, the last royal inhabitant of the château, died in 1660. Only Princess Marie-Casimire, widow of the Polish King John III Sobieski, later lived in the château for a short time. Both château and town were badly damaged by German bombing in June 1940.

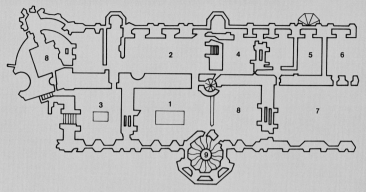

Blois, château (after Lesueur) **A** Salle des Etats **B** Tour du Foix **C** chapel **D** NE wing (Louis XII) **E** NW wing (Francis I) **F** SW wing (Gaston d'Orléans)

Layout of rooms on the second floor in 1588
1 council chamber **2** King's chamber **3** old cabinet **4** new cabinet **5** château chapel **6** gallery of honour **7** Queen's chamber **8** guard rooms **9** staircase

A bloody drama was played out in these rooms on December 23 1588: a king, supported by prayers for success from two clergymen, assassinated his rival. Henry III selected 20 impoverished members of his entourage to kill the Duc de Guise, one of the leaders of the Catholic party in the Huguenot Wars, a driving force behind St.Batholomew's Eve and a founder member of the league with Spain. At 8 o'clock in the morning he ordered the Duke to leave the council in the council chamber and attend him in the old study. The route led through the King's chamber, in which eight of the hired assassins were apparently chatting casually, and allowed the Duke to pass with a courteous greeting. But as he stepped into the study de Guise became uneasy. The sight of 12 armed men made him fear the worst. He turned on his heel, but was seized and disarmed by the men from the King's chamber. Although outnumbered, he managed to tear himself free and ran away, but collapsed, mortally wounded, in front of the King's bed, and Henry III ran to tell his mother, Catherine de Medici, the good news: 'The King of Paris is dead, I have no more rivals!' The following day the murdered man's brother, the Cardinal of Lorraine, was also murdered.

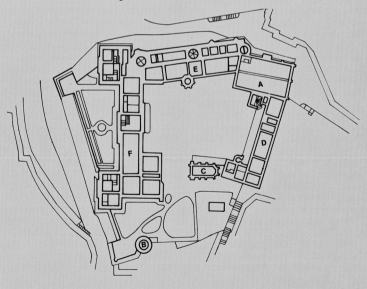

Château: Built in a dominant position on high ground between the valleys of the Loire and Arrou, the château displays all the developments in French architecture from the time of St.Louis to that of Louis XIII. The oldest sections of this château (built around an irregular, rectangular courtyard) are the 13C Salle des États in the N. corner and the round Tour du Foix, also 13C, in the S. The chapel and NE wing were built by Louis XII; the NW wing with its very fine Renaissance architecture was built by Francis I. The SW wing dating from the 17C was built by F.Mansart for Gaston d'Orléans. Thus the architectural history of the complex stretches from the feudal period in the 13C to the classicism of the early 17C.

The first builder of significance after the de Châtillon family was Charles d'Orléans who from 1440 onwards attempted extensive rebuilding of the medieval fortress on the site today occupied by the SW wing of Gaston d'Orléans. A drawing by Androuet du Cerceau dating from 1579 shows the appearance of the building before it was torn down in the 17C. All that has remained of the efforts of Charles d'Orléans is the gallery NW of the chapel. However, his endeavours were followed by those of his son Louis XII, who constructed the L-shaped, two-storeyed wing built of ashlars and brick and adjoining in the SE the 13C Salle des États. Like his father, he made use of a continuous gallery running along the side overlooking the courtyard and from which there is access to every room in the wing. This was a great advantage compared to the system employed in medieval buildings, in which it had previously been necessary to go through all the rooms to arrive at the last one. Building began in 1498 and ended in 1503 under C.Biart, who was also the architect of the Château d'Amboise. The Chapelle St-Calais was built as a completely new structure at this time. Originally single-aisled, with a choir somewhat narrower but of approximately the same length, today only the choir survives (rebuilt in the 19C), the nave having been torn down in the 17C to make room for the wing built by Gaston d'Orléans. In parallel with the construction of the large wing of château and the chapel, Pacello da Marcoliano laid out the park on three large terraces. Today the railway station occupies the site of the park.

The finest part of the château from the architectural point of view is that built by Francis I, who had ascended to the throne in 1515 at the age of twenty one. He later married Claude de France, daughter of Louis XII and heiress of Blois and immediately after his father-in-law's death began expanding Blois into the chief royal residence. In 1515 work on rebuilding the 13C NW wing was begun under the guidance of the Italian architect D. da Cortona and the architect J.Sourdeau. Not all of the old structure was torn down for this purpose, in fact as much use as possible was made of older sections of the building. Thus a massive wall reaching up to the roof still separates the large rooms on the courtyard side from the smaller, outer ones; this wall dates from the 13C and formerly surrounded the old counts' castle. Even the round defensive towers at both ends were integrated into the new building. Firstly the rooms facing inwards together with the splendid façade overlooking the courtyard and the famous octagonal tower were built. The King was disturbed by the contrast between the unusually beautiful loggia facing the courtyard and the unadorned defensive wall on the outside, so a second row of rooms was then built on the outside, and these had a completely new façade with loggias. Francis I's building activities were terminated by 1524 at the latest because the King began his Italian campaign at that time and there was no longer any money for building. It

Louis XII, portal in the château ▷

Blois, château, detail of staircase tower

was not until some hundred years later that the most recent wing of the complex, on the SW side of the courtyard, was built by F.Mansart for Gaston d'Orléans. Mansart, the famous architect employed by Louis XIII, began his work in 1635 by tearing down the SW wing built by Charles d'Orléans. The architect had planned to tear down the old complex completely and to build a regular new structure with four wings but this plan was thwarted by Richelieu who cut off funds for the work. Hence only the three-storeyed wing with a central pavilion named after Gaston d'Orléans was built. The King's brother received sufficient money for three years, 1635–8, and then the building work had to be terminated abruptly. The interior remained incomplete and was not inhabited until last century. The stairwell was only finished in 1932. At the time of the Revolution

the château, regarded as a symbol of royal dominion, was badly wrecked. The completely run-down building was used as a barracks from 1788 onwards. Restoration, begun in 1845 under the supervision of F.Duban, is today by no means complete.

The *Louis XII wing* (1498–1503) still clearly shows late Gothic characteristics. The rich decorations on the ashlars, and the bricks which are skilfully worked in a contrasting style, show that the owner and the architect both had good taste. The importance of the round-arched portal leading to the inner courtyard is emphasized by a superb niche containing a life-sized figure of the King on horseback. The original of this statue was broken to pieces in 1792 and the present one was built in 1857 based on old diagrams. Under this niche there are the initials L (for Louis) and A (for Anne de Bretagne) with the porcupine (the King's emblem) in between, but originally there was a Latin inscription, dating from 1498 and reading as follows: 'Here, where Louis was born by favourable chance, he received the royal sceptre with a dignified hand. Happy the day which beamingly brought forth the news of such a king. Gaul was not worthy of such an exalted ruler.' The courtyard façade of this wing is flanked by two dissimilar staircase towers; on the ground floor there are arcades with flat arches. Arabesques on the columns of the arcades and capitals decorated with dolphins, eagles, grotesque faces, and plant ornaments, show a clear Italian influence. The interior was at one time decorated with splendid tapestries, but of these nothing has survived. Today there is a *museum of religious art* on the ground floor; the upper storey has a *fine art museum* with a collection of paintings, tapestries and sculptures from the 15C–20C. The finest items are two frescos from the time of Louis XII, a rare series of 16C silk paintings and works by Flemish and Dutch artists.

The *Chapelle St-Calais* was consecrated in 1508, although only the choir has survived, Mansart having torn down the nave in 1635. The chapel was comprehensively restored in 1957, when the present windows were installed by M.Ingrand.

Although the *Francis I wing* (1515–24) was begun only 12 years after the completion of the Louis XII wing, the progress attained in architectural and artistic terms is nowhere so significant as here, where the full bloom of Italian-inspired Renaissance architecture is seen for the first time in France. The *outer façade* has a loggia, two arcaded storeys, and a gallery on the storey above these two. The distribution of the windows, balconies and pilasters shows a striking lack of symmetry. Neither the loggias nor the single or paired pilasters are of rhythmic design. Instead, their position is determined by the spatial arrangement of the interior, which is entirely dictated by the French imagination. The loggias are not joined to one another—rather they are designed as deep frames around the windows. Individual balconies, oriels and bays provide additional features, while an astonishing spiritedness results from an abundance of carved decorations including some very fine gargoyles. Describing this façade, La Fontaine wrote: 'The whole has something splendid about it that greatly pleases me.' The main point of interest of the inner façade is the splendid *staircase tower* with the Grand Escalier, which was used as a kind of tribune at royal receptions. Five sides of this octagonal tower project into the courtyard, and these sides are themselves divided into rectangular sections. The pillars and parapets are decorated on the inside and outside with impressive arabesques, some of which are so finely worked that it is as if they were in ebony and not stone. The profusion of plant ornaments and animal and human figures combine to bring out the real purpose of this spiral staircase which was built to impress: the court took up positions in the vaulted

Blois, château, staircase tower

panels of the five outer sides in order to receive the King, while the guard of honour paraded on the balconies. The rest of this wing's façade is also richly ornamented. The balustrade is decorated with the coat-of-arms of Francis I and Claude de France, and the building is guarded by statues of children which stand above the windows on the roof. The windows are framed with pilasters decorated with salamanders. The ground floor of this wing was originally occupied by domestic rooms and servants' quarters, while the royal apartments were on the first and second floors. However, it should be remembered that what is visible today is by no means the original furnishing, for Duban gave free rein to his imagination in his 19C restoration efforts. The brightly-coloured decorations are impressive, but bear little relation to the building's former state. Furni-

Blois, château, heraldic animal

ture, tapestries and paintings seen in the château today derive from widely differing sources. On the first floor, the *Great Hall* behind the staircase tower has two gorgeous fireplaces and door frames which are originals from the time of Francis I. One splendid fireplace is decorated with wonderful arabesques and the symbolic royal animals of Francis I and Claude de France. The most interesting room is the *Cabinet of Catherine de Medici* the walls of which are completely faced with wooden panelling decorated with flowing arabesques. The coffered ceiling and the fireplace were rebuilt in the 19C. A total of 237 panels on the walls conceal various wall cupboards, including secret compartments which can only be opened by a hidden mechanism in the skirting board. The oratory and Catherine's bedroom, in which she died in 1589, are also to be seen.

The *Salle des États,* the oldest part of the château, was the great hall of the former castle of the Counts of Blois and connects the Francis I wing with the Louis XII wing. The Counts of Blois gave their audiences and feasts in this 13C hall where they also sat in judgement. Some 100 ft. long and 40 ft. wide, wooden columns and pointed-arched arcades divide the hall into two aisles. The tapestry, designed by Rubens, depicting the life of Alexander the Great, has occupied this room since the 17C. The room takes its name from the States General which assembled here inm 1576 & 1588.

The *Gaston d'Orléans wing* (1635–8) is the most recent part of the château. The three-storeyed building consists of a central pavilion with asymmetrical wings extending both into the courtyard and towards the garden. The *façades* are symmetrically

Blois, St-Nicolas

designed. The slight asymmetry resulting from the terrain is skilfully compensated by the stairwell in the central pavilion. The façades themselves are subdivided with pilasters in Doric, Ionic and Corinthian orders and there are sparse carved ornaments. The courtyard side derives its accent from the central axis which is designed to appear as a projection of the main pavilion. Double columns, triangular pediments and coats-of-arms are symmetrically arranged around the central bust of Gaston d'Orléans.

Pavillon d'Anne de Bretagne: Once the summer house in the queen's garden. Surrounded by a wooden gallery with plants, the pavilion itself was built of ashlar and brick in *c.* 1500. The octagonal middle section is flanked by short cruciform terraced wings, one of which was a chapel where Louis XII and his queen held nine-day devotions to pray for the birth of a successor to the throne. Nothing has survived of the large gardens around the pavilion.

Church of St-Nicolas: This, the most interesting church in the town, formerly belonged to the Benedictine abbey of St-Laumer, whose classical buildings are today used as a hospital. The church itself was built in the 12&13C and is mainly of interest for the happy manner in which Romanesque and Gothic have been united. The choir apse is entirely Romanesque and reminiscent of that of St-Benoît; the choir itself, the transept, and the first bay of the nave, present an outstanding example of the transitional style dating from 1138–86. The bays of the nave date from the early 13C and are obviously modelled on the cathedral of Chartres. The façade, which makes a somewhat sober impression, is flanked by two towers which were given their slender helm roofs in the 19C. The Gothic nave has narrow aisles and an elegant triforium. The cylindrical dome over the crossing has pointed vaulting.

Cathedral of St-Louis: This dates back to the original 9C church which was expanded into a cathedral in the 16C. A hurricane led to the collapse of the whole church in 1678 apart from the W. front and the apse. The church was rebuilt in Gothic style in the late 17C; the ambulatory was added in 1867. The W. tower is the town's dominant feature. Its lower sections are 12C. Work on this tower continued in the mid 16C, and it was given its crowning double lantern in 1609. Of particular interest is the *crypt of Saint-Solenne* discovered by M.Cauchie in 1928. The E. section of

this crypt, which is 72 ft. long, dates from the 10C; the W. section from the 1st half of the 11C. It occupies the nave and apse of a 9C Carolingian church dedicated to the Apostles Peter and Paul. The side walls of the crypt also date from this Carolingian church. Columns and vault were inserted in the Romanesque period when a funerary church for St.Solenne, Bishop of Chartres, was required. The *former bishop's palace* was built in the early 18C by J. Gabriel, father of the builder of the Place de la Concorde in Paris. Today it is the town hall.

Basilica of Notre-Dame-de-la-Trinité: This modern building, completed in 1939, is by P.Rouvière, who was also responsible for all the decorations, with the result that the building is surprisingly uniform for a modern structure. The façade is

Blois, St-Vincent-de-Paul

Blois, former bishop's palace

adorned by a large relief of the Virgin and the Trinity by the Martel brothers. The choir gable is decorated by a statue of St.Michael by Gualino. A magnificent Annunciation by Roux-Colas embellishes the entrance, while a monumental *Stations of the Cross*, which Lambert-Rucki carved straight into the fresh cement, dominates the interior.

Museum Robert Houdin: Devoted to Jean Eugène Robert Houdin (1805–71), a famous 19C illusionist and quick-change artist.

Hôtel d'Alluye: Florimond Robertet, Baron d'Alluye, and minister of finance under Charles VII, Louis XII and Francis I built his town house at No. 8 Rue St-Honoré in the early 16C. The front was built in ashlar and brick modelled on the Louis XII wing of the château. The large inner courtyard has an Italianate arcade; two storeys have loggias with flat-arched arcades. The loggia parapets are decorated with medallions of the twelve Caesars and Aristotle. A palm vault graces the spiral stone staircase.

Old town: Despite extensive devastation in the last war, there are still numerous picturesque old alleyways between the cathedral and the Loire. The following sights are especially worth seeing: *Hôtel des Guise* (No. 18 Rue Chemonton), *Hôtel de Jassaud* (No. 5 Rue Fontaine-des-Elus), *Hôtel Sardini* (No. 7 Rue du Puits-Châtel), *Hôtel de Condé* (No. 3 Rue des Juifs) and the church of *St-Vincent-de-Paul*.

Environs: Bury (10 km. W.): From 1511 onwards this small village to the W. of the great forest of Blois was the residence of Florimond Robertet. Baron D'Alluye and royal finance minister, he owned one of the most beautiful early Renaissance châteaux, a regular structure with a tower at each of its four corners. Unfortunately, only ruins of this splendid

building survive. The church of *St-Secondin* (1 km. N.) dates from the 11C and was given its present form in the 16C; fine stone font and two 16C wooden statues of Christ and the Virgin.
Chapelle Vendômoise, La (13 km. NW): 11&12C church.
Chaussée Saint-Victor, La (3 km. NE): Small ceramics museum of Adrien Thibault. The church has a brightly painted and gilded wooden panel of the hunt of St.Victor (late-16C).
Coulanges (10 km. SW): Site of the former *Abbaye de la Guiche*, an abbey for aristocratic ladies founded by Jean I de Châtillon in 1272. Apart from ruins, all that remains of the monastery is part of a gallery and a Gothic room with two aisles. The *village church* contains a fine 16C prayer desk which, along with its carved walls, came from Guiche abbey.
Fossé (7 km. NW): 12C *church;* castle in the style of Louis XIII, temporary home of Mme. de Staël, best known for 'De l'Allemagne' (1810), her book about Germany and Romanticism.
Herbault (16 km. NW): The *church* was completed in 1790 and contains an altarpiece dating from 1633 and 16C choir stalls.
Orchaise (11 km. W.): The *church* of the small village on the right bank of the Cisse dates from the 17C, but a Carolingian sculpture from the previous church survives above the portal. Interior decorations are 17C. 13C *barn* beside the church.
Saint-Lublin-en-Vergonnois (8 km. W.): Church dates from the 11&15C and has a figure of Christ and a wooden Virgin (15C).

Boumois
49 Maine-et-Loire   p.136☐G 4

Château: Late 15C or early 16C structure entered through the gate in the ramparts surrounding the town. This gate is flanked by two towers with machicolations. The W. outer

Bourgueil, St-Germain, vault

façade makes a similarly martial impression, with a parapet walk and the two large towers (also with machicolations) which formerly stood in the water of the moat, which is now filled in. However, the inner façade, pierced by numerous windows (including large dormer windows), shows that this building of bright, amiable tufa stone was a comfortable place to live. The style is typical of the transition from the late Gothic Flamboyant to the Renaissance with the added refinement of the spirited, high dormer window in the octagonal staircase tower.

Bourgueil
37 Indre-et-Loire   p.136☐H 4

This town is as well known to wine-lovers for its good, fruity red wines as it is to the lover of literature for the Renaissance authors Ronsard and Rabelais.

Church of St-Germain: The façade's pre-Romanesque gable and the fine late-12C Plantagenet choir with a pointed vault borne on four tall columns have survived the 19C rebuilding of the church.

Benedictine abbey: The 'cellar'—an imposing 13C building today used as a chapel by the sisters of St-Martin—survives from the abbey founded in *c.* 990 and made famous through Rabelais. Other remnants include a 15C section of the cloister, the former 17C 'abbot's château', the 18C priory building, a large building dating from 1730 which houses the refectory, kitchens, monks' cells, and an unusually spacious staircase.

Also worth seeing: A 15C *house* opposite the church. *Medallion* by the town hall, depicting Rabelais (1494–1553).

Environs: Chevrette (2 km. N.): A *wine museum*, with a wine-press and cooper's tools from the 16–18C, occupies a former quarry near the village.
Réaux, Les (5 km. S.): Late-15C *château* surrounded by a wide moat fed with flowing water. Much altered in the 18C, only the rectangular keep and the gate flanked by two round towers remain unchanged.
Restigné (small wine-growers' village, 5 km. E.): Old *church* with an 11C nave and a 15C wooden vault. The straight-ended choir has a tall vault reminiscent of that in Bourgueil.

Brissac-Quincé
49 Maine-et-Loire   p.136☐F 4

A small town standing on a gently rising hill with an extensive view of the countryside. A terrace half way up is flanked by two massive round towers

Brissac, château ▷

with parapet walks and set back upper storeys. Wedged between the towers is a five-storeyed pavilion with the entrance and, at right angles to this, an elongated wing.

Château: Despite all the beautiful detail, this is an asymmetrical and stylistically very heterogeneous building whose history dates back to the 11C. The present château was built in the 15C on the foundations of the original fortress, an old citadel. This was so severely damaged in the Wars of Religion (1562–98) that work on rebuilding the E. wing began in 1606. However, the owner died in 1621, and instead of having the two old round towers torn down and the E. wing completed symmetrically, his son added the elongated N. wing with a pavilion which almost resembles a tower block. Hence the château today presents a somewhat confusing aspect. Two round defensive towers from the 15C call to mind the former function of the château as a forward defence for Angers. Between them we see half of the planned E. wing with the domed entrance pavilion (originally intended to form the middle of the wing), an elegant structure in the style of Henry IV, with three bays. Round-arched niches, pilasters and large decorative strips clearly indicate the influence of the Renaissance (construction was supervised by J.Corbineau and J.d'Angluze). The N. wing is in the style of Louis XIII.

The *interior* is richly decorated. The *grand drawing-room* is 18C, with a richly-carved, gilded wooden ceiling. There are sumptuous tapestries in the dining room and Mortemar room.

Parish church: Rebuilt and extended in 1532. Fine 16C windows.

Candes-Saint-Martin, St-Martin, detail

Environs: Aubigné (17 km. S.): Beside the church are the ruins of a large 15&16C *château*. The square defensive tower with a parapet walk also survives in good condition.
Château de Fline (12 km. S.): 18&19C.

Martigné-Briand (14 km. S.): Early-16C *ruined château*.
Notre-Dame-d'Allençon (6 km. S.): 12C *church* with 16C nobleman's house opposite.
Thouarcé (10 km. S.): The *church* has a 16C Madonna and Child.

Candes-Saint-Martin
37 Indre-et-Loire   p.136□H 4/5

One of the most attractive spots in the Loire valley at the confluence of the Loire and the Vienne. Like Tours it owes a great deal to St.Martin who founded the monastery and later died while paying it a visit.

Pilgrimage church of St-Martin: Built at the end of the 13C and the beginning of the 14C on the spot where the saint breathed his last,

lying in prayer on the ash-strewn floor. In the 15C, during the Hundred Years War, the W. façade was fortified with tower-like corner buildings and with battlements and machicolations on the N. porch. As the church is built around the chapel of St.Martin (complete in itself) and because the remains of a thick wall between the chapel and the N. arm of the transept were also incorporated, the three aisles of the choir and the four-bayed hall nave have a slightly distorted ground plan. The vault is supported by tall, slender, clustered columns decorated with figures and is a typically Angevin vault with a complex pictorial scheme, as in St-Serge in Angers or in Le Puy-Notre-Dame. The N. portal, protected by a porch, and the outer façade of the porch itself are also lavishly decorated with figures; the upper storey of the porch accommodates a chapel of St.Michael.

Château: Set above St-Martin, this building with a fine octagonal staircase tower was commissioned in 1485 by the Archbishop of Tours.

Environs: Petit-Thouars (4 km.

SE): *Château*, dating from the late 15C.

Saint-Germain-sur-Vienne (2.5 km. SE): Romanesque *church* with a square 12C bell tower. The choir has a fine Angevin vault and dates from the early 13C.

Thizay (6.5 km. SE): *Dolmen*.

Chambord
41 Loir-et-Cher   p.138□M 3

Château: Emperor Charles V was of the opinion that this unorthodox building commissioned by Francis I in the depths of the forest of the Sologne was 'the epitome of the finest products of man's art'. It is 511 ft. long, 383 ft. wide and has 440 rooms, making it the largest château on the Loire, and hinting at the future splendours of Versailles. This château of superlatives overwhelms the visitor with its endless turrets, gables, belfries and chimneys. Among the labyrinth of the roofs there are over 800 capitals and 365 chimneys. As well as a staircase tower there are 14 large and 70 smaller flights of stairs.

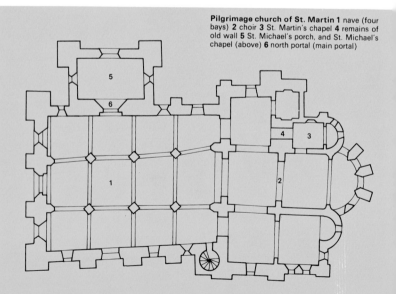

Pilgrimage church of St. Martin 1 nave (four bays) **2** choir **3** St. Martin's chapel **4** remains of old wall **5** St. Michael's porch, and St. Michael's chapel (above) **6** north portal (main portal)

Chambord, Louis XIV outside the château, painting by Van der Meulen

Chambord, château (after an engraving by the French architect and engraver Du Cerceau dating from 1576) **A** corner towers **B** donjon with roof terrace **C** central staircase (a double spiral staircase)

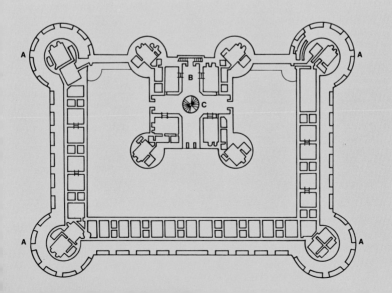

The château replaced an earlier building which was demolished. In 1519 Francis I pulled down a Blois hunting lodge in the forest of Boulogne to make room for his own château, intended for hunting and feasting. More than 13,750 acres were enclosed by a wall 32 km. long and declared a royal hunting ground. On September 6 1519 François de Pontbriant became the supervisor of building. The architect may have been D.da Cortona; the master builders were J.Sourdeau, his son Denis, P.Trinqueau and J.Coqueau. Laying the foundations caused great difficulties, because the marshy land would not take much weight. In 1524 the Italian campaign caused the king to break off work until 1526. This was followed by 12 years of intensive activity with an average workforce of 1,800. The inner part of the château, the keep, was completed by 1533. The towers and the pavilions on the corners of the roof terrace were completed in 1537. By 1539 work had progressed to the extent that it was possible to receive Emperor Charles V. However, the private royal apartments were not completed until 1547, the year of the death of Francis I. Henry II continued the work, but the Wars of Religion and the king's early death (1559) meant that the palatial château remained incomplete, although François II and Charles IX often stayed here to hunt.

Louis XIV was the first to realize the château's potential as a backdrop for glittering feasts. In 1670 it was used for the first performance of 'Le Bourgeois Gentilhomme' by J.B. Poquelin, better known as Molière. Finally Louis XV placed the château at the disposal of his father-in-law, Stanislaus Leszcynski, the dethroned King of Poland. In the 18C Marshal Moritz of Saxony was given the château in recognition of his victory at Fonte-

Chambord, château ▷

Chambord, château, detail

noy. The marshal made the château the centre of an extravagant court life based around two regiments of cavalry, which consisted of negroes dressed as tartars riding on white stallions. When the marshal died in 1750 (it was never clear whether or not this was the result of a duel with the Prince Conti), the huge building was left unoccupied. During the Revolution some of the furnishings were plundered, some auctioned. The building itself only survived because no-one could afford to pull it down. In 1820 the entire château was put up for sale. As the result of a fund-raising campaign by Count Adrien de Calonne it was acquired for the Duke of Bordeaux, the grandson of Charles X, and presented to him. The rest of the money which had been collected was used for the restoration of the château, and this prevented its falling further into disrepair. In 1930 the state bought the château from the Duke's heirs.

Building: As in the château of Vincennes the buildings are based on the medieval castle pattern: a large rectangle with round corner towers and largely incomplete sides forms the inner courtyard, the NW side of which is dominated by the massive, square *keep*, which also has round corner towers. Although the keep was built on the medieval pattern, the Renaissance building is delicately articulated with pilasters, cornices, arches and windows and is not at all like a fortress. The core of the three-storey keep—and thus of the whole château—is the central staircase, which was originally free-standing and rises directly to the level of the roof. A special feature of the staircase is that it has two intertwining flights, which mean that someone ascending the stairs never has to meet someone

Chambord, detail of ceiling in château

descending. Each storey has large cruciform halls adjacent to the steps. In their turn these halls enclose gigantic corner apartments which extend into the round towers. It is said that the basic conception for the staircase and articulation of the keep came from Leonardo da Vinci, although nobody has been able to prove this. It is true that Francis I summoned him to his court in Amboise in 1516, i.e. during the period in which the king was keenly involved in the planning of his château and it is also certain that Leonardo produced drawings of double spiral staircases. It seems the plan of the keep existed when building began and when Leonardo died in the same year it was retained unaltered.

The *decorative additions* to the roof of the donjon are a miniature town in themselves.

The *440 rooms* in the château seem at first to be a never-ending labyrinth, but the whole building can be seen to have an overall plan if the purpose of this bewildering mass of rooms is considered. It was never intended that one should be able to live here in a normal fashion, and certainly not in comfort. The intention was rather to express absolute monarchy in stone, to give an idealized vision of a rule ordained by God. This will was also the driving force behind the state rooms, but only a shadow of that intention remains, as no restoration, however lovingly carried out, could make good the plunder of the Revolution. Much of the furniture and decoration consists of conscientiously assembled museum pieces, although in some places attempts have been made to copy items of which plans are still extant. Thus the so-called *hall of the sun* (sunflower emblem on the shutters) is now decorated with paintings and a large Brussels tapestry depicting the Call of Abraham. The so-called *hunt room* reminds us of Francis I's passion for hunting; it now contains a sequence of tapestries manufactured in the late 17C in Paris to designs by L.Guyot. They show scenes from Francis I's history of hunting. On the first floor of the keep, in which Louis XIV had recently established himself and where in 1669 Molière's 'Monsieur de Porceaugnac', and a year later 'Le Bourgeois Gentilhomme', had been performed, it has been possible to assemble parts of the original furnishings, such as wall hangings and paintings. In the *parade room* the state bed is a copy; the carved panelling, which originally came from Versailles and which was presented by Louis XIV to the marshal of Saxony, is original. There is also an interesting portrait of Henry

III by F.Clouet and a portrait of Anne of Austria by P.Mignard. The *chapel*, intended from the inception of the project for the NW tower, was not started until the reign of Henry II and completed under Louis XIV by F.Mansart. Baroque furnishings were added under Louis XV. The second floor, originally meant as a hunting museum, houses weapons, trophies and works by 17C Flemish painters of animals. One room contains a series of tapestries on the life of the Greek hero Meleager and a room on the first floor in the SE corner is dedicated to the memory of the Count of Chambord; his refusal to accept a proposed constitution led to the foundering in 1873 of the movement to restore the monarchy. The guardroom in the main façade was rebuilt in 1748 by G.N. Servandoni as a theatre for the actress Favart.

Chambord, painting in château

Park: The park, with an area of 13,750 acres and surrounded by a 32 km. wall, is a state hunting ground.

Champigny-sur-Veude

37 Indre-et-Loire   p.136☐I 5

Château: This splendid building was commissioned by Louis I and Louis II of Bourbon in the early 16C on the site of a medieval fortress. It was pulled down on the orders of Richelieu; the great cardinal, jealously determined to be the greatest in the land after the king, countenanced no rivals. He bought all the châteaux in the immediate area whenever he could and pulled them down or, as in the case of Chinon, allowed them to fall into disrepair. Only the farm build-

ings survived of Champigny-sur-Veude, along with the *Sainte-Croix chapel,* so called because it housed a splinter from the True Cross; the chapel was saved by the intervention of Pope Urban VIII. It was built 1508–1543 and is a single-aisled building with four bays and a triangular choir. Despite all its Gothic features its exterior columns and pilasters, cornices, and the allegorical figures on the entrance portal make it one of the jewels of French Renaissance architecture. Most famous of all are the *stained-glass windows,* (*c.* 1550) which fill the interior (empty except for the marble statue of Duke Henri de Bourbon-Montpensier) with colour of extraordinary richness and splendour.

The *present château,* an elegant and spacious building of attractive design is based on the former farm buildings

Chambord, staircase tower and lantern

Champigny-sur-Veude, Sainte-Croix chapel

Champigny-sur-Veude, Sainte-Croix chapel

which were taken away from Richelieu's heirs.

Château de Landifer
49 Maine-et-Loire   p.136☐G 3

This lonely little château, a square building with four protruding towers, is only recognizable as a Renaissance building by its windows and roof lights and the high chimneys decorated with pilasters and gables. It was restored *c.* 1900 and extended by the addition of a modern wing in the same style. The building is well balanced, with the exception of the windows, which are rather clumsily arranged and suggest the hand of an inexperienced architect; the building was in fact designed by local masons. The many embrasures and the entrance, tiny for a château, show the builders' preoccupation with defence at the time of the Wars of Religion (1562–98).

Environs: Bocé (2.5 km. SE): Old *church*; 11C nave; the choir and left transept arm are 12C, the right transept arm is 13C. 5 17&18C retables.
Cuon (4 km. S.): Romanesque *church.*
Jumelles (9.5 km. S.): Heavily restored 12C church.
Longué (15.5 km. S.): This little town, set among green fields and famous for the breeding of horses, has a church built in 1850–60 in 13C style. E. of this is the **Manoir de la Cirottière** with a 13C chapel and a large 15C tower. 3 km. W. is the **Manoir d'Avoir,** a fine Renaissance building in which Françoise de Maridort, the 'Madame de Montsoreau', ended her days. 6 km. SE is **Blou:** fine 11&13C *church* with a remarkable bell tower.

Châteaudun, St-Jean-de-la-Chaîne

Châteaudun

28 Eure-et-Loire   p.138☐M 1

The settlement belonged to the counts of Blois from the 10C until 1391 when it was sold to Louis d'Orléans, the brother of Charles VI. The bastard of Orléans, the natural son of Louis d'Orléans, born in 1403, lived here until he was 15. He fought against the English with Joan of Arc and is buried in Notre-Dame-de-Cléry. The town, set on a plateau above the Loir, burned down to a large extent in 1723, but Dodun, the king's chancellor at the time, made sure that his home town was rebuilt on generous lines. Jules Hardouin, the royal inspector of buildings, was commissioned to do the work and the geometrically designed part of the town was built to his design. Despite

all this there are some old houses in the Old Town, the two oldest dating from the 16C.

Ste-Madeleine: This church built directly on to the town wall dates from the 12C and is the oldest church in the town. The crypt still dates from the time of the church's foundation. The portal on the S. side is lavishly decorated with human figures and fabulous animals. Parts of the former fortifications can still be discerned in the W. façade.

St-Valérien: The church was begun in the late 12C, completed in the 13C and rebuilt in the 15C. The square tower also dates from the latter period. The trefoil tympanum on the S. portal is worth seeing. Interesting features of the interior are the alternating pilasters supporting the vault of the nave.

Chapel of Notre-Dame-du-Champdé: Destroyed at the end of the last century, when only the façade dating from 1520 with its late Gothic filigree decoration survived. It is now the entrance to the cemetery.

St-Jean-de-la-Chaîne: This church on the right bank of the Loir is Romanesque in origin but was altered in the 15C, when the vaulting in the nave and aisles was added. The massive tower was completed in 1506. Worthwhile features of the furnishings are a Crucifixion with statues of Mary and John and the Temptation of St.Anthony in the right transept. There is a painting by J.Restout of Rouen in the left transept.

Châteaudun, château **1** entrance **2** old 12C keep (one of the first round donjons in France) **3** 15C chapel **4** 15C Dunois wing **5** 16C Longueville wing **6** Renaissance steps **7** Gothic steps **8** terraces

Château: Set steeply above the Loir, the château was built at various times and is in excellent condition. The oldest parts date from the 12C. The most important sections were added in the 15&16C.

Keep: Built in the early 12C as one of the earliest round keeps in France. Without its roof the three-storey building is 102 ft. high and is architecturally unusual in having a lavatory oriel in each storey.

Chapel: The chapel, built in the 15C for Count Dunois, has a square bell tower and choir with three-sided apse. There are two oratories beside the choir and the nave. The two-storey church has an upper room intended for the servants; this upper room has a wooden tunnel vault and the lower room has rib vaulting. The S. oratory contains a late-15C fresco representing the Last Judgement. 15 very fine life-size statues are evidence

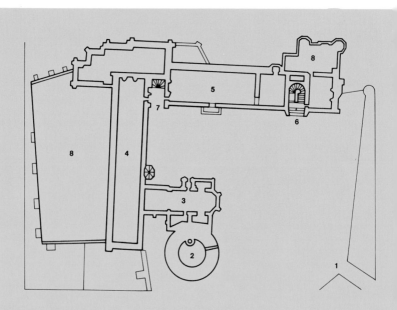

of the high standard of achievement in sculpture of the period. They represent St.Elizabeth, Mary, Radegund with sceptre, Apollonia with her forceps, Barbara with her tower, Geneviève, Catherine with the wheel, Mary Magdalen and also John the Baptist, John the Evangelist and Martha with the dragon. A Madonna and Child complete the collection. Three smaller statues are later additions and were placed here by François d'Orléans-Longueville, the son of Dunois; they represent Dunois himself, St.Agnes and St.Francis.

Dunois wing: The Gothic S. wing of the château was started in 1460, but was finally completed by the son of Count Dunois. He was mainly responsible for the Gothic staircase, which has some Renaissance features.

Longueville wing: This wing was built 1511–32 on older foundations by Cardinal Longueville and the son of Count Dunois, but it remained incomplete. Distinctive exterior features are Italian moulding and the Flamboyant balustrade. The staircase is decorated with lavish Renaissance ornament. The finest items among the furnishings are numerous tapestries and 16C carved chests, particularly in the great reception room on the first floor. The several splendid fireplaces are partly Gothic, partly Renaissance.

Museum: This houses a collection of prehistoric exhibits and medieval sculpture, as well as ceramics and three mummies from Egyptian graves. A collection of birds and their nests, some of which are mounted in glass cases in simulated natural habitat, is a most attractive feature.

Environs: Bonneval: A little town on the left bank of the Loir, along

Châteaudun, château, Renaissance decoration

Châteaudun, château, courtyard

Châteaudun, Ste-Madeleine, detail of portal

which still runs the old *town wall* with moats fed by the river. The *Porte de Boisville* and the four-arched *bridge* over the Loir by the swimmimg pool date from the 13C. *Notre-Dame*, in the purest Parisian Gothic style with nave and aisles, was built in the early 13C. The nave is unusually high, and the 213 ft. bell tower with a slate roof and the fine rose window above the triforium in the straight-ended choir are also interesting. Left of the church is the 15C *Porte St-Roch* with two towers, and next to this is the large *Tour du Roi*, part of the old town wall. In the street to the right of the church are a number of *old houses*; in the *Rue de la Grève* by the bridge are a Gothic house and the *Benedictine abbey of St-Florentin*, founded in 857 and now used as a psychiatric clinic.

Brou (*c.* 20 km. NW): 12&16C *church* with a wooden figure of St.Roch.

Ruins of the 11C *St-Romain*. Remains of 16C *fortifications*.

Clois-sur-le-Loir (12 km. SW): *Church* with 12C apse and 15C bell tower. The pretty turret in front of the church dates from the 16C. 16C *houses*. Only the 12C church with wall paintings of the same period has survived of *Yron priory*, founded in 1114. Emile Zola's novel 'La Terre' was written in Cloyes-sur-le-Loir.

Dangeau (about 14 km. NW): Fine 11&12C Romanesque church with nave, two aisles, radiating chapels and ambulatory.

Jallans (3 km. E.): 13&14C *church*.

Ouzouer-le-Doyen (16 km. S.): 12&16C *church* with fine painted 17C wooden vaults.

Romilly-sur-Aigre (15 km. SW): Small 16C moated *château*.

Varize (15 km. E.): In 1939 Romanesque frescos were discovered in the

Châteaudun, Ste-Madeleine

Châteauneuf-sur-Loire, St-Martial

little Romanesque *church*. John the Baptist, the Descent from the Cross and the Holy Women at the tomb can be made out.

Châteauneuf-sur-Loire

45 Loiret   p.138☐O 2

The town was named after a little *château* extended in the 17C by Louis Phélypeaux de la Vrillière, Louis XIV's secretary of state and master of ceremonies. By 1803 little remained of this 'little Versailles'. The only surviving parts are some of the domestic buildings, the orangery and an octagonal building with a dome which is now part of the Town Hall.

St-Martial: This church dates back to the 12&13C, but the present building was largely constructed *c.* 1600.

The *marble tomb* of Louis Phélypeaux de la Vrillière, who died in 1681, is a notable feature of the interior. The tomb was made in Rome by a pupil of Bernini and shows the theatricality of Roman baroque.

Musée da la Marine de la Loire: This Loire shipping museum is housed in the ground floor of what remains of the château. Exhibits include river boatmen's equipment from boathooks to porcelain from the captain's cabin, model ships, and peasant furniture.

Château park: Famous for its rhododendrons.

Environs: Jargeau (7 km. W.): The site of Joan of Arc's victory over the English in 1429. Her statue (Lanson, 1898) is in the Place du Martroi. The former fortifications have been made

15C Pietà in Autrèche (Château-Renault)

into boulevards. The old **collegiate church** has a very old nave renovated in the mid 12C and a choir rebuilt in the 16C. There is a chestnut fair in Jargeau on the 18/19 October.

Châteauneuf-sur-Sarthe
49 Maine-et-Loire   p.136☐F 2

Church: 12&13C building with fine Angevin vault.

Also worth seeing: *Bronze statue* of Robert the Strong, Count of Anjou in the Place de la Mairie; he fell in the battle against the Normans in 866. A *ruined tower*, also associated with Robert the Strong.

Environs: Abbey (2.5 km. upstream on the left bank): 16C buildings with

chapel. 4 km. NE of the abbey in **Brissarthe** is a notable 10&12C church.

Château-Renault
37 Indre-et-Loire   p.138☐K 3

Small tanning town and birthplace of the painter André Bauchant (1873–1958).

Château: Built by Geoffrey de Château-Gontier in the early 11C for his son Renault. The château was rebuilt in the 12C by Thibaut de Champagne and again rebuilt in the 14&18C; large parts of the outer walls and a fine gate have survived from the 14C and a round donjon from the 12C. The residential buildings date from the 18C and the side buildings from the 16C.

Church (16C): Fine 15C Madonna.

Environs: Autrèche (13 km. SE): 10C *church*. Several old statues, including a 15C **Pietà**.

Chaumont-sur-Loire
41 Loir-et-Cher   p.138☐L 3

Château **Chaumont** is one of the few Loire châteaux set directly on the river. In the 10C Eudes I Count of Blois built a fortress on what was then a bald mound (calvus mons = Chaumont) above the Loire. The castle was intended to defend his territory against his aggressive neighbour Foulques Nerra, Count of Anjou. In 1026 the buildings passed to Count Gueudoin. In 1154 the Count of Blois had the building razed, and then shortly afterwards rebuilt it. In 1170 the newly built castle was the scene of a confrontation fit for an antique tragedy, the meeting between Henry II of England and Thomas à Becket,

Châteauneuf-sur-Loire, château ▷

Archbishop of Canterbury. The archbishop was scarcely home before proclaiming the excommunication of the king. The king replied by arranging the murder of the archbishop.

The château was once more in the firing line three years later. Louis XI razed it again in the course of his conflict with the allied feudal lords. Count Pierre d'Amboise, lord of the château made a public apology, was pardoned by the king and allowed to start rebuilding. The first phase, the N. section (now disappeared) and the W. section were completed by 1475. The two remaining wings, forming the courtyard, were built 1498–1510 for Charles d'Amboise, admiral, general and lord chamberlain to Louis XII. Supervision of the building work was entrusted to his uncle, Cardinal Georges d'Amboise, who was among other things Louis XII's prime minister. In 1560 the château was acquired by Catherine de Medici, widow of Henry II; she intended to swap it for the Château de Chenonceau. The château on the Cher was claimed by Diana de Poitiers, the late king's mistress. By making the exchange Catherine compelled her rival to leave her favourite residence and to make do with Chaumont. The angry Diana moved to Anet, and left Chaumont to her brother-in-law, the Duke of Bouillon. After that it changed hands frequently; finally in 1740 one of its owners, Nicolas Bertin de Vaugyen, had the idea of pulling down the N. wing, thus opening up the splendid view across the valley of the Loire and establishing the building in its present form. The château escaped damage or destruction at the time of the Revolution because in the second half of the 18C Jacques Le Ray had made it into an arts and crafts centre, making glass and ceramics.

In 1810 the château was made over to Madame de Staël, who had been forbidden by Napoleon to live within 40

Chaumont-sur-Loire, tapestry in the château ▷

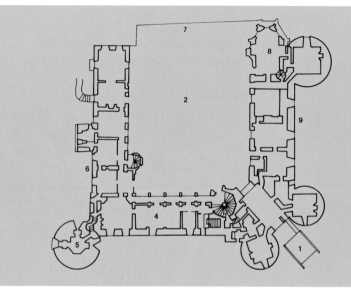

Chaumont-sur-Loire, portal decoration

Chaumont-sur-Loire, château

Chaumont, château **1** main entrance **2** cour d'honneur **3** staircase tower **4** S. wing (early 16C) **5** Amboise tower **6** W. wing (2nd third of the 15C) **7** N. wing (removed in the 18C) **8** chapel **9** S. wing (early 16C)

miles of Paris. She wrote 'De l'Allemagne' here and gathered a circle of literary figures around her, including A.W. Schlegel and Adalbert von Chamisso.

After this the Count of Aramon made great efforts to restore the château and to make it the scene of lavish feasts. In 1938 it was finally taken over by the state.

The *buildings* of Chaumont are in the shape of a horseshoe, open to the NE and on an almost square ground plan. The E. and W. corners have massive round towers, and the main entrance at the SE corner is protected by 2 round towers. It is these four mighty towers which give the château its somewhat daunting appearance. The

oldest section is the NW wing. It originally had fewer and much smaller windows. The two other wings also have the intimidating look of a former fortress, but with suggestions of the Renaissance. The two round portals in the main entrance have the same decorative frieze as the outer walls. It consists of two intertwined Cs (for Charles de Chaumont), alternating with stylized blazing hills. Above the portal are the coat-of-arms of France and the initials of Louis XII and Anne of Brittany. The whole is framed by the French lily and the ermine spots of Brittany. The left entrance tower carries the coat-of-arms of Cardinal George d'Amboise. All the machicolations are decorated with the symbols of Diana de Poitiers, sometimes two intertwined Ds, and sometimes hunting horn, bow and quiver, the symbols of Diana, goddess of the

hunt. The dominant feature of the older, NW wing is the tower built by Pierre d'Amboise, the largest and also the most solid of all the buildings. This colossus, also known as the *Amboise tower*, with walls almost 12 ft. thick, was intended as the last refuge for the inhabitants of the castle. Although it is connected with the W. corner of the château it is completely independent of the residential wings because access is only possible via an extremely narrow spiral staircase inside the massive curtain wall. The tower diagonally opposite is the *St-Nicolas tower*, which houses the study of Ruggieri, the royal astrologer. If tradition is to be believed, Catherine de Medici shut herself up here with the astrologer in order to consult the stars about the fate of her sons. It is said that Ruggieri predicted the dark destiny which awaited all three of them, and the rise of the Bourbons under Henry IV. In the 19C a long balcony with tracery balustrade was erected along the front of the upper storey; this enabled the inhabitants of the château to enjoy the view over the valley of the Loire. The polygonal staircase tower on the left of the main entrance is of architectural interest. In its lower parts at least late Gothic ornamentation has survived; there is scarcely a trace of the influence of the Italian Renaissance.

The interior of the château was originally divided up in a quite different way. The rooms are now predominantly small and often interconnected, whereas formerly there were broad halls taking up the entire width of the building. As each of the owners made alterations to suit his own taste, there is now very little left of the original interior. Much was reassembled in the 19C, but even that has not survived complete. The 16–18C features on view today were collected and arranged by the authorities concerned with the preservation of ancient monuments. The museum-like character is underlined by the collection of *Aubusson carpets* exhibited on the ground floor and the glass cases with examples of portrait medallions by Nini. The first floor has Brussels carpets, embroidered silk wall hangings, faience, and Italian, Spanish, Portuguese and French furniture from various periods. The *Salle du Conseil* has a 17C Italian floor made of coloured faience tiles and depicting a lively hunting scene. The floor was brought to Chaumont from a palace in Salerno by Prince Amédée de Broglie.

Park and stables are now only a shadow of their former splendour. At the beginning of the present century the park had an area of 2500 hectares and now only 17 of them remain.

Environs: Mesland (7 km. NW): 11C *church* with portal decorated with grotesques, 12C font, 15C wooden figure of Christ and an early-16C marble Virgin and Child. 15&16C *houses*.
Monteaux (7 km. W.): 16C *château*. 16C *country house* in which Descartes' father lived.
Onzain (3 km. N.): 15&16C *church* with Renaissance portal and four 18C terracotta statues.

Chenonceaux
37 Indre-et-Loire   p.138□L 4

Château: A small, graceful building in the river, a long gallery over the Cher, an old keep on a terrace, two canals and two large, beautifully designed gardens on the bank—that is Chenonceau; in the 16C feasts of unimaginable splendour were held here, showing a degree of imagination which the modern mind would think bizarre. The château was in the possession of the lords of Marques from the 13C. In 1411 the castle was razed because the lord had risen against the king and, with the excep-

Chaumont-sur-Loire, drawbridge in the château▷

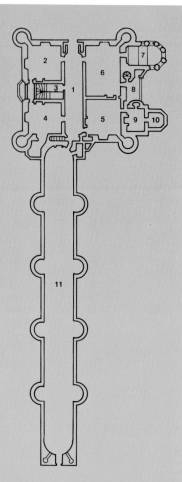

Chenonceaux, château (Parterre) **1** vestibule **2**
Louis XIII room **3** steps **4** François I room **5** Diana
of Poitiers room **6** guard room **7** chapel **8** terrace
9 green study **10** library **11** gallery. This ground
plan gives an impression of the size of the château
conceived by Catherine de Medici, who wanted
to set a pavilion corresponding to Bohier's building on the other bank of the river, to complete
Delorme's 196 ft. gallery over the Cher. If her plan
had been realised it would have made Chenonceaux, as can be seen from Du Cerceau's
engraving, published in 1607, into the largest
building of its century.

tion of the keep, it was then rebuilt
and pulled down again in the early
16C by its new lord Thomas Bohier,
the king's deputy treasurer. Bohier
was interested in art, had spent much
time in Italy, and wanted the château
to be a memorial to himself. His
motto, still visible on the tiles of the
luxurious floor in the vestibule, was
'S'il vient à point me souviendra'
('When it is complete it will be a
reminder of me'). And so in 1513 the
ambitious project began under the
direction of Bohier's wife Catherine
Briçonnet. Even the choice of site is
revealing. Instead of building the château on the terrace of the old castle, by
the keep, it was decided to place it in
the middle of the river on the foundations of the old mill. However, only a
few years after its completion (1521)
the son of the taxgatherer, who had
died in the meantime, had to hand the
château over to the crown to pay off
debts incurred by his father which
had been discovered when the
accounts were checked. Chenonceaux
under Henry II (1547–59), now a
royal château, became the residence of
the beautiful Diana de Poitiers, the
notorious mistress of Francis I and
Henry II. She, hardly less ambitious
than her predecessor, commissioned
Philibert Delorme to build a 197 ft.
bridge over the Cher, and laid out the
larger of the two garden terraces. The
second was laid out under her successor at Chenonceaux, Catherine de
Medici. Gardens of this kind not only
looked attractive but also produced
fruit and vegetables. In 1559 Henry II
was killed at a tournament and Diana,
who so enjoyed her morning bathe in
the Cher, had to put up with being
sent to Chaumont by the rival who so
hated her, Catherine de Medici, the
king's widow. Catherine, possibly the
most ambitious of all the owners of
Chenonceaux, commissioned a design
which, had it been carried out, would
have made the little château de plai-
sance the largest castle in 16C France.

Chenonceaux, château ▷

Chenonceaux, château, detail of portal   *Cheverny, château*

The only part of this grandiose project to be realized was the two-storey gallery over Diana's bridge (*c.* 1580). However, the feasts which now took place in Chenonceaux left nothing to be desired. No opportunity was ignored, and no part of the château was left unused: the gardens, already a popular setting for parties, the canals, from which singing sirens were made to emerge, and the galleries, which in the Renaissance became the centre of court life.

The river was used for pleasure outings, the re-enactment of naval battles and for magnificent firework displays; the gardens for keeping exotic birds, for strolling and even for little hunting parties.

Yet only a generation later the château became a place of mourning. After the murder of Henry III all festivities were discontinued. His widow, who devoted the rest of her life entirely to her sorrow, had her room painted black and decorated with white tears, crowns of thorns, death's heads and bones. Chenonceaux was revitalized in the 18C by the art-loving wife of Farmer-General Dupin, whose salon was adorned by the illustrious figures of Voltaire, Grimm and Marivaux, and who appointed J.J. Rousseau tutor to her children. She enjoyed such universal respect and affection that she was allowed to live peacefully in her château during the Revolution—a rare exception. The most important periods in the history of the château are depicted in the *Musée de Cires* (waxwork museum) located in the garden of the so-called Bâtiment des Dômes.

Chenonceaux has a special place in the history of architecture because of its various innovations. It does not have 'cattle yards' and instead of a spiral staircase has straight flights of

steps and landings in the Italian style. The most revolutionary feature, however, is the much-copied new arrangement of the rooms, which do not lead from one into the next, but into a common vestibule, which made service at receptions considerably easier. The arrangement is identical on each of the residential floors: in the centre and occupying the entire width of the building is the vestibule, with a fine, somewhat unorthodox rib vault, and to the left and right of this are 2 rooms. On the ground floor in the W. is Louis XIII's room and separated from it only by the staircase, that of Francis I. On the E. side is Diana of Poitier's room and the guard room with its magnificent majolica floor, much of which has unfortunately been destroyed; the fine 16C Flanders tapestries are a later addition. On this side two other buildings were added to the basic square: the chapel, which

can be reached from the guard room, and the Green Cabinet, joined to it by a terrace; this room is so called because of its ceiling, which was once covered with green velvet and which is still green today. Adjacent is a tiny library with a fine carved wooden ceiling dating from 1521. The kitchen and other domestic rooms are housed on the lower floor of the old mill; its attic once provided temporary accommodation for a Capuchin nunnery.

The strict symmetry of the N. and W. façades—characteristic of the clarity and balance of the Italian Renaissance—is the striking feature of the exterior. (The S. façade, now hidden by the gallery, used to look exactly the same.) The only concession made to the taste of the earlier period is on the E. side, but even here the buildings protruding from the main section are symmetrical. Equally typical of the Renaissance style of Bohier's building is the handling of ornament: the four round towers on corbels which emphasize the corners and which clearly no longer have a defensive function, and the lavishly decorated balustrades and roof lights, which emphasize rather than blur the articulation of the building.

Cheverny

41 Loir-et-Cher   p.183☐M 3

Hardly any other château on the Loire has a history stretching back as far as that of Cheverny, and there is certainly no other which owes its enlargement to a tragedy of passion ending in a double murder.

The history of the building can be traced back to 1392, when Jean Hurault bought the estate of Cheverny with 'buildings, wine presses and

vineyards'. It is not known what the château looked like at that time. The earliest picture, a drawing by Martel-lange, dates from the early 16C and shows an extensive residential complex with a striking number of round towers with conical roofs. This was built from 1510 by Raoul Hurault, the secretary of Louis XII. In 1564 it passed to his son Philippe, later chancellor to Henry III and Henry IV and first chancellor of the Order of the Holy Spirit. Together with his brother Jacques, the Lord of Vibraye, he further extended the château. In 1577 the king raised Cheverny to the rank of count, and in 1625 to that of marquis.

In 1589 Henri Count Hurault, heir of Cheverny, married the daughter of François Chabot, the Master of the French stables, when she was just 11 years old. While the young count was away in the service of the king his wife

Cheverny, staircase

Cheverny, guard room

looked for and found a substitute. It was the king himself who suggested to the count that his wife might not be faithful. Hurault surprised Françoise with her lover, killed his rival in a rage and forced his wife to choose between poison and the sword. She chose poison. According to an entry in the parish register she was six months pregnant. The king was lenient in his punishment for the double murder, probably because he considered himself partly responsible for it. He banished the count to Cheverny for life. Shortly afterwards the count married Marguerite Gaullard, daughter of the local governor, and he began to build the present château, probably to take his mind off the tragedy. He pulled down most of the old building. The new château was designed by J.Bougier of Blois and building started in 1626. Neither the architect (d. 1632) nor the countess

(d. 1635) nor the count himself (d. 1648) saw the project completed. The much-admired set of buildings was completed under their daughter, Cécilie Elisabeth, Marquise de Montglas.

Until 1755 the château remained in the possession of the Cheverny family, then it had to be sold to count Henry d'Harcourt because of a quarrel over inheritances. He left the château empty and 9 years later sold it to Jean-Nicolas Dufort, the Count of Saint-Leu, who wrote the following description of the building: 'In the outer courtyard, where the walls had been completely pulled down, corn was growing right up to the steps. The paving had been covered with earth and planted. Only five rooms were habitable all told.' But the count remained undaunted and within 12 years he had made the château into 'one of the most comfortable in the

Cheverny, tapestry

country.' There is evidence that within a single year he bought 27 marble fireplaces and 60 copper locks. Because the count lived in the château himself, and was apparently extremely popular in the neighbourhood, the buildings survived the Revolution relatively undamaged. Finally in 1825 the château was acquired by the Marquis de Vibraye, a member of the Hurault family, and so the château came back into the possession of the family.

The *exterior* of the château stands confident in the unruffled dignity of the 'Grand siècle'. It is basically a simple building, symmetrical but never dull; it consists simply of a single two-storey section with a narrow flight of steps in the middle and two massive three-storey pavilions to balance the ends of the building. Because their plan is square they protrude by the width of a window axis on the N. side, and thus form a vestigial courtyard. There used to be a paved cour d'honneur here, framed by a wall with urns and statues at its ends, and enclosed by a moat. Traditional building principles were followed in the design of the façade. It is structured by means of hoizontal lines, broken by busts of emperors on the first floor. The arrangement of the roofs is the most important feature of the design. Each section of the building has a roof of its own, in one of three designs. The central pavilion has a narrow and thus relatively high hipped roof with its long axis cutting though the main axis of the building. The two intermediate sections have hipped roofs with the long axis parallel to the main axis of the house, and the two outer pavilions have vault-like roofs with lanterns, and it is these roofs which give the château its 'à l'impériale' appearance. The carefully designed roof lights further emphasize this aspect of the building. The *interior* has remained largely unchanged. It was an unusual piece of luck that except for short periods the château was always lived in and was never plundered and that the Dufort and Hurault families complemented each other so well in their work on the furnishings. The atmosphere of museum-like sterility which is all too common in other châteaux is thus avoided. The valuable furnishings were brought here over the centuries because the owner of the château felt that they were a necessary part of a living whole, not just furnishings for a museum. The dominant style is that of the Louis XIII period, and no other château shows off the style so completely and with objects in such good condition as at Cheverny.

The central building is the *staircase* which, as at Chenonceaux, is in two sections with vaulted flights on central pillars. The bottoms of the staircase is in the relatively cramped vestibule, hung with tapestries designed by Vernet. The straight flights of steps, the pillars and pilasters are deeply fluted and decorated with garlands of fruit. On the first floor the pilasters are decorated with attributes of war and the arts. The astonishly wide range of motifs reaches its peak in the finely modelled little musketeer with his hat in his hand. On the top floor the pillar frieze is decorated with partridges and snails.

The *dining room* and the *gallery* on the ground floor are among the small number of rooms restored in the 19C. The dining room still has its old beams, although the paintwork has been restored. The panelling, originally painted by J.Mosnier, shows scenes from 'Don Quixote'. The gallery contains valuable portraits of members of the Hurault family. There are two particularly interesting portraits by Clouet and four by Rigaud. The *grand salon* on the ground floor is in Luois-Quatorze style, the wall panelling with grisaille love games is 17C, and the furniture is upholstered with Aubusson material with a pattern of red flowers. Fine portraits by Mignard, Titian and Raphael of Marie Johanne de la Carre

Cheverny, king's room

Saumery, Cosmo de Medici and Jeanne d'Aragon. The *petit salon* also has valuable furniture and an outstanding set of Flemish genre tapestries. On the first floor the guard room and the king's room have survived almost intact.

The *guard room* serves as an antechamber to the king's room and is the largest room in the house, occupying the entire right half of the main building. The most prominent feature is a monumental *fireplace* with Mercury and Venus. In the middle is a painting by J.Mosnier of the death of Adonis, and the sides as well are decorated with scenes from the story of Adonis. On the wall opposite the fireplace is a *tapestry* depicting the abduction of Helen. It was woven as a copy of a painting by F.Franck dating from 1621. The remaining walls are decorated with fine weapons and armour. The ceiling beams are painted with

arabesques, flowers and the coats-of-arms of the Hurault family. A low wainscot runs round the whole room; its panels are outstandingly well painted by J.Mosnier. The panels depict various flowers, carefully painted in cartouches against a landscape background in green grisaille. By each picture is a Latin saying, for example by the blue campanula: 'Though I am small I am the colour of the sky'. These allusions are thought to have been pictorial riddles intended to amuse scholarly visitors. Other panels are decorated with mythological figures personifying muses, arts and gods, and they too are related to the symbolism of the flowers. This kind of precious game was taken so seriously in the 18C that it has a literature of its own.

The *king's room* was intended for visits from the king or other high-ranking guests. There is no part of the room which is not decorated with carved, painted or woven figures in the haraldic blue, gold and red of the host. Everything is linked, both in design and in symbolic content, down to the smallest detail. The artist responsible for this room was the painter J.Mosnier, who showed absolute mastery in his use of pastel shades of white, grey and blue to set off the three heraldic colours. The rectangular coffered ceiling, the fireplace picture and the area above the door tell the story of Perseus and Andromeda in numerous individual scenes (final picture over the fireplace). Even more successful are the 30 *wainscot panels*, also by J.Mosnier. They represent the amorous adventures of Theagenes and Charikleia from the Greek novel 'Aithiopika' by Heliodor of Emesa (3C AD). This romantic novel had been discovered by courtly society in the 16C and had been a powerful influence on the development of the baroque love novel. The choice of this material for the decoration of the king's room is an indication of the Count of Hurault's strong artistic sense. The painter's art is equalled by the lavish tapestries, made in Paris *c.* 1640. The six tapestries show scenes from the Odyssey and were woven after pictures by S.Vouet. In the midst of all this splendour is the *state bed*, also called the 'king's bed'; its canopy and cover are in Persian silk embroidered with pearls. This is not the original bed, but an accurate copy. The chapel in the central pavilion pales in contrast with all this splendour. It has undecorated rib vaulting. The only decoration of any importance is a stained-glass window from the building period representing Jacques Hurault. The *park* is now only a shadow of its former splendour. The once splendid flower beds have disappeared, as have the statues in the manner of Versailles and the canal running though the park. The most important outbuilding to survive is an 18C orangery, set precisely on the central axis of the

château. There is a *hunting museum* in part of the former domestic buildings, with a collection of trophies (*c.* 2,500 sets of antlers); the 80 hounds belonging to the lord of the château (the pack has been in existence since 1825), housed in another of the outbuildings, ensure that it is never too quiet around the Château de Cheverny.

Chinon
37 Indre-et-Loire   p.136□H 5

Archaeological finds confirm that Chinon is one of the oldest settlements in France. There was an oppidum here in Celtic times, and a castrum under the Romans. Clovis (481–511), the founder of the Frankish kingdom, made *Caino* into one of the most important fortresses in his empire, and in the 10&11C the counts of Blois and Anjou fought over this strategically vital rocky spur on the Vienne, and in the 12&13C even the kings of France and England were in dispute over it. New lords added new buildings, and so over 5 centuries the massive fortress, 1312 ft. long by 229 ft. wide, came into being; the remains are still to be seen today, and are a textbook example of medieval defensive architecture.

The most important parts of the castle, or to be more accurate the three castles, date from the 12&13C. The counts of Blois, lords of Chinon until 1044, did build a castle in the 10C, but it was not effectively fortified until the time of Henry of Anjou. He, as Henry II of England, secured the entrance with a bulwark, the Fort St-Georges, so called because of its chapel dedicated to the patron saint of England, of which only the crypt has survived. The 590 ft. long and 262 ft. wide ring wall around the so-called middle castle, the central part of the building, also dates from the 12&13C. In the 14&15C work was confined lar-

Chinon, Fort St-Georges clock tower ▷

gely to improvements and rebuilding of the residential sections. From 1205 the château was the residence of the kings of France. After a siege lasting almost a year Philippe Auguste reconquered the fortress for France, and in the Hundred Years War (1339–1453) it was to be one of the last bases of the French crown. In 1428 Charles VII summoned the States General to Chinon and on March 9 1429 he received the Maid of Orléans in the great hall of the château. In 1633 the building passed to Cardinal Richelieu, who deliberately allowed it to fall into disrepair, so that his nearby Château Richelieu would shine the more brightly. It was not until the 19C, when the walls threatened to collapse on to the town, that Prosper Mérimée intervened and the reinforcement of the walls began.

Château: The 10–15C buildings consist of three fortresses separated from each other by deep ditches: Fort Saint-Georges in the E., the Château du Milieu in the middle and the Château du Coudray in the W. The main entrance is via the *Fort St-Georges*, the latest of the three fortresses, which was later removed; a bridge then leads to the clock tower 115 ft. high but only 16 ft. wide, which contains a somewhat uninspiring Joan of Arc museum. This tower with an old clock and a bell is the gateway to the *Château du Milieu*, which contains the late 15C Argenton tower, semicircular on the outside but straight on the inside and used as a prison, the likewise semicircular Dog Tower, and opposite, on the other side of the curtain wall, the royal apartments. All that has survived of these are the rooms on the ground floor, which now house Gallo-Roman sculpture, tapestries, paintings and a statue of Joan of

Chinon, château

Arc by Dubois, and also a few steps and the W. gable with the fireplace from the great hall. It is separated from the *Château du Coudray* by a deep ditch; this too is enclosed by a curtain wall reinforced with towers, parts of which date from the 10C. The round keep or Coudray tower was built in the 13C by Philippe Auguste and was used as a residence tower but also as a prison. Joan of Arc was accommodated here, but 100 years earlier it housed templars, members of the knightly Order founded in 1119

Chinon, château A Château du Coudray **B** Château du Milieu **C** Fort St-Georges **1** clock tower **2** Argenton tower **3** dog tower **4** royal chambers **5** Coudray tower

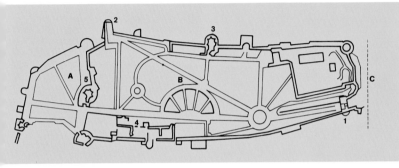

Chinon, old town

to protect pilgrims to Jerusalem.

St-Etienne: This five-bayed single-aisled church with a choir and two bays (1477–83) has an impressive double portal in the Flamboyant style.

St-Maurice (below the château): The church has a fine nave in the Plantagenet style lavishly decorated with figures and a bell tower with Romanesque stained glass and a 15C stone spire. In the 12C it was extended by the addition of a N. choir chapel, in the 14C by a S. choir chapel and in the 16C by a S. aisle.

St-Mexme: In 1817 the crossing tower collapsed, destroying the 12C transept and choir, and now only the 10C nave remains; during the Revolution it was used as a saltpetre factory and it later became a school. The

vestibule and N. tower are 11C and the S. tower (reconstruction) is 15C.

St-Radegonde chapel: This chapel cut in the rock dates from the 6C, although it has been much altered between the 12C and the present day. A 12C fresco of a hunting scene was discovered in 1964.

Old Town: The narrow streets and twisty alleyways have survived in remarkably good condition and provide a very charming walk. At the centre of life in the Middle Ages was the *Grand Carroi*, the most picturesque part of the whole town, with 11C half-timbered and brick buildings and smart 15C houses with protruding upper storeys, gables and turrets. The *Rue Voltaire* and its continuation, the *Rue J.-J. Rousseau* also give a most pleasing impression of old Chinon.

Also worth seeing: *Maison des Etats Généraux*, a fine patrician house with corner turrets, the meeting place of the States General summoned by Charles VII in 1427&8. In the fine chambre d'honneur on the first floor is a portrait by Delacroix honouring the town's famous son Rabelais, on the second floor is a kind of local history museum with Gothic chests etc. *Raidillon du Pitoche*, a little stairway leading from St-Mexme to the St-Radegonde chapel past cliff dwellings.

Environs: Avoine (8 km. NW) 15C *château*.
Avon-les Roches (20 km. E.): *Church* with 12C Romanesque porch and Romanesque font and stoup. 2 km. NE: Renaissance façade of the *collegiate church of Roches-Tranchelion*, founded in 1527 but now in a poor state of repair.
Coudray-Montpensier, Le (9 km. SW): *Château* surrounded by deep ramparts with wall passage, a large rectangular tower and 2 fine cylindrical towers, acquired in 1927 by the

Chinon, St-Etienne, portal

Belgian dramatist Maurice Maeterlinck and restored by him.

Cravant-les Côteaux 8 km. E.): Wine-growing village. 1 km. N. in the old part is a former *church*, the side walls of which date from the early 10C. It now houses an *archaeological museum*, which exhibits 2 Merovingian columns, sarcophaguses from Touraine etc.

Devinière,La (7 km. SW): *Rabelais museum.* This is the house in which the greatest French satirist and famous Renaissance writer, also a doctor and professor of anatomy, (1494–1553) grew up. The heroes of his novels, Gargantua and Pantagruel, still live in the imagination of the French people.

Panzoult (12 km. E): Old *church* with a 10C façade and a 12C choir in the Plantagenet style. Numerous *caves* in the rock, of which one is said to be the famous grotto of the Sybil of Panzoult from Rabelais' 'Gargantua and Pantagruel'.

Rivau, Le (10 km. SE): 13C *château*, rebuilt in the 15C. Medieval buildings with residence in Renaissance style. Furniture Gothic and Renaissance.

Saint-Louand (2 km. NW): Small *pilgrimage chapel* with a vault containing the mortal remains of St.Louand and three of his pupils in 4 old sarcophaguses. The saint had come to found a small abbey (7C), of which the Romanesque crypt has survived.

Seuilly (8 km. SW): Ruins of the *Benedictine abbey* in which Rabelais was educated. Mentioned in his novels.

Cinq-Mars-la-Pile

37 Indre-et-Loire   p.136☐I 4

Village at the confluence of the Loire

and the Cher with ruins of an old feudal château. When its owner Henri Coeffier de Ruzé, Marquis de Cinq-Mars and favourite of Louis XIII, was accused of conspiracy and executed, Cardinal Richelieu took the opportunity to destroy the castle (like that of Champigny-sur-Veude).

Château: 2 12&13C cylindrical towers (windows not pierced until the 15C) and two vaulted rooms have survived of the former square fortress with 4 towers. The extremely large moats are a striking feature.

Church: 10&12C Romanesque building with 15C stone spire.

Environs: Pile Romaine (so-called Roman column): 0.5 km. outside the village is a curious object, a massive tower 16 ft. thick at the base and 65 ft. high; its date and function are unknown.
Point-de-Bresme (3 km. N.): *Château d'Andigny*. Numerous *caves* at the foot of the mound.

Cléry-Saint-André

45 Loiret   p.138☐N 2

Basilica of Notre-Dame-de-Cléry: This church was originally a small chapel in which peasants set up a statue of Mary *c.* 1280. Because the statue was said to have miraculous powers, a popular pilgrimage developed, and a larger church was built. In 1428 however the English leader Salisbury destroyed the church on his march to Orléans. Charles VII and Dunois, Joan of Arc's comrade in arms contributed to the rebuilding of the church. The strongest supporter of the rebuilding, started in 1449, was Louis XI, who at the siege of Dieppe in 1443 had sworn to sacrifice his weight in silver to the Madonna of Cléry if he won. Even after his coronation he did all he could to encourage the church and made no important decisions without first praying there. At his own request he was buried in the church in 1483, in a tomb designed and commissioned by himself (he had even tried it out).
Building: The seven-bayed basilica has a transept which does not protrude, and a two-bayed polygonal choir with ambulatory. The tower on the N. side was built in the early 14C and surprisingly not destroyed by the English. The church was built from 1449 by P.Chauvin, but not continued until 1460 by P.Le Paige, who completed the building in 1485. There is no triforium between the arches and the windows and this gives the interior breadth, but the missing capitals and plain furnishings give a feeling of austerity. It may be that the church looked different with its original tapestries and stained-glass windows. Only the window on the axis of the choir still has the original glass, as well as the Flamboyant tracery. All the windows of the church used to give the same lighting effect as this one.
Tomb of Louis XI: The king's splendid tomb is under the E. arch on the N. side of the nave. Its oblique position is explained by the fact that it was originally oriented towards the Mary altar with the miraculous image. The memorial consists of a marble slab resting on four columns, on which a life-size statue of the king kneels in prayer to the Madonna. The corners of the marble slab are decorated with 4 putti. The marble statue is the work of the sculptor M.Bourdin of Orléans, who completed it in 1622 to replace the original bronze statue melted down by the Huguenots in 1562. Even though La Fontaine thought that 'the statue looks like a rogue, but then the king probably had such qualities too', the sculpture is nevertheless very impressive.
Louis XI vault: The bones of Louis XI and his queen Charlotte of Savoy are in their own vault by the tomb. Body and skull were not buried

Cléry-Saint-André, basilica, portal ▷

*Cléry-St-André,
Notre-Dame-de-Cléry*

Cormery, abbey church

together. The skulls were removed, embalmed and are kept in a glass shrine. The black mourning strips on the walls bore the arms of the dead, and their height shows the high rank of the deceased. Beside the king Tanguy du Châtel is buried; he was struck by a cannonball in 1477 at the siege of Bouchain, while watching the fighting with Louis XI. His last wish was to be buried before an image of the Madonna. The king fulfilled the request by having him buried beside his own tomb. The heart of Charles VIII is buried on the right of the tomb.

Miraculous image: The enthroned Madonna and Child are carved in oak, and are the central feature of the high altar built in the 19C. It cannot be ascertained whether the sculpture is the 12C or 13C original or a new version made in the 16C.

Chapel of St-Jean: Built in the right aisle from 1464–8 as a grave chapel for the Dunois family. The count was the natural son of Louis d'Orléans and the companion at arms of Joan of Arc. The chapel was built by Simon du Val, who felt compelled to include a buttress supporting the nave in his building. Thus the right-hand side of the vault has 3 and 12 bays, and the apex runs in a zig-zag.

Chapel of St.James: Built from 1515–18 by church deacon Gilles de Pontbriant and his brother François, the chamberlain of Francis I. The Renaissance chapel is decorated with an extravagant rib vault. Knots, ropes, pilgrims' staves and beggars' sacks alternate with ermine spots (from the arms of Anne of Britanny). The pilgrims' symbols are a reminder that the chapel was visited by pilgrims on their way to Santiago de Compos-

Notre-Dame-de-Cléry, choir stalls

tella in Spain. The two keystones in the vaults bear the coat-of-arms of the alliance between France and Brittany and the arms of the Pontbriant family. The *grave niches* in the chapel are decorated with carved canopies. The carved statues of St.James dressed as a pilgrim (16C) and St.Sebastian (17C) are particularly striking. The stone Virgin Mary dates from the 17C.

Choir: The central window in the clerestory was endowed by Henry III. Its upper part shows the miracle of Pentecost and the lower part shows Henry III with the Evangelists founding the Order of the Holy Spirit. All the other stained glass was destroyed by the Huguenots. The *choir stalls* were endowed by Henry II, and are lavishly carved.

The ends of the second row on the right carry the initials of the founder and his lover, Diana de Poitiers. In the second bay of the ambulatory is a magnificent door in the Flamboyant style, on the right-hand side. It used to lead to a grave chapel, now used as a sacristy.

Cormery
37 Indre-et-Loire   p.136☐K 4

The core of this little village on the left bank of the Indre was a Benedictine abbey founded in the 8C by Ithier, abbot of St-Martin in Tours and extended by his famous successor Alcuin. It was in existence until the time of the Revolution. Another abbot, Pierre Berthelot, fortified the little town in 1450; two towers and other fragments have survived. The abbey had its own walls, as can still be seen from the 15C St-Jean tower.

Abbey: Very little has survived. The 11C bell tower has survived from the church. It has unusual scale and lozenge decoration, Romanesque bas-reliefs on the W. façade and a choir chapel. Surviving residential buildings are the prior's house (15C), the abbot's house and the large former refectory (a very fine room 105 ft. long with two aisles and six bays and pointed vaulting), the kitchens and cellars and a few arches from the 14&15C cloister.

Parish church of Notre-Dame de Fougeray: An interesting 12C building with one aisle with a crossing tower above a squinch dome; its effect is drawn largely from the majestic apse with three radiating chapels. In the interior there is a 13C fresco on the N. wall and a large 12C font decorated with strange masks.
The cemetery has a 12C altar and a lantern of the dead.

Cunault
49 Maine-et-Loire   p.136☐G 4

Cunault grew up around a monastery; it was founded in 857 by monks who had been driven by the Normans from the island of Noirmoutier with the corpse of St.Philibert. 15 years later however they had to leave Cunault and fly further, to Burgundy, where the saint was finally laid to rest in St-Philibert-de-Tournus. Although the monks took the coffin with them, several valuable relics remained in Cunault (a small bottle of dried milk from the Virgin's breast and her wedding ring), and they attracted many pilgrims. And so in the middle of the 11C a pilgrimage church was built, a fine building which had an ignominious fate in store in the age of enlightenment: after the dissolution of the priory in 1741 it was split into two by a wall and the choir allotted to

Cunault, Notre-Dame, portal ▷

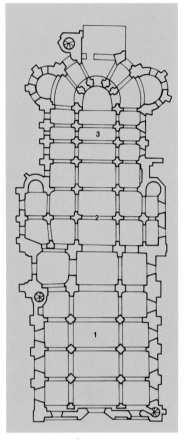

Cunault, Notre-Dame pilgrimage church
The ground plan shows a hall with nave and three aisles (**1**) with a pseudo-transept (**2**) and a long choir with ambulatory and semicircular apse (**3**) with radiating chapels

a private individual as a barn. The nave was used for worship by the parish, as the church had collapsed in a hurricane in 1754. About the middle of the 19C the building became public property and was thoroughly restored on the instructions of the writer Prosper Mérimée.

Pilgrimage church of Notre-Dame: This hall church is character-

Cunault, Notre-Dame

ized by a long semicircular choir, a nave and two aisles and a false transept. It is one of the most remarkable buildings on the Loire. The old bell tower with its ornate articulation is a striking feature: it has round arches in the upper section and massive blind arches in the lower part with two impressive capitals showing the Annunciation and a Temptation scene. Another fine feature is the tympanum above the main entrance in the W. façade dating from *c.* 1200 and representing Mary with the infant Jesus, framed by angels on banks of clouds swinging censers.

In the *interior* there are different vaults corresponding to the various building periods: in the bell tower a domical vault, in the nave a tunnel vault, in the aisles groin vaulting, and Angevin vaulting in the last three bays, which were obviously added at a later date. The most impressive

Cunault, Notre-Dame

Cunault, reliquary shrine

feature of all of the interior, 236 ft. long, 62 ft. wide and 66 ft. high and articulated with massively tall clustered pillars, is its overwhelming perspective, with an abundance of widely differing *capitals* (223 in all, which present a wonderful picture of the development of Romanesque art in the 12C. The motifs decorating these capitals are by no means all biblical. There are also animal pictures with moral implications, scenes of knights and wars, some of which are based on the Chansons de Geste and show heroic deeds in the struggle with the Saracens in Spain. The wall paintings, which have unfortunately survived only as fragments, are also of interest; they were a medieval device used to emphasize the articulation of the building.

Also of interest: a 16C Pietà, a 13C carved reliquary shrine, a wooden sta-

tue of St.Catherine (15C) and 14C recumbent figure.

Also worth seeing: In front of the church are a fine Francis I *house* (1515–47) and a modern *château* with a 17C portal.

Environs: Gennes (3 km. NW): Small market town with two churches: *St-Vétérin*, on the right of the valley, 11C (only evidence brickwork on the S. façade of the bell tower) rebuilt in the second half of the 12C (transept, choir and apse) and in the 13&14C; *St-Eusèbe*, on the other side of the valley, largely 11C (choir, transept and bell tower 12C, spire 15C, the wall adjacent to the aisle is pre-Romanesque and dates from *c.* 1000). Nearby are 4 *dolmens* and 2 *menhirs*, including one 36 ft. long, 13 ft. wide and 10 ft. high.

Durtal
49 Maine-et-Loire   p.136☐G 2

Château: The little town grew up around this château, built in the mid 11C high on a hill on the right bank of the Loire by Geoffroy Martel, Count of Anjou. For a time it was in the hands of the La Rochefoucauld family and is now used as a hospital. 2 imposing towers with machicolations and fragments of the rampart

which used to join them remain of the massive old fortress. The S. wing and the W. pavilion were added under Henry IV and Louis XIII.
There are still some faience vessels decorated with vignettes in the hospital pharmacy, and the old guardroom and vaulted cellars have survived in the basement.
The *Porte Verron*, a 15C gate, leads along the old town wall into the little town, which still has a 14C bridge.

Environs: Cheffes (30 km. W.) on the right bank of the Sarthe: *Church* with 12C choir and octagonal crossing tower. Frescos in the apse.
Daumeray (10 km. NW): Renovated Romanesque *church*. Remains of the *St-Martin priory*.
Huillé (7.5 km. SW): Fine *Renaissance house*. 17C *château*.
Seiches-sur-le-Loir (20 km. SW): Partly 13C *church* with windows dating from 1509 and a 14C stone Pietà. 3 km. N. of Seiches-sur-le-Loir remains of the magnificent late 15C **Château du Verger**: 4 round towers (2 with machicolations), guardrooms,

stables and moats. Nearby ruined *Ste-Croix priory*.

Villevêque (26 km. SW) 15–19C *château* of the bishops of Angers.

Ferté-Saint-Aubin, La

45 Loiret p.138□N 2

Little old town on the left bank of the Cosson with a 12&16C *church* (St-Aubin).

Château: The broad moats used to be fed by the Cosson. The present château dates largely from the 17C, although many improvements were made in the 19C. It was designed by F.Mansart. The pavilion in the domestic quarters was added in the 18C under Louis XV (1715–74).

Fontevraud-l'Abbaye

45 Loiret p.138□N 2

Abbey: This is one of the great attractions of Anjou; it was founded in 1099 by Robert d'Abrissel, a famous preacher, who was so popular that he decided to give up his hermit's life and found a home for his congregation, and so this extraordinary monastery came into being. It was an enormous complex, divided into a nunnery and a monastery (the latter no longer exists), a leper colony, a hospital for incurables and a home for sinners, or fallen women, as we might say today (this also no longer exists). It was led by a woman as the representative of Mary, following Christ's words on the Cross 'Son, behold your mother'). Shortly after its foundation the abbey acquired wealthy patrons, above all the counts of Anjou, later kings of England, who chose it as their burial place; the abbey thus became increasingly devoted to the nobility. The Order itself, which followed the Rule of St.Benedict, was known throughout the country. It started to become rather slack, however, and so three rigorous abbesses from the Bourbon

Fontevraud, Romanesque monastery kitchen

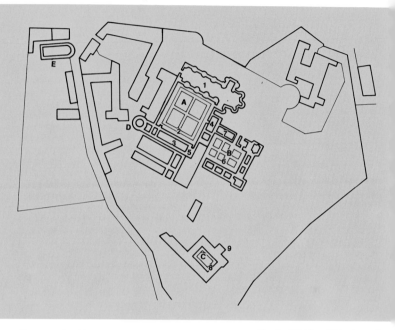

Fontevraud, abbey **A** convent **B** St-Benoît hospice for incurables **C** lepers' courtyard **D** monastery kitchen **E** St-Michel without the gates **1** abbey church **2** Mary cloister **3** refectory **4** chapterhouse **5** Renaissance steps **6** cloister court **7** Benedict chapel **8** cloister court **9** Lazarus chapel

Tomb of Richard Lionheart ▷

royal family, Renée (1491–1534), Louise (1534–75) and Eléonore (1575–1611) carried out sweeping reforms. This reorganisation also led to a great deal of rebuilding. The abbey lost its open social character, and its institutions for the sick were only used for members of the monastic community. The rich abbey went through a difficult period at the time of the Revolution: it was plundered, pillaged and wrecked, and many of the noble nuns were executed. The buildings were altered in revolutionary style in 1804 (a typical example of this is the low entrance portal in the W. walk of the cloister, with columns in the Egytian style) and equipped as a prison under Napoleon. This unworthy situation persisted until 1963, when restoration work began.

Abbey church: One of the most impressive Romanesque churches in Anjou. After being secularized and used as a prison for more than a century, it has gradually been restored to its original character. The 276 ft. long building with a single aisle 52 ft. wide and a 131 ft. transept was built in the first half of the 12C. The use of the round arch and the lavishly decorated capitals are particularly impressive in the first section of the basilican ambulatory with radiating chapels and massive columned arches, in the transept, built a few years later but already in a slightly different style, and in the four-bayed nave with its enormous domes.

The main attraction however is the so-called *royal cemetery*, or more correctly, what remained of it after the

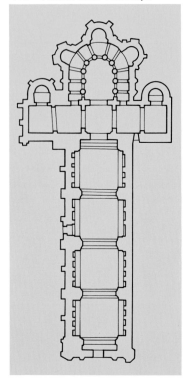

Fontevraud, abbey church

Fontevraud, abbey church The ground plan shows the influence of SW French Romanesque (Périgord, Angoumois, Saintonge). The single aisle with 4 domes is a typical feature

Revolution: three painted tufa grave slabs, larger-than-life representations of Henry II (1154–89), the first Count of Anjou, who came to the English throne by dint of skilful marital policy and founded the English house of Plantagenet, his queen, Eleanor of Aquitaine (who spent the last years of her life in Fontevraud and died here in 1204) and their son, the legendary Richard the Lionheart. The fourth figure, later than the other three and made of wood, cannot be identified with any certainty. It seems probable that it is Isabella of Angoulême, the third wife of the unhappy King John Lackland, the second son of Henry and Eleanor.

The great cloister of the *convent* is adjacent to the S. but very little has survived of the original building. The massive nine-bayed rib vault in the refectory in the S. wing was added in 1515, and the E. wing with chapter-house, Renaissance staircase and dormitory in the upper storey, was built in the mid 16C under Louise de Bourbon. The notable feature here is the tent-like rib vault on decorative columns in the two-aisled chapterhouse. The E. wing of the convent leads into the former *St-Benoît hospital for incurables*, like the other buildings set around a cloistered courtyard of which only the single-aisled Benedict chapel (*c.* 1180) has survived from the period of building.

A little further away is *St-Lazare*, the

Fontevraud, abbey cloister

Fontevraud, abbey church

former leper house, which like the other parts of Fontevraud originally had its own church, chapterhouse and refectory, but only the 12C chapel has survived. The rest of the buildings date largely from the turn of the 16&17C.

The most famous of all the abbey buildings however is the *monastery kitchen*, a most unusual construction; it is octagonal, with radiating apses and a pyramidal stone roof. For a long time no-one could work out what its function had been, but finally old engravings enabled it to be identified and restored. The apse-like sections were fireplaces with conical roofs and smoke flues; smoke and other fumes also escaped through chimneys on the edge of the pyramidal roof and into the hollow pyramid above the main room. Thus what was originally thought to be the funerary chapel of

the Plantagenets was revealed as an ingeniously designed kitchen, which in the Middle Ages provided meals, mainly of meat and fish, for a good 500 people; the main room was used for preparation of the food.

St-Michel parish church (almost directly in front of the abbey gates): By 1170 there were so many people living around the abbey that Abbess Audebruge built a single-aisled church with lavish architectural ornament and a fine Angevin vault. The interior was also not skimped. The church has valuable altars, numerous paintings, reliquaries and fine wooden statues, including a 15C figure of Christ.

St-Catherine chapel (on the right of the avenue of limes starting at the main entrance to the church): This

Fontgombault, detail of portal

early-13C building was once a cemetery chapel.

Fontgombault
36 Indre   p.136□L 7

This little village on the right bank of the Creuse, which here thrusts between picturesque chalk cliffs, was named after a hermitage founded by a spring by a hermit known as Gombault and is famous for its Benedictine abbey, built in the late 11C by Pierre de l'Etoile (Petrus a Stella) and occupied by monks again since 1948.

Monastery church: Built 1091–1141, a massive building 269 ft. long, 59 ft. high, 59 ft. wide and with a 98 ft. transept, this is one of the most beautiful Romanesque churches in central France. The nave and façade with three round-arched portals, fine carvings and the lion supporting the columns, are largely the work of 19C restorers, who found only ruins on the site. The transept and choir have survived intact, however, and show wonderful purity and harmony of line.
The present *monastery* consists of a 15C building with a machicolated round corner tower at the rear and a much-rebuilt cloister with the old chapterhouse, refectory and a vaulted room (the last two 15C) grouped around it.

Caves (on the right bank of the Creuse): probably once used by hermits.

Environs: Lurais (4.5 km. N.): Romanesque *church*, with two Flamboyant chapels. Remains of a medieval *château*, altered in the 16C. 17C *château*.
Bénavant (3 km. SE): ruined *Château Rochefort*.
Mont-la-Chapelle (5.5 km. SE): remains of a 13&16C *priory*.

Fougères-sur-Bièvre
41 Loir-et-Cher   p.138□M 3

This château in the middle of the village is surprising at first; it has none of the Renaissance excess of Chambord or the severe classicism of Cheverny, but the visitor has a sense of the medieval period, when buildings were designed without an eye for artistic effect.
The château dates from the 11C, but only parts of a defensive tower have survived from then. In the 14C the Black Prince, the son of Edward III, took the king of France prisoner at the battle of Poitiers, then had him taken to London, and ordered that all the fortresses in the area were to be razed. In Fougères only the square keep survived. A little later the château came

Fougères-sur-Bièvre, château, portal decoration

Fougères-sur-Bièvre, courtyard

to Jean de Refuge by marriage. His son Pierre was Louis XI's minister of finance, and in 1470 the king gave him permission to rebuild and fortify the château. Pierre de Refuge did not follow the example set by others of his period, who had replaced older castles with rather more comfortable châteaux. He built a veritable fortress, including the square 11C keep, and naturally there were a moat, a drawbridge, embrasures, machicolations and all the other paraphernalia associated with a castle. Refuge died without issue, and the castle passed to his brother-in-law Jean Villebresme, who found the château too gloomy and fortress-like. He replaced the embrasures with windows, and added roof lights. He too died without issue, and in 1686 the castle was bought by the Marquis d'Effiat, but its history was not destined to become any more

peaceful. It changed hands frequently; a spinning mill was established after the Revolution, and then it became accommodation for workers on the land until it was finally acquired by the state in 1932.

The *buildings* are a textbook example of a rural medieval castle. There is no sense of comfort or even the desire to impress, but much more of the need to protect family, crops and stores from attackers. The multiple function of the building as the centre of the owner's farming activities, his home and his fortress evolved quite naturally from this need. The buildings around the farm courtyard in front of the château proper have disappeared now, and so have the moats and drawbridge, but the entrance façade has survived in its original form. It consists of the 11C keep and a thick round tower. The portal leading to the courtyard has slender integrated round towers on either side. One of these towers contains a spiral staircase, and both have a wall passage with machicolations. The actual residential buildings are on the S. side of the *courtyard*, which seems surprisingly domesticated. There is a shallow-arched gallery with unexpectedly elaborate pillars and cornices. The portals are decorated with ogee arches and the roof lights with finials and coats-of-arms. This is all the more astonishing when one remembers that the whole of this part of the building came into being without an overall plan. There is no section which pulls the design together, no uniform roof and not a single hint of symmetry. Everything seems to have been put together to fulfil particular needs, with the result that walls of different types and roofs of differing heights are juxtaposed, and it is just this which gives this late medieval castle its appeal.

Inside, unfortunately, none of the furniture has survived. The only interesting features are the large carved *fireplaces* and a wooden ceiling in the form of an inverted ship's keel.

Fougères-sur-Bièvre, château

Germigny-des-Prés
45 Loiret   p.138□O/P 2

Church: The unassuming exterior of
this building gives away nothing of
either its history or the treasure which
it contains, and yet it is a major work

of Western architecture. The church
was founded *c.* 800 by Bishop Theodulf, abbot of Saint-Benoît-sur-
Loire, who built a private chapel and
a house here, 5 km. from his monastery. The chapel was consecrated in
806. When Theodulf died in 818 the
building began to fall into disrepair
and it was badly damaged by the Normans in the second half of the 9C. As
time passed the house disappeared
completely, and the church was
extended in the 15C by the building
of a nave and some smaller additions.
Building: Bishop Theodulf's chapel
was a square, centrally-planned
building, with sides just over 34 ft.
long. Originally each side had a horse-
shoe-shaped apse, and on the E.
side there were two additional small
side apses; their foundations were
excavated in 1930. The W. apse made
way for the 15C nave. Four square
pillars form a central area crowned

with a dome set on arches. The side areas have tunnel vaults, and the corners have domes and groin vaulting. This subdivision meant that there was no impression of a single large space, but rather one of a series of individual cells. The model for this building is the Byzantine cross-in-square design, familiar to Theodulf from his home in Spain. Tradition maintains that Theodulf intended the building as an imitation of Charlemagne's palatinate chapel in Aix-la-Chapelle; the bishop was adviser to Charlemagne. It is reported that Theodulf did everything he could to outdo the furnishings of the chapel in Aix, hence the lavish standards which once prevailed here. It is said there used to be a marble floor, stucco and mosaics, but all of this seemed to have disappeared, until in 1840 some children were found playing with pieces of coloured glass. Research then led to the discovery of the only surviving Carolingian mosaic.

Mosaic: This was discovered under several thick layers of plaster in the vaults of the E. apse and consists of 130,000 coloured cubes of glass in gold, silver, blue, green and red. It represents the Arc of the Covenant, watched over by 2 cherubim. 2 large archangels, whose figures are adapted to the curve of the vault, are also pointing to the Arc of the Covenant, and between them the hand of God appears through the clouds. The Latin inscription defines the theme and also invites the visitor to include Theodulf in his prayers. It is possible that the mosaic, by no means the only one originally in the church, was created by an artist from Ravenna. In the 19C mosaics were discovered above the arch of the main apse, the tunnel vault in front of the apse and in the dome, but the fragments were not

Germigny-des-Prés, church, interior

Germigny-des-Prés, church

restored and only water-colour copies survive. Their most striking feature is that they consist only of cherubim and ornaments. This can be explained by the philosophy of Theodulf, who in his book 'Libri Carolini' denounced the Byzantine cult of images and demanded that there should be no pictorial representations of Christ or the saints. It thus makes sense that in his own chapel he placed the Arc of the Covenant at the most important point, rather than a Majestas Domini. This background adds to the chapel's significance as a major phenomenon in the history of art.

Gien

45 Loiret   p.138☐P/Q 2

The most easterly of the Loire châteauteau towns was built for the most part by Countess Anne de Beaujeu, the eldest daughter of King Louis XI. Her father said of her: 'She is the least mad of all the women in France, I know none saner'. It was perhaps for this reason that he made her a present of the little town, together with a small earlier château. The countess, who for a time was regent for her brother Charles VIII (he being only 13 at the time of his father's death) commissioned new fortifications for the town, built the present château and the arched bridge over the Loire, and founded a monastery. 2 years later Anne of Austria, Mazarin and the young Louis XIV took refuge here when they had to flee from Paris at the time of the Fronde.

Ste-Jeanne-d'Arc: A church was built in the late 15C by Countess Anne of Beaujeu, but only the tower has survived of this building. The

Germigny-des-Prés, mosaic in the church

church itself was rebuilt after the war as a skeleton concrete building clad in brick, and is considered one of the few successful post-war ecclesiastical buildings. The stained glass, which tones precisely with the colour of the bricks, is by M.Ingrand. The church itself is by the architect A.Gélis. The new building was dedicated to Joan of Arc because she spent a lot of time in Gien, and set off from here with Charles VII for his coronation in Reims in 1429. Interesting interior details are a Way of the Cross in Gien faience and the terracotta capitals depicting scenes from the life of Joan of Arc.

Château: This somewhat irregular late 15C building was also badly damaged in 1940, but has been restored in its original form. Its red brick walls are decorated with dark brick lozenges, the corners of the building and window reveals are in ashlar. Since 1953 the building has housed

Gien, hunting museum, detail from a tapestry ▷

Gien, hunting museum, detail from a tapestry

Gien, château

the *Musée International de la Chasse.* The collections on hunting and falconry are unique in many respects. Weapons and mementoes, paintings and engravings explain the history of the hunt, over 500 hunting trophies give an impression of the wide range of game, and there is a collection which probably is unique in the world of buttons with hunting motifs (the oldest dating from the time of Louis XIV). The *great hall* has impressive chestnut beams and contains an interesting collection of paintings by F.Desportes (1661–1743), Louis XIV's court animal painter.

Environs: Château de la Bussière (12 km. NE): This 16C building was the first stage on the Jacques Coeur route, which used to lead along a chain of châteaux and houses to Bourges. The building, which was partly rebuilt after the Wars of Religion, was provided with its surrounding lake by Louis XIV, and Le Nôtre laid out the park. The château now houses an *international fishery museum* and a notable art and craft collection. There is anything and everything with a fishy motif, from an Iranian jug decorated with carp to plates from China, and in the kitchen there are fish kettles, fish plates and fish-shaped moulds.

Grand-Pressigny, Le
37 Indre-et-Loire   p.136☐K 6

This tiny market town of just under 1500 inhabitants at the confluence of the Claise and the Egronne stands on a site rich in history. Excavations in 1862 revealed that it was one of the most important centres of prehistoric flint working. The flint is found in yellow clods and is ideally suited for

Grand-Pressigny, general view

shaping; it was mined in the Stone Age, above all in the New Stone Age, on an almost industrial scale and exported, usually in the form of blades up to 15 inches long, throughout Europe, and even to Africa. Finds from this period are exhibited in the extraordinarily interesting *Musée préhistorique* in the Renaissance building of the château.

Château: Above the village on a hill to the N. are the ruins of the old castle, a medieval fortress extended *c.* 1550 by Honorat II of Savoy, Marquis de Villars and Baron de Pressigny, as an elegant residence in Italian Renaissance style. It has massive castle walls, with several 14C towers, a huge, unusual octagonal tower with machicolations and a dome (the Tour Vironne) and the oldest part, a particularly fine square 12C keep 111 ft. high and with 15C machi-

colations. The Renaissance building, the so-called Château neuf, set between two courtyards, has a splendid gallery on the ground floor; it has very fine groin vaulting and is now used as a museum.

Musée préhistorique (in the Château neuf): The museum is arranged chronologically and shows techniques for splitting stone and the most important stone tools from the Old and Middle Stone Ages, and in very large quantities indeed from the New Stone Age, and also bones, and sandstone and flint polishing tools.
There are also pieces of equipment and craft objects from the New Stone Age which give an insight into the development of social life.

Church: Rebuilt and extended in the 15&16C, and dating from the 12C. In the present sacristy, a former chapel, there are wall paintings attributed to C.Dubey, Louis XIII's court painter.

Environs: Betz-le-Château (15 km. NE): Remains of an enormous 14C *fortress. Church* with a 12C choir.
Celle-Guénand,La (8.5 km. NE): Old *church* with a simple façade dating from the first half of the 12C, and an interesting 11&12C nave (12C font). 14,15&16C château with machicolated corner tower and lower storeys.
Ferrière-Larçon (11.5 km. NE): Fine *church* with 11C Romanesque nave, elegant 12C crossing tower and 13C choir.
Ligueil (15 km. NE): 12–15C *church* (St-Martin; gilded wooden 17C retable) and old 14&15C *houses.* 2 km. W. of Ligueil: 17C **Château Epigny**.
Paulmy (7.5 km. NE): *Château;* late 16C *church.* 2 km. downstream: **Châ**-

teau **du Châtellier,** a massive 12&13C fortress with a fine 14C keep surrounded by a moat and a complete wall with drawbridge and portcullis. Downstream: *Dolmen.* 4.5 km. from Paulmy: **Neuilly-le-Brison:** Romanesque church portal, ruined château.
Petit-Pressigny,Le (9.5 km. E.) 12–15C *church.* 1.5 km. downstream: **Château de Ray**, late 15C château with 2 frescos. 2 km. E. of Le Petit-Pressigny: Remains of 13C **Ste-Radegonde priory**.

Guérande
44 Loire-Atlantique   p.134☐A 4

If you have followed the Loire to its mighty estuary at Saint-Nazaire, it is worth making a small detour into the so-called 'white country', the salt gardens on the Atlantic coast, to

Grand-Pressigny, château, detail

Guerche-sur-Creuse, La Roche bell tower

which the formerly heavily fortified town of Guérande owes its wealth. Everything seems devoted to defence, from the curtain walls and ten massive towers down to the 2 town gates.

St-Aubin: Even this church, (12–15C), with its late Gothic double portal looks somewhat daunting, mainly because of the enclosed, relatively unornamented porch. The carved round capitals of the fine Romanesque pillars are also in this style; the motifs depict the torments of hell. After all this the colourful stained glass in the choir seems all the more life-enhancing; it depicts scenes from the lives of the saints.

Musée du vieux Guérande: In the machicolated St-Michel town gate (15C) is a local history museum dealing with the history and art of the town.

Guerche-sur-Creuse, La
37 Indre-et-Loire   p.136□K 6

Château de la Guerche: The château is on the right bank of the Creuse, and its machicolated corner towers are most charmingly reflected in the deep water. The 15C building owes its special reputation to its two storeys, dug deep into the earth, and enormous rooms with groin vaulting supported by massive square pillars; these were used as corn stores, and as casemates in the basement. From the bridge leading to La Petite-Guerche there is a fine view of the château.

Church: 12C building.

Roman baths: Remains in La Petite-Guerche on the other side of the Creuze.

Guerche-sur-Creuse, château

Environs: Chaise, La (7.5 km. N.): 14&16C *château*.

Descartes (10 km. N.): Birthplace of the great French mathematician and philosopher René Descartes (1596–1650), who moved from deep-rooted doubt to the conclusion 'I think, therefore I am'. Descartes was baptized in the 11&12C *St-Georges*. The *former church of Notre-Dame* (1104) is no longer used for divine service.

Leugny (3.5 km. N.): Romanesque *church*; Romanesque chapel.

Mairé (3 km. SW): 12C *church*; remains of a *Gallo-Roman villa*.

Roche-Posay, La (14 km. SW): Picturesque little spa (skin diseases) with remains of the old *12&14C town walls*, an old *town gate* with machicolations and a square 12C *keep*. Fine view from the bridge of an old mill and ruins of a Gallo-Roman bridge. The mineral springs, known as early as 1573, were very popular in the 17C. The 14–16C *church* has an 11C Romanesque bell tower and two strange square machicolated towers to the left and right of the N. transept. The retable in the chapel to the left of the choir with a bas-relief of the birth of Christ dates from 1685.

Saint-Rémy (9 km. N.): Romanesque *church*.

Ile-Bouchard, L'

37 Indre-et-Loire   p.136□I 5

Nothing has survived of the fortress to which the little market town at the confluence of the Vienne and the Manse owes its name. The building put up *c*. 880 on an island in the Vienne by a certain Bouchard was completely destroyed in the 17C. The barony fell to Cardinal Richelieu. All that remains are the two parts of the town which gradually grew up around the fortress: Saint-Gilles on the right bank of the Vienne and Saint-Maurice on the left.

Saint-Gilles: Built *c*. 1069, extended in the 12C; the Romanesque portals with geometrical decorations and the Romanesque font now used as an

Ile-Bouchard, L', St-Maurice bell tower

aquamanile date from the latter period.

Église des Cordeliers (in Saint-Maurice): Ruins of the 11&12C Franciscan church with Romanesque nave and apse.

St-Maurice (in Saint-Maurice): 15C building with nave and two aisles with 14C choir. Elegant soaring hexagonal bell tower; interesting bishop's throne in the choir (early-16C).

Former Priory of St-Léonard: Interesting ruins of the 11C buildings. Unfortunately all that has survived of the church is the wonderful

Romanesque *apse* with ambulatory and radiating chapels; its large arches have supports built in the following century in the form of smaller arches inserted between the columns, a most unusual feature.

The splendid carved foliate *capitals* depicting scenes from the Life of Christ (from the Annunciation via a particularly remarkable Last Supper to the Resurrection), and with monsters and creatures rising from the deep, are outstanding.

Environs: Crouzilles (2.5 km E.): 12C *church* with Romanesque statues on the façade, in the right transept and in the apse.

Lamottoe-Beuvron
41 Loir-et-Cher   p.138□O 3

This little town on the Beuvron has made a name for itself as the starting point for hunting parties in the Sologne. The church and Town Hall date from the Second Empire.

Château: The buildings date from the 16&17C. Napoleon III (1852–70) used the extensive grounds as a model farm which has been a penal colony since 1870.

Environs: Pierrefitte-sur-

Sauldre (17 km. SE): 12, 15&16C *church*. Old half-timbered *country house*.
Souvigny-en-Sologne (10 km. NE): 12, 15&16C *church* with a fine 16C wooden gallery.

Langeais
37 Indre-et-Loire   p.136□I 4

This little town on the right bank of the Loire, the old *Alangavia*, known for its Roman citadel, has had a long and stormy history. In the 4C the castle protected the church founded by St.Martin, it was extended towards the end of the 10C by the counts of Anjou as a fortress against the counts of Blois, and then razed in the Hundred Years War, leaving only the keep.

Another fortress was built under Louis XI in 1465 to protect the Crown Territories, and this remained in the possession of the French crown until 1631. After that one lord followed another until the last, Jacques Siegfried, left the château to the Institut de France, after restoring the interior to its original condition.

Château: Langeais is one of the most

Langeais, courtyard of château

interesting of the Loire châteaux, even though it is not as imposing as Chambord and does not have the grace and harmony of Blois. It is unusual in its setting, not on a hill but amidst a sea of houses, and because it was built so quickly, over a period of 4–5 years, it has remarkable uniformity of design.

The *keep*, built in 900 by Foulques Nerra, exuberant both as a builder and in his belligerence, it is considered to be the first stone defensive tower, and therefore an innovation in fortress architecture, which had previously been confined to wood. Unfortunately very little remains of the once massive and gloomy building.

The *new château*, built *c.* 1465 by J. Bourré, is a different matter altogether. Its defensive function is still inescapable: three thick round towers with conical roofs, a drawbridge in front of the two entrance towers, a lower storey without windows and a protruding wall passage with 270 machicolations above the fourth storey—all this makes the exterior look defiant and warlike. On the other hand the open garden side with its narrower, more slender polygonal staircase towers and dormers above the window axes actually looks comfortable and even welcoming, and it does indeed herald the transition from the fortress to the château.

In the *interior* this impression is even stronger. J. Siegfried took the advice of scholars and artists for his restoration, (using as far as possible originals from France and Italy; if no originals were available, as in the case of wainscots and floor tiles, copies were made of contemporary designs). This means that the visitor is given a clear idea of 15C château life. All the lavishly decorated cupboards and

Langeais, château, portal

Langeais, church

chests, the costly wall hangings, paintings and sculptures, the wilful fireplaces (one is in the form of a castle with wall passage) the four-poster bed (one of the first of its kind) or the magnificent Renaissance carpets—all show the Renaissance inclination towards the good life. Reports of the celebrations of the wedding of Charles VIII and Anne de Bretagne in this château sound like a fairy tale (1491), although it was the occasion of an important pact: the unification of France and Brittany. The *château gardens* were laid out in 15C style, using contemporary miniatures.

Church: The church was unfortunately spoiled in the 19C, but still has a Romanesque apse and tower; the latter has a spire added in the 15C, as so often happened. The crypt is said to date from the time of St.Martin, the founder of the church.

Also worth seeing: In the square in front of the château is a pilastered *Renaissance house* in which the famous writer Rabelais (1494–1553) is said to have lived. There are two more 16C *houses* in the Rue Anne-de-Bretagne.

Environs: Chapelle-sur-Loire,La (16.5 km. SW): This little market town on the Loire suffered constantly (even in the 19C, as next to nothing was done about regulating the river) from disastrous flooding. The *church* dates from the 16C.
Saint-Michel-sur-Loire (5 km. SW): Ruins of a 14C fortified *château*.

Lavardin
41 Loir-et-Cher   p.138□K 2

This old and picturesque Loir village was the scene of much fighting in the

Hundred Years War. It was the site of an important castle of the counts of Vendôme, and possession often passed from the Capets to the kings of Anjou and back again. In 1589 the fortress was taken by the troops of the Catholic league. A year later Prince Conti reconquered the castle and had the buildings razed to the ground.

St-Genest: Built in the early Romanesque period by the monks of the abbey of St-Georges-des-Bois. The priory was founded in the 9C by Salomon, a liegeman of Bouchard the Elder, Count of Vendôme. The church itself was begun in the second half of the 11C. The choir was completed c. 1080, the nave in the first half of the 12C. The nave and aisles are not vaulted, but separated by rows of square pillars with oustandingly well-crafted capitals. The choir is separated from the nave by a triumphal arch, and the apse has domical vaulting.

The church's greatest treasure is its 12–16C *wall paintings*. The oldest show the baptism of Christ and the Tree of Jesse and are to be found on a pillar at the entrance to the left choir chapel. The frescos are particularly well preserved in the choir and apse. The Passion is depicted on the right, on the left is the Washing of Feet and in the centre Christ as Ruler of the World with symbols of the Evangelists. The right choir chapel has a St.Christopher; the outstanding Last Judgement with heaven and Hell dates from the 15C. The pillars in the nave and aisle are decorated with pictures of saints. On the left is the crucifixion of St.Peter and on the right the martyrdom of St.Margaret.

Château: The oldest part is the 85 ft. high *keep* (11C). It was strengthened

Lavardin, Montoire-sur-le-Loire, St-Gilles chapel, frescos

by towers in the 12C. The 3 sets of
curtain walls were added in the
13&14C, and they were finally consolidated as an outer castle. The underground passage under the first curtain
wall dates from the 14C. Within the
second curtain wall are remains of a
15C building with interesting vaults.

Environs: Montoire-sur-le-Loir
(3 km. W.): In the 7C the St-Gilles
priory was founded here, and in the
9C a fortress against the Normans. In
1940 Hitler and Marshall Pétain met
in Montoire, and Hitler tried to convince Pétain of the necessity of joining
the war against England. The *St-
Gilles chapel* is Romanesque and was
part of a Benedictine priory once led
by the poet Ronsard. The nave of the
chapel has been destroyed in part, but
fine frescos have survived in the transept and the apse. The oldest dates
from the first quarter of the 12C and

is in the vault of the apse. It
represents Christ announcing the
Apocalypse. In his hand he holds the
book with the seven seals, and he is
surrounded by the four symbols of the
Evangelists. In the transept the subect
is Christ handing the key to St.Peter.
Unfortunately Peter is no longer
recognisable. Byzantine influence
shows in the symmetry of the folds in
the garments depicted in the fresco,
which dates from *c.* 1180. The fresco
in the N. transept is somewhat later.
It dates from the early 13C and shows
Christ with the Apostles. The scene is
thought to represent Pentecost. The
four crossing arches are also painted.
On the arch on the nave side Christ is
shown crowning the virtues of
patience and chastity, while vice is
destroyed. The *ruined castle* has an
11C *keep*. There is a model in the
Town Hall which shows how the
castle once looked.

Lavardin, château

Lavardin, St-Genest, capital

Le Liget, ruined church

Troo (9 km. NW): The 'cave dwellers' town' with its houses built on terraces is set above the porous tufa slopes above the Loir. Often the houses have only a façade, the rooms being hollowed out of the soft tufa. A complex network of underground passages, the Caforts (from 'caves fortes') is a reminder that Troo was part of a medieval fortress, most of which was underground. *St-Martin* was founded in the 11C as a collegiate church and rebuilt in the 12C in Angevin style. A new choir was added in the 14C. The oldest part of the church is a Romanesque apse with Gothic windows. The crossing has good Romanesque capitals. The square Angevin tower is an interesting feature; its window niches have little decorative columns in the reveals. Much of the interior dates from the 16C, including the well-

carved choir stalls, a communion table, an equestrian statue of St.Martin and a wooden statue of St.Mamas. The marble font was carved in 1687. Close by the church is the old *puits qui parle* (talking well) with a shingle roof. It is over 147 ft. deep and has a magnificent echo. On the E. edge of the town is the *Ste-Catherine* hospital. It dates from the 12C and has impressive Romanesque arches. Sick pilgrims on their way to Santiago de Compostela were received here. The *grotte pétrifiante* is an interesting limestone cave. *St-Jacques-des-Guérets* is late 11C. It has impressive wall paintings revealed in 1890; they were painted between 1130 and 1170 and show clear Byzantine influence. The individual scenes are framed and connected by ornamental bands, and thus the 13 individual pictures form a single composition. On the left, in the

Le Liget, St-Jean chapel, fresco

apse, are the Crucifixion, the Resurrection of the Dead, St.George and St.Augustine, and on the right God the Father with symbols of the Evangelists and Christ with the twelve Apostles (Last Supper). On the right wall of the apse is the martyrdom of St.James with Paradise above it. The S. wall of the nave has the legend of St.Nicolas in its upper part. The saint is seen throwing three gold pieces to three young girls to rescue them from dishonour. Below this is the resurrection of Lazarus. Also on this side is Christ in Limbo redeeming Adam and Eve. The latest frescos are on the N. wall of the nave; they represent the Birth of Christ and the Massacre of the Innocents. Interesting furnishings are three painted 16C wooden figures. In a niche on the left is St.James, in the choir St.Peter and on the right another apostle.

Liget, Le
37 Indre-et-Loire   p.138☐L 5

On the edge of the forest of Chinon, away from heavily populated areas, are the ruins of the Carthusian monastery which Henry II Plantagenet, the Count of Anjou on the throne of England, is said to have built to expiate the murder of his chancellor Thomas à Becket. When he became Archbishop of Canterbury and Primate of England Becket took the side of the Pope and the clergy, and by his resistance to the king's political wishes forced Henry to make an angry remark which was interpreted as a challenge to dispose of the chancellor.

Monastery: Only the 18C gate in the curtain wall, the ruins of the late-12C church, a walk from the cloisters of

1787 and some 18C buildings remain of the monastery built in 1176 and later continually altered and extended.

St-Jean-du-Liget chapel: A few hundred yards further N. in the open fields there appears for no very good reason a somewhat clumsy-looking late-12C Romanesque building built in ashlar with round-arched windows and a low conical roof. It is presumably the first monastery chapel of the Order (only a minute fragment of masonry remains of the nave added *c.* 1200). The building may have an unpromising exterior, but the interior has a great deal to offer, in particular the *wall paintings*, which like the nave are presumed to date from around 1200 and which are among the finest of the period. They include scenes from the Life of Christ, the death of Mary and the Tree of Jesse. Above them is a meander frieze with prophets, and there are saints in the window reveals. The pictures in the dome have unfortunately not survived.

La Corroirie: 1 km. NE on the road to Montrésor in beautiful countryside is a fortified estate which used to belong to a Carthusian monastery. The parchment used by the monks was made here. Three of the buildings date from the 12 or 13C (one has a chapel with Anjou vaulting in the basement), and there are a 15C house and a 15C square tower with machicolations containing the main gate.

Limeray

37 Indre-et-Loire   p.138☐L 3

Attractive old town with courtroom

Le Liget, St-Jean chapel, fresco

and a 14C bridge which has survived in part.

Church: This building with a Romanesque tower and fine Angevin vault contains, above all in the Mary chapel on the left of the nave, a series of remarkable old statues, including a late 16C Magdalene of the Tours school. There is a 15C château on the hill.

Environs: Cangey (2 km. upstream): *Church* with Romanesque nave and 16C choir.
Fourchette (4 km. downstream): Charming 18C *château*.

Loches

37 Indre-et-Loire   p.138□L 3

This little town, crowded around the massive fortress on a rocky plateau above the Indre, is one of the the most impressive historical towns in the whole of France. The strategic importance of the site meant that there was a castle here from the 6C onwards, and in the Middle Ages Loches became one of the most important citadels in the Loire valley. Foulques Nerra of the house of Anjou, who built so many châteaux and monasteries, was involved in this; he built the stone keep on the S. side. When the counts of Anjou came to the English throne as Plantagenetso (1154) Loches became English too, but it was returned to France as part of the ransom for Richard Lionheart, who had been taken prisoner on his return from the Crusades. Richard had hardly been released, however, when he took the fortress in a surprise raid, a heroic deed which occasioned much admiration at the time. 10 years

Limeray, church

Loches, Porte des Cordeliers

later Philippe Auguste managed to reconquer the castle for the French crown, but he had to lay siege to it for a year.

From then on the fortress was a notorious state prison, and then in the 15C became a source of scandal as the residence of Agnes Sorel, the mistress of Charles VII. Agnes was a pretty peasant girl and, as the king's favourite, she soon developed a taste for pomp and circumstance, and probably for intrigue as well; she was a thorn in the flesh for the Dauphin (later Louis XI) and for many of her contemporaries, who were offended by a degree of openness in the liaison which was unheard of in those days. The lords of the church also made this the reason for refusing to allow the 'sinner' to be buried in the St-Ours castle chapel, which she had so lavishly endowed with gifts. They felt that the king should remove her mortal remains to the château, and Charles VII was prepared to do this, provided that the gifts were returned with her. Nothing could have made the clerics change their minds more quickly, and until the French Revolu-

tion Agnes lay in St-Ours. Her tomb may be visited in the château.

Fortifications, keep and château: The entire plateau is taken up by a fortress surrounded by a curtain wall; the fortress consists of the old keep in the S., the later Logis du Roy in the N. and the medieval Cité with the former collegiate church of St-Ours between them. There is only one means of access to this so-called upper town, the *Porte Royale*, a 15C fortified gate with two 13C round towers.

Keep: The most imposing building of all is the old 11C keep, the great Loches landmark; its massive walls, over 9 ft. thick and with very few openings, are supported by semicylindrical buttresses and tower, brooding and gloomy, 120 ft. into the sky. On the N. side is a gateway, and staircase tower leading directly to the upper storey. The ground floor is not accessible from outside. The stairs in the E. wall lead from the first to the second floor. There are also blind passegeways in the walls to confuse anyone entering the castle illicitly.

The fortifications were continually

Loches, château, tomb of Agnes Sorel   *Loches, château, painting* ▷

extended. In the 15C the round tower and the Martelet tower were added, but they shortly became prisons, and gave the castle a most sinister reputation.

The *Round Tower* (Tour ronde), also called the Louis XI tower, was originally intended as a new donjon with four rooms one above the other, but made history because of its torture chamber and the cellar beneath it. Cardinal La Balue, the adviser of Louis XI, who betrayed his king to Charles the Bold, apparently languished here for eleven years in one of the notorious cages which he is said to have invented himself. This is the traditional view; historical research has cast doubt on the existence of these cages, about which so much has been written. They were apparently so small that the prisoner could neither stand, nor sit, nor lie down in them. It is more likely that the prisoners were prevented from leaving the open rooms usual in the Middle Ages by means of heavy chains. According to the historian Pierre Champion Cardinal Balue was never shut up in a cage, but simply pursued his studies under a kind of house arrest.

In the *Martelet tower*, which consists largely of underground dungeons, there is still evidence of the prisoners' suffering today. See for example the paintings and inscriptions on the wall of the first dungeon, in which Lodovico il Moro, Duke of Milan and patron of Leonardo da Vinci, spent 8 years paying for his betrayal of Louis XII, or the little altar and the Way of the Cross scratched on the walls of the cell below it, in which the Bishops of Autun and Le Puy were imprisoned for their involvement in the rebellion of the Constable of Bourbon.

Logis du Roy: Opposite on the N. side is the later residential section, two connected and somewhat dissimilar buildings consisting of the 14C *Vieux Logis* and the *Nouveau Logis* built to extend it in the 16C. The older part is still fortified with an open battle-mented wall passage and 4 semicircular towers in the façade, but the slightly lower later building does not have such war-like attributes, but elegant dormers with gables and finials instead.

The *interior* of the two buildings has relatively little to offer. An exception is the late Gothic *prayer chapel* of Anne de Bretagne on the first floor of the Nouveau Logis. Its walls are decorated with a pleasing design of knotted ropes and ermine spots. (The ermine was Anne's heraldic animal, and the knots indicate her worship of St.Francis.) Also worth seeing are the *triptych* (school of J.Fouquet, 1420–1477/81) in the fourth room, depicting the Bearing of the Cross, the Crucifixion and the Descent from the Cross, and the *tomb of Agnes Sorel* in the so-called Charles VIII room, where she has been interred since 1970, when her bones were found after being scattered in the French Revolution. The badly damaged recumbent figure of the king's mistress, erroneously thought to be a saint, has also now been restored, and so Agnes rests as the sculptor J.Morel first made her, with her head supported by angels and her feet by gentle lambs (a play on the name Agnes: Latin agnus = lamb).

A wall connects the Vieux Logis with the *Tour Agnès Sorel*, known since the 16C as 'Beautiful Agnes' Tower', and in which her tomb was found from 1809–1970. A remarkable feature of this tower is the relief of a pair of lovers on the base of the adjacent staircase tower.

St-Ours: The former collegiate church of Notre-Dame has only borne the name of the saint who converted the area around Loches in the 5C since 1806, but it has looked as confusing as it now does since the 12C; it has a line of four towers, which make it one of the oddest churches in the whole of France. In reality only the

Loches, south town gate ▷

Loches, château

two outer ones are towers. The two smaller ones between them are pointed octagonal vaults over the bays of the nave, as a glance into the interior will show; they were added in the late 12C on the orders of Prior Thomas Pactius to prevent the collapse of the nave, which was imminent. There is a similar extension of Romanesque vaulting in the kitchen at Fontevraud. *Porch and portal:* (11&12C, altered in the 14&15C, restored in the 19C): The spacious porch with rib vaulting and a former Gallo-Roman altar used as a stoup, leads to a magnificent Romanesque portal in the Aquitaine style; it is round-arched, and its archivolts are decorated with with fantastic figures, half man, half animal. Above the arch, and to a certain extent replacing a tympanum, is an Adoration of the Magi with column statues at the side.
Interior: The portal leads to a tunnel-vaulted vestibule with striking archaic capitals. This is the oldest part of the church, and consists of the lower part of a tower, which is the link with the nave and the pyramidal vaulting which has already been mentioned. The church originally had only one aisle, and a second was added on the right in the late 12C, and a third on the right in the 14&15C. The choir with three apses and most of the transept also date from the 12C.
Crypt: In this little room under the S. choir chapel is a fine fresco dating from the second half of the 11C and depicting St.Bricius, St.Martin's successor as Bishop of Tours.

Museums: *Lansyer Museum* (Rue Lansyer). A collection of paintings by the local artist Lansyer and objects from the Far East. *Musée du Terroir et du Folklore* (in the Porte Royale), a local history museum.

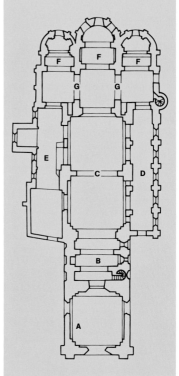

Loches, St-Ours castle church A narthex **B** vestibule **C** nave **D** r. aisle **E** l. aisle **F** choir **G** transept. The plan clearly shows the various building phases.

Lower town: There are many enticing alleyways and picturesque old buildings; the following are outstanding: 2 gates from the old town fortifications: the *Porte des Cordeliers* (Franciscans' gate) with round corner towers and parapet walk, definitely a military building but still an elegant one; the *Porte Picoys*, a 15C watchtower in the middle of the road with interesting frescos in one of the rooms.

Next to this is the *Hôtel de Ville*, the four-storey Renaissance Town Hall dating from 1535–43; Francis I gave permission to build it in 1519. The architect J.Baudouin was faced with a problem which is familiar today, that of making sensible use of a restricted space, and he solved it most skilfully. Nearby are the *Maison du Centaure*, also a Renaissance building, named after a statue showing Hercules (Francis I) killing a centaur, and next

to that the *Maison de la Chancellerie* dating from 1551 with stone medallions on the façade. The *Hôtel Nau* and some of the buildings in the Rue St-Antoine and the Grande Rue are also worth seeing. The most impressive of all the Renaissance buildings is the *Tour St-Antoine* (1529–75) with balustrades, protruding turrets and a dome reminiscent of Tours cathedral; it is all that remains of a chapel which was probably used as a watch-tower.

A *statue of Alfred de Vigny* at the junction of the Rue des Jeux and the Rue Victor Hugo commemorates the great son of the town who achieved immortality as a Romantic poet.

Environs: Beaulieu-lès-Loches (1 km. E., on the right bank of the Indre):

This little industrial town with about 2000 inhabitants once had an important abbey, altered in the 18C and now used as Town Hall and school. There is still an exterior pulpit on the façade of the old 16&17C abbot's house (Logis Abbatial). Very little indeed remains of the *abbey church* (1007–12), founded by that exuberant builder Count Foulques Nerra of Anjou, who wished to be buried here, but it is still possible to imagine how large and beautiful the original building must have been from the large 12C bell tower with its dwarf galleries, dormers, small belfries and octagonal spire, the Romanesque transept, and the ruins of the Romanesque apse, which used to have

an ambulatory with radiating chapels, and which can still be seen below the Gothic apse. Nave and choir of the present church date from the 15C. The nave in its present form is considerably smaller than its Romanesque predecessor, and was built in the E. part of the earlier building; the choir has fine Flamboyant windows. The gable of the N. transept is decorated with large allegorical bas-reliefs. The interior dates largely from the 16–18C: the choir stalls are Renaissance, the wooden figure of Mary above the portal is 16C, the retable on the high altar is 17C and the lectern 18C.

Also worth seeing: The church of *St-Laurent* with its elegant nave in Plantagenet style. The remains of the old church of *St-Pierre* dating from the late 12C. The *Maison des Templiers* (the house of the Order of Knights Templar, founded in 1118 and dis-

Loches, St-Ours, portal

solved in 1312), a late-12C fortified building and some other old buildings, including the so-called *Maison d'Agnès Sorel* and the 15C *Vieille Poste* with its double gable (Rue Basse).
Further E., on the road to Montrésor, are the ruins of the 12C **Tour Chevaleau**.
Ferrières-sur-Beaulieu (2.5 km. NE): 11&12C church in Plantagenet style.
Fretay (4.5 km. SW): 18C *château*.
Mauvière (2 km. S.): Square 14C tower.
Verneuil-sur-Indre (9.5 km. SE): Square 15C *keep* with round tower beside it.

Luynes

37 Indre-et-Loire   p.136□I 4

Some of the densely-packed houses of

the old *Maillé*, as the little market town, one of the first baronies in Touraine, used to be called, are cut into the rock beneath the fortress high above the Loire. In 1619 the Pair de France, Charles d'Albert, Duke of Luynes acquired the barony, which was raised to the status of a dukedom named after him. Since then the château has been in the possession of this family, who still live in it, which means that it is not open to the public.

Château: There was a Gallo-Roman citadel on this strategically important rocky spur above the Loire, and a medieval castle, which was destroyed by the counts of Anjou in 1096. Hardouin de Maillé rebuilt the castle in 1106, and the present buildings are largely based on this. The entire château still looks medieval, particularly the defiant W. façade with its four round towers, which used to look

Loches, St-Ours, detail of portal

Luynes, château

even more threatening, as the windows were not pierced until the 15C. The two 13C outer towers and the 15C inner ones still have their original conical roofs, but the tops were removed from the N. and E. sides. The keep was pulled down in 1658. At about the same time the architect Le Muet added a wing on the S. side of the château; this was removed in the 19C, with the exception of the two outermost pavilions, in order to open up the view over the Loire, as in Chaumont and Ussé. It has been replaced by a fine terrace. The elegant late-15C W. building, with its octagonal staircase turret, survived and was thoroughly restored in the 19C.

Convent church: This 15C single-aisled building is notable for its simple beauty.

Also worth seeing: Opposite the church are 3 16C *houses*. The 15C wooden *market halls* are also interesting.
1.5 km. N. of Luynes are significant remains of a Gallo-Roman *aqueduct*, which is said to have been built before the 4C and probably supplied the citadel with water.

Environs: Chatigny (2 km. NE): 15C *château*. There was a villa on the site in the Roman period.

Fondettes (3 km. NE): 12,13&15C *church*.

Saint-Etienne-de-Chigny (3.5 km. SW): This *church* built in 1542 by J.Binet has fine 16C beams with carved ties. There is an old baptismal chapel, and a fine stained-glass window (Crucifixion) in the choir dome.

straight flights, with a magnificent coffered ceiling in white stone. It is decorated with over 130 realistic, allegorical and mythological individual motifs, and the artist responsible works with remarkable elegance, sharpness of detail and conceptual sweep. The large *pigeon loft* is also of interest.

Ménars
41 Loir-et-Cher   p.183□M 3

Château: Guillaume Charron started the building in 1637. It was extended by his nephew Jean-Jacques Charron, who also added a large garden. In 1760 the Marquise de Pompadour, Louis XV's mistress and the real ruler of Versailles, bought the château and estate and commissioned court architect J.A. Gabriel to extend it and make it into one of the few baroque châteaux on the Loire. Gabriel, who was responsible for the Place de la Concorde and the Petit Trianon in Versailles, had the side buildings pulled down and surrounded the courtyard with single-storey buildings to emphasize the two-storey main section with its new wings. The Marquise was only able to enjoy her new château in the country for four years; she died of tuberculosis in Versailles on April 15 1764, at the age of 42. Her brother, Abel Poisson, the Marquis de Marigny, inherited the château and ordered further work on the building, still far from complete. He engaged J-G Soufflot, the architect of the Panthéon in Paris; Soufflot doubled the size of the main building on the courtyard side, built a single-storey terraced section and replaced the flat roofs with the present ones. He also added the orangery and the Temple d'Amour, a domed rotunda with columned and pilastered side sections. The Marquis de Marigny's principal preoccupation, apart from the extensions, was redesigning the gardens. He built a series of symme-

Manoir de la Poissonnière
41 Loir-et-Cher   p.136□K 2

This early-16C house, charmingly sited on a slope near Couture-sur-Loir, was built in the Italian style by Louis de Ronsard, an educated soldier. The poet Pierre de Ronsard was born here in 1524. There are Latin sayings and maxims on the façades of the house and outbuildings, and one of the attic windows is decorated with the coat-of-arms of the Ronsard family, three fishes on a blue ground. The outer façade of the house has Louis XII mullioned windows on the ground floor, but the windows of the upper storey are decorated with medallions and pilastered frames in the early Renaissance style.

Environs: Poncé-sur-Loir (3 km.NW): The *Renaissance château* originally consisted of two pavilions with access from a central staircase tower. In the 18C one of these pavilions was replaced by a building in no particular style. The plain façade is relieved by protruding cornices and Ionic pilasters. The original main façade is now at the rear. Its most prominent feature is an Italian gallery, which also serves as a terrace for the upper storey. What makes the château really worth seeing is the Renaissance staircase, which is one of the most important in France. It has six

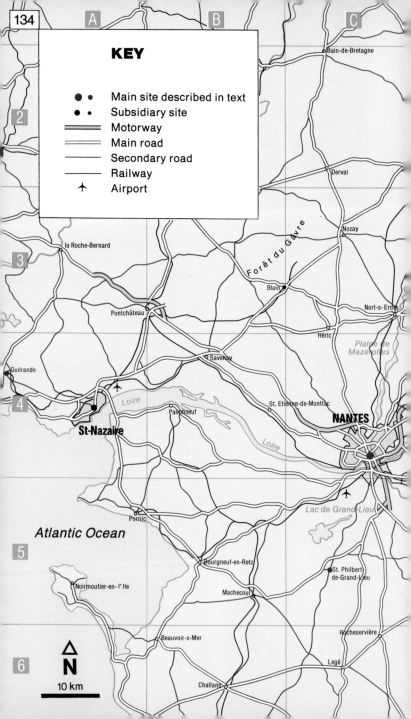

A B C

KEY

- Main site described in text
- Subsidiary site
- Motorway
- Main road
- Secondary road
- Railway
- ✈ Airport

2

3

4

5

6

Bain-de-Bretagne

Derval

Nozay

Forêt du Gâvre

la Roche-Bernard

Blain

Nort-s-Erdre

Pontchâteau

Héric

Plaine de Mazerolles

Savenay

Guérande

Loire

St. Etienne-de-Montluc

NANTES

✈

Paimboeuf

St-Nazaire

Loire

Lac de Grand-Lieu

Atlantic Ocean

Pornic

Bourgneuf-en-Retz

St. Philbert-de-Grand-Lieu

Noirmoutier-en-l'Ile

Machecoul

Rocheservière

Beauvoir-s-Mer

△
N

Legé

10 km

Challans

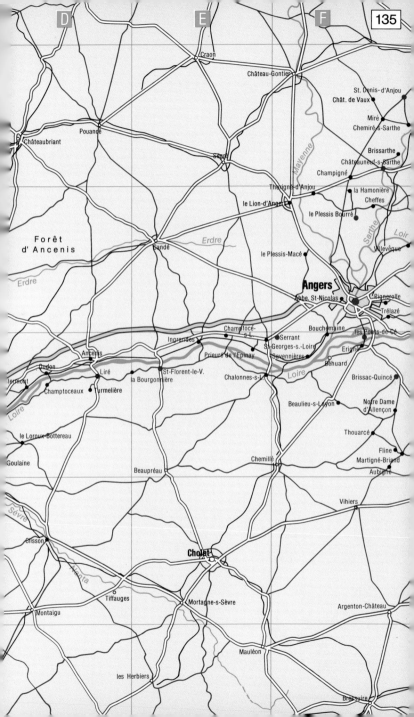

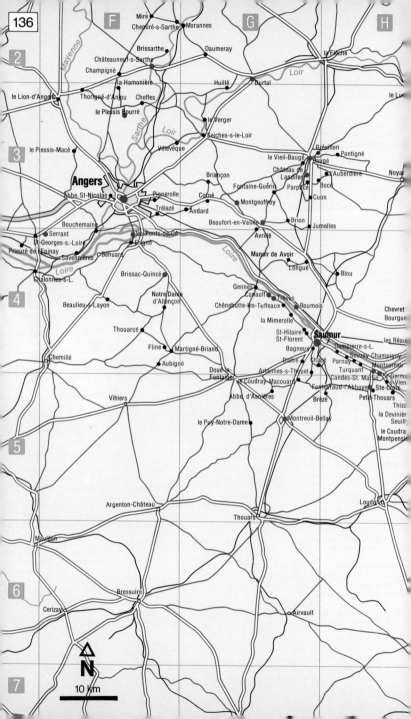

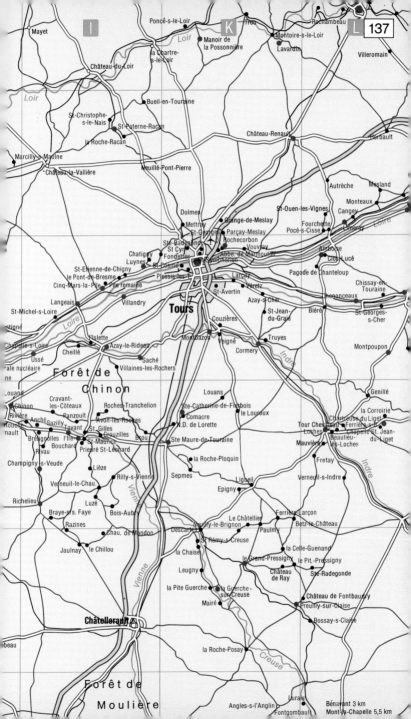

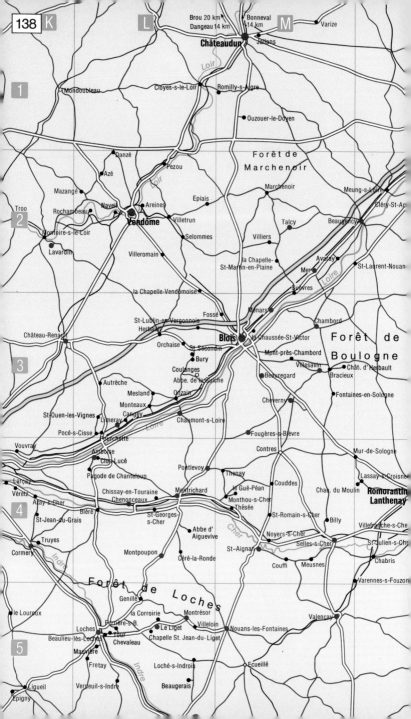

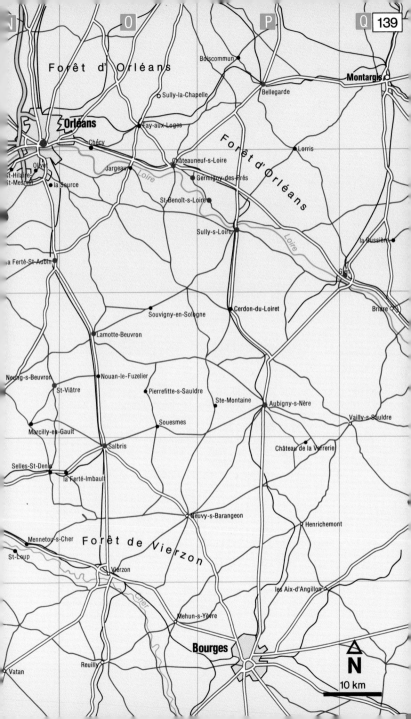

Ménars, château

trical ramps which extended the garden down to the Loire. In 1771 the final building was added, the fountain grotto in the style of Palladio. Marigny also had part of the garden made into a 'jardin anglo-chinois' and completed the double avenue of limes on the bank of the Loire; this is over a kilometre long, and had been started by Madame de Pompadour. By the time the Marquis died in 1781 the château had developed to its full splendour. It was considered 'one of the finest estates in the kingdom' and 'certainly the most pleasant in Europe'. After the death of the Marquis its decline was equally swift. Furniture and art treasures had to be sold just to put into effect the most important bequests in the will of Madame de Pompadour, and none of the later owners came anywhere near to providing for the maintenance of the huge building; it was finally

acquired in 1939 by the Compagnie de Saint-Gobain, who had supplied window and mirror glass to Madame de Pompadour; they restored the building thoroughly and used it as a conference centre.

Environs: Suèvres (5 km. NE): This little town is on the site of a Roman settlement, and has two interesting old churches. *St-Lubin* dates from the 10C, but only the crossing and the tower have survived from this period. The choir is 12C. The nave has not survived, and the S. aisle was rebuilt in the 16C. The apse was not added until the 19C. The plain Romanesque tower is particularly attractive. It has two storeys with double louvres and a simple, squat stone spire. In the interior the two 16&17C carved altar panels are of interest; they show scenes from the Life of Christ. The portal in the S. aisle dates from the 16C and is decorated with coats-of-arms of the lords of the château of Forges. *St-Christophe* dates from the early Romanesque period.

Mer
41 Loir-et-Cher　　　　　　p.138☐M 2

An old town which had to defend itself in the past, as the remains of the *fortifications* show.

Church: This single-aisled building was rebuilt and extended in the 15C and enlarged by the addition of the tower in the 16C. Some of the wooden vault dates from the 11C; the pulpit and pews are Louis XIV.
In the suburb of Aunoy is a 12&16C church with a free-standing bell tower.

Environs: Avaray (5 km. NE): *Château* in the style of Louis XIII with four 13C corner towers, still surrounded by broad moats with water in them.
Chapelle - Saint - Martin - en - Plaine, La (6.5 km. W.): 12C Romanesque *church* (the bell tower over the crossing and the transepts were not added until the 15C). *Saint-Vincent-du-Villers* (late-11C/early-12C); late-12C frescos were discovered after the Second World War.

Montbazon
37 Indre-et-Loire　　　　　　p.138☐K 4

It is assumed that this charming little town on the right bank of the Indre was originally associated with the great warrior and builder Foulques Nerra, Count of Anjou, who built a massive keep on the narrow plateau above the river towards the end of the 11C. Foulques is also said to have taken up quarters in the abbey of Cormery and to have supervised the building of a defensive tower person-

Louroux (Montbazon), church

ally. Whether this is true or not, local people still point out the remains of his former home, 1 km. SE of the little town.

Keep: This massive, almost windowless square tower resembles its fellow in Loches, with which it also shares a characteristic site at the extreme S. end of a narrow plateau. It is still 91 ft. high. Since the Second Empire (1866) the largely 12C building (parts of it are older) has been crowned by a 30 ft. statue of the Virgin Mary. Traces of the 12C wall and two of its towers have survived; in the 15C a curtain wall was built around the whole of the plateau, including the N. area. At the same time a château was built in the N, but this has now completely disappeared, though two towers and the main gate (Rue des Moulins) have survived from the second wall.

Environs: Louans (17.5 km. S.): *Church* with 12C sections, with a 16C fortified building at its side.
Louroux, Le (18 km. S.): 11C **church;** next to it are the picturesque buildings of a 15&16C *priory*, now used as a farm.
Veigné (2 km. SE): Romanesque *bell tower*. 2 km. further N. is the *Château de Couzière*, with 2 15C side towers; this has been the residence of the dukes of Montbazon since the 16C.

Montgeoffroy

49 Maine-et-Loire   p.136☐G 3

The château is set among its own grounds and the fruit plantations of the right bank of the Loire as if in a geometrical park. One of the most successful examples of the Louis Seize style in Anjou, it is in the administrative region of Mazé.

Montbazon, donjon

Château: The present château was built by Marshal Louis-Georges-Erasme de Contade, governor of Alsace in Strasbourg, who commissioned the Paris architect N.Barré to build him a country seat in 1773. The strictly symmetrical 18C building, almost entirely devoid of decoration, was completed within two years; its straight lines are broken only by chimneys and the few roof lights. The slightly protruding central section has a pediment containing the building's only three-dimensional decoration, the Contade coat-of-arms framed by two trophies. The two-and-a-half-storey central building has two wings set at right angles, followed by two single-storey pavilions which are set back and lead to the stables and coach houses. On the right-hand side of the courtyard which they form, which has two round towers, is a late Gothic chapel, which, like the two towers,

was part of an earlier medieval building. At the far side of the courtyard on the château side is a semicircular pool with a balustrade; from its centre leads a dead straight, broad path which stands out clearly from the gardens on either side; it runs towards the central part of the building and is the principal axis of this geometrically lucid complex.

The *interior* of the building will come as a surprise to the visitor: the furnishings are still pure 18C. As the château has been in the possession of the Contade family ever since it was built, very little change has been made to the interior, which the Marshal seems to have ordered complete from Paris. The fine furniture, made by well-known 'designers' such as Gourdin, Garnier and Durand and conceived to fit precisely into certain rooms, is still in the settings for which it was intended. There are also paintings by Rigaud, Drouais, Pourbus the Younger, Van Loo, Desportes and others, and beautifully matched wall panelling, carpets, curtains and tapestries. In short, the whole of the furnishings, for which there is an inventory which almost serves as a guide to the château, is, in contrast with most châteaux, genuine, and therefore gives an unusually vivid picture of the living conditions of 18C noblemen of an artistic cast of mind. Only certain rooms on the ground floor are open to the public (billiard room, large and small salon, Mme Hérault's apartment and the dining room).

The *stained glass* in the chapel, dating from 1543, is also worth seeing; it represents God the Father, the Birth of Christ and the founders of the chapel. The collection of old coaches and carriages in the stables and the saddle room in the round tower are other interesting features.

Environs: Andard (12 km. SW): 11C *church*. **Corné** (9 km. W.): 15&16C *church*. **Briançon** (3 km. N.): 18C *château*.

Montpoupon
37 Indre-et-Loire   p.138☐L 4

Château: Between the valleys of the Cher and the Indre, far from noisy main roads and set on a slight eminence, is the Château de Montpoupon, now part of the parish of Cerélä-Ronde, a 15&16C building, completely restored with great sensitivity after the First World War. Of a still earlier' date is the fine cylindrical keep, part of the old 12&13C fortress. The wall passage with machicolations in the upper part was not added until the 15C, at the time of the major building programme. The fortified entrance leads through a square pavilion framed by round turrets which emphasize the defensive character of the building.

Environs: Genilé (4.5 km. SW):

Montgeoffroy, château

Montpoupon, château

The present church dates partly from the 12C and partly from the Renaissance. It has a particularly fine carved wooden vault, a white marble stoup (1494), a 17C pulpit and an 18C altarpiece.

Montrésor

37 Indre-et-Loir   p.138☐L 5

This little town on a picturesque site on the right bank of the Indrois has an interesting château and an equally remarkable church. 17C wooden market halls and a house with Renaissance-style turrets complete the picture. Montrésor has a similar history to a number of other larger and smaller places in the present department of Indre-et-Loire: like Loches or Chinon, Montrésor was a bastion of the counts of Anjou in their struggle for Touraine with the counts of Blois, and like Touraine it became part of the Angevin-English empire when the counts of Anjou came to the English throne as the House of Plantagenet; again like Touraine it was reconquered for the French crown by Philip-Augustus (1180–1223). Later it was privately owned by various families, and since 1849 the château has been the property of the Branickis, a Polish family who completely restored and refurnished it.

Château: Very little remains of the square keep built on the rocky plateau above the Indrois by the notorious Count Foulques Nerra d'Anjou. The curtain wall dates from the 12C, the outer walls, fortified with round towers and including an increasingly dilapidated gatehouse, are late 14C. The actual château was not built until the early 16C by Imbert de Bastarnay,

Montrésor, Imbert de Bastarnay tomb

the grandfather of the beautiful Diane de Poitiers, mistress of Francis I (1515–47) and Henry II (1547–59). Despite the two machicolated corner towers on the outside above the Indrois valley, this so-called new château does not fulfil any defensive function. As the high dormers, the small protruding round turrets and the smart polygonal tower on the courtyard side suggest, it is a building intended as a comfortable home. In the *interior*, which is open to the public, is a kind of Polish national museum. There are also valuable Italian pictures, ('The Adultress' by Paolo Veronese, a portrait of a man by Caravaggio) and 16C Italian furniture. The small gold and silver collection is particularly notable.

Church: Founded in 1519 by Imbert de Bastarnay and destined to be his final resting place (now the parish church). The building is one of the finest Renaissance churches in France, although the rib vaulting and Flamboyant traceried windows are still late Gothic. The façade with its elegant round portal and large window is particularly impressive. In the interior of the single-aisled building, completed in 1541, a striking feature is the *tomb of Imbert de Bastarnay* (d. 1523) with wife and son, destroyed during the Revolution and restored in 1875; it is an extremely expressive marble sculpture attributed to the great French Renaissance sculptor Jean Goujon (1510–66). The 16C *stained-glass windows* representing the sufferings of Christ are also very attractive, and the *choir stalls*, also 16C with head medallions, are another fine feature. Note also the 16C pictures of the Italian school in the nave and the 'Annunciation' by the Flemish painter P. de Cham-

paigne in the first chapel by the choir
and a 16C wooden Virgin in the sacristy.

Environs: Loché-sur-Indrois (8.5
km. S.): 12C *church*. 4.5 km. SSW:
ruined **abbey of Beaugerais** (the
nave of the church is 12C).
Villeloin (2.5 km. SE): remains of the
old *fortifications* and 15, 16&18C
towers. Traces of a *Benedictine abbey*
founded *c*. 850 and the ruins of the
church attached to it. In the *parish
church* is a 16C wooden figure of
Christ and J.Boucher's Adoration of
the Shepherds. 2.5 km. SW: remains
of *Villiers priory*, now used as a farm.

Montreuil-Bellay
49 Maine-et-Loire   p.136☐G 5

The name of this picturesque little
town on the Thouet, which winds
lazily past the château and spreads out
like a pond in front of it, is a combination of *monasteriolum* and Berlay, later
reduced to Bellay. It points to the fact
that there was probably once a small

Montrésor, château ▷

Montrésor, church, Annunciation

Montreuil-Bellay, château

monastery here, and that the du Bellay family, the ancestors of the Renaissance poet Joachim du Bellay (1522–60) were the first lords of the château. The fortress was built in the 11C by the tireless builder and warrior Foulques Nerra, Count of Anjou, on the site of a former Roman oppidum. It was razed in 1150 by one of his successors, Geoffrey of Anjou, known as Plantagenet because of his habit of wearing a broom sprig (plante genêt) in his helmet. The château was destroyed because the du Bellays, proud of owning one of the most powerful fortresses in the whole of Anjou, had intrigued against their feudal lord. Geoffrey was unable to take the fortress by storm, but laid siege to it for three years, and starved out the occupying forces. Rebuilding did not start until the 13C, when the castle mound was surrounded by an irregu-

lar wall with protruding round towers. The so-called Vieux Château or Châtelet, a strongly fortified gatehouse, was built at the same time. The new and the small châteaux were added two centuries later.

Château: This unusual set of heterogeneous buildings, enclosed by a curtain wall and cut off from the town by a deep ditch, is reached by two bridges. There are three sections, the Châtelet, the Nouveau Château and the Petit Château.

The *Châtelet,* is the oldest section and dates from the 13–15C; it has a massive portal with two towers which used to be protected by a drawbridge. The three massive protruding round towers, reaching up to roof level and with high parapets, make the exterior of the *Nouveau Château* (1485–1505) look like a medieval fortress, but the

Montreuil-Bellay, château

Montreuil-Bellay, Notre-Dame, detail of portal

two lighter and more elegant octagonal towers on the courtyard side with their many windows make the building look rather more welcoming.

The *Petit Château* is the strangest and in some ways the most modern of the buildings; the two sections accommodate four individual dwellings, each with its own entrance and staircase tower. It is assumed that they housed four canons from the nearby collegiate church, who held services and looked after the archives; even today it is said that they knew rather more about drinking than writing. The spires, gables and chimneys give the building a feeling of loftiness, but it is aptly named the small château; on the courtyard side is a remarkable *kitchen*, with a central fireplace on a square plan expanding to an octagon, reminiscent of the famous monastery kitchen of Fontevraud. This central fireplace, a massive pyramid with a chimney, supported by round piers, was probably intended to remove smoke and kitchen smells. Provisions were delivered through the broad window in the main façade.

There is little of artistic worth in the *interior*. In the Nouveau Château attention should be drawn to the paintwork in the two-bayed chapel, which unfortunately has been damaged, the fireplaces in the Flamboyant style and some old furniture and objets d'art, including a German Renaissance sideboard (1647) and Aubusson tapestries designed by Lancret (18C), the elegant vaulting in the cellar and the large staircase in the first tower, which the Duchess of Longueville is said to have ascended on horeseback. In the Petit Château the four bathrooms are an impressive feature.

Notre-Dame (former collegiate church, now parish church): Despite its spaciousness and Flamboyant decoration, the single-aisled building (1460–81) with Plantagenet vaulting and a polygonal choir seems modest and restrained.

Prieuré des Nobis: Below the castle, protected by three curtain walls which connect the fortress wall with the river, is a building reached via the Porte du Moulin (mill gate) between the mill and the old mill house. On the left after a second gateway are the ruins of *Saint-Pierre*, consisting of part of the 15C nave with 12C Romanesque apse and side apse and, on the right, two walks from the 17C cloister with an additional building dating from the same period.

Town: Large parts of the wall,

Puy-Notre-Dame
(Montreuil-Bellay), church

particularly on the N. side, and 3 fortified gates have survived of the 15C town wall. The *Porte Nouvelle* is by the Rue Nationale in the N. and the *Porte St-Jean* or Thouars gate, with two towers in massive ashlar decorated with 16 rows of cannon balls, is in the S. Nearby is the secularized *hospice chapel* dating from thr 15C. In the Rue Nationale itself is a *house* with a Renaissance turret (No. 62) and a fine 17C house, the *Hôtel Mallerais*.

Environs: Asnières abbey (8 km. NW): The abbey was founded in 1129 by Giraud de Berlay, lord of Montreuil-Bellay, destroyed by the Protestants in 1569 and struggled on after that until 1746. Only the transept and choir have survived of the *church*. The S. arm of the transept and the crossing were built between 1150 and 1180, the crossing tower is 13C. The rectangular *choir,* built between 1210 and 1220, is one of the finest examples of the Plantaganet style, along with the famous church of St-Serge in Angers. The vaults with their beautifully carved and painted keystones stretch like sails between the fine ribs on their slender columns and seem to soar effortlessly. The pictorial decoration shows Christ as teacher, surrounded by angels and the four Evangelists, with scenes from his ministry. **Coudray-Macouard, Le** (7.5 km. NE): 12C *church* with a crypt carved into the tufa. 3 km. NE: **Artannes:** old *cemetery church,* parts of which date from the 12C, with a 13C font. N. of this is a *menhir* in an open field.

Puy-Notre-Dame, Le (7.5 km. W.): This little town was fortified until 1784, and is in a well-known winegrowing area. It was formerly known as Le Puy-en-Anjou, and was the seat of a priory, of which a covered well and a church have survived.

Church: This hall church, 173 ft. long and 65 ft. wide, with three aisles and a 65 ft. transept, is one of the most perfect examples of 13C Angevin architecture, even though the façade with its three rows of arches, two rectangular buttresses and two bell towers is reminiscent of Poitiers cathedral. On the other hand the nave and two high aisles have typical Angevin vaulting, and the arrangement of the square choir with six windows in the ribs of the vaulting and the lavish design with figures in the vaults themselves are characteristic of the Plantagenet style.

The interior has fine 16C choir stalls with carved saints and Apostles and various works of art, including an Assumption on the high altar by J.Boucher of Bourges (1620). Most famous of all is a relic, the so-called *girdle of the Virgin* (la ceinture de la Vierge), a piece of oriental linen and silk brought to France at the time of the Crusades, and still an object of pilgrimage today. It is said to have the power to allay the pains of childbirth.

Anne of Austria, Louis XIII's queen, sent for the relic in the course of a difficult birth, and it was brought with great ceremony to Saint-Germain-en-Laye and placed around her body; she recovered, although still in great pain, and gave birth to a healthy boy, who went down in the history of Europe as le Roi Soleil.

The old town also has an old *Franciscan convent*, the chapel of which is now used as a barn, several 16C houses and limestone tufa quarries with underground workings, some of which are now used for mushroom growing.

Montrichard

41 Loir-et-Cher   p.138☐L 4

This little old town on the Cher has

Le Puy-Notre-Dame, stalls

Montrichard, half-timbering

managed to preserve much of its character. There are some particularly fine old houses in the Rue Nationale. The oldest is the 11C *Maison du Prêche*. The 16C *Maison de l'Ave Maria* has a corner post with a carved Annunciation. The *Hôtel Jacques de Beaune* is also 16C and is now used as a hospice.

Keep: This keep built in 1010 is one of the best-known in France. It was built of wood by Fulques Nerra, Count of Anjou and Lord of Amboise, Loches and La Haye, as a bastion against the threat from the lords of Saint-Aignan and Pontlevoy. The site was well-chosen for strategic purposes, because the roads from Tours to Bourges and Blois to Poitiers crossed at the foot of the castle mound. The wooden keep was replaced by the present stone building

between 1110 and 1130. It was built on the pattern of the keep in Loches. In 1461 Louis XI acquired it from the lords of Amboise as a base for his visits to the miraculous image of the Madonna in the church of Nanteuil. In 1589 Henry IV had the top 13 ft. of the keep pulled down to reduce its defensive capability. Nobody lived in the building from the end of the 17C and it fell into disrepair. Despite this the three-storey keep has survived remarkably well, and shows the 12C technique of defensive tower building very clearly. The ground floor was not lived in, according to the usual custom, but used as a storeroom. Only the middle floor with its pointed windows had people living in it. The upper storey with battlemented wall passage was used for defensive purposes. The stone staircase connecting the various levels has survived in its original form, and is still used by visitors to the tower.

Sainte-Croix: The former château chapel at the foot of the keep mound dates from the 12C, but only the pillars and arches on the S. side of the nave have survived from this period. The N. side of the nave is 16C and the choir 18C. The remainder of the S. part of the nave and the tower are 19C additions. In 1476 Duke Louis d'Orléans married Jeanne de France, the daughter of Louis XI, as a favour to the king. When he came to the throne himself he rejected the daughter of his predecessor and married Anne de Bretagne. Jeanne de France was canonized by Pope Pius XII in 1950.

Nanteuil church: This dates from the 12C. The apse and the crossing still date from this period (the central tower is modern, however). The nave was built in the 13C, the façade in the 15C. The chapel dedicated to the Blessed Virgin is a place of pilgrimage, and was built in the 15C and largely paid for by Louis XI. The ground floor serves as a vestibule and the actual chapel is on the first floor and directly accessible from the interior of the church.

Environs: Former abbey of Aiguevive (7 km. SE): Parts of the 12C abbey church have survived; the abbey was founded in the 11C. The vaulting has disappeared in the nave and aisles, but the crossing is largely intact. The choir with one large and two small apses is also of interest. There are still traces of 15C paintwork on the walls.
Céré-la-Ronde (9 km. SE): the *church* dates from the 12C. The plain Romanesque tower of this period, but the rest of the church was altered in the 16C.
Chissay-en-Touraine (4 km. W.) 15,16&17C *château*.
Monthou-sur-Cher (9.5 km. E.): 11,13&15C *church* with a Romanesque façade.

Montrichard, stone cross

Saint Georges-sur-Cher (8 km. W.): 11C *church*. Good wine.

Montsoreau
49 Maine-et-Loire   p.136☐H 4

There has been a château in this village at the attractive confluence of the Loire and the Vienne on the strategically important road from Chinon to Saumur since the 11C. The present building is based on the mid-15C château built by J. de Chambes, which was divided among many owners after the French Revolution, much altered, and then neglected until it was bought and restored by the state. Its owners made it rather more famous than its architecture; they have gone down in history and literature as bloodthirsty intriguers. A lady

Montsoreau, château, detail of façade

a high base, with moats cut into the rock, once fed with water from the Loire. On the other hand the large windows of the two-storey main building show signs that this was meant to be lived in; the two-storey dormers above the wall passage, with gables and Gothic ornaments, and the lavish Renaissance décor (arabesques, medallions, putti) on the E. staircase tower, which dates from 1520, show awakening artistic sensibilities. Even so, the entire castle is still dominated by the somewhat clumsy defensive design, particularly outside. The main section has prominent side pavilion towers, which must have seemed even more prominent in the days when their pitched roofs towered above the central part of the building. On the courtyard side the octagonal staircase towers with many windows make a much lighter impression.

In the *interior*, rooms with the original beamed ceilings and old fireplaces can be visited (the two large rooms on the second floor of the main building, and the wall passage are particularly interesting) and in the *Musée des Goumsâ marocains*, moved here from Rabat in 1956, there are memorabilia of the knights (Goums) of Lyautey and the conquest of Morocco.

from Montsoreau conspired against the king with the brother of Louis XI in the so-called Ligue du Bien Public; another provided Alexandre Dumas with material for an exciting horror story: Françoise de Maridor, the beloved of the governor of Anjou, Bussy d'Amboise, was compelled by her husband, Jean IV de Chambes, to make a rendezvous with her admirer at the château Coutancière, two miles away, and thus made it possible for him to be stabbed to death. The same Jean IV played a cruel part as a leader in the Massacre of St.Bartholomew in the Wars of Religion (1562–98).

Château: Montsoreau is one of the first feudal castles to show the transition from medieval fortress to Renaissance château. The façade on the river side in particular looks very fortress-like, with its heavy towers, wall passages and machicolations; it is set on

St-Pierre: Much renovated in the 18C; the 13C Plantagenet-style transept and choir have survived in their original form. In the choir are 6 carved choir stalls (15C) and an altar panel (16C) from Fontevraud.

St-Michel chapel: This old Gothic building is now used as a house.

Also worth seeing: The village, which is well-known for its fine white wines and pretty little streets on the hillside overgrown with wild vines, has a number of 15&16C houses.

Environs: Parnay (3.5 km. NW): There is a fine *church* with a Romanesque nave on an attractive site at the

Montsoreau, château, hall

top of the hill (excellent view). The portal dates from the Renaissance period and the apse is 15C. The church has a 15C wooden Madonna and the tomb of Jehan du Plessis.

Turquant (2 km. NW): Late 15C

church with some 12C parts. The altars are 18C, and the bas-reliefs from Fontevraud in the choir are 17C. *Château de la Fessardière*, used by Ben Bella in 1961. There are numerous *cave dwellings* on the road to Montsoreau.

Nantes

44 Loire-Atlantique   p.134□C 4

Nantes has 264,000 inhabitants, and is the seventh largest city in France; with its harbour of St-Nazaire it is also the fourth largest port in the country; all this comes from its position on the Loire. In fact the river played (and still plays) a more important role in the history of Nantes than in any other town in the Loire valley. The old *Condivincum* of the Gallic Namnetes was rechristened

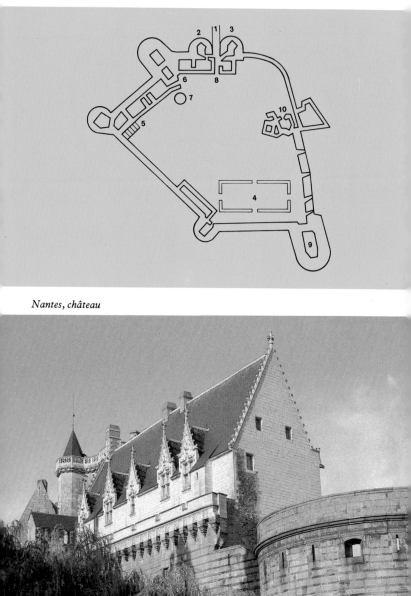

Nantes, château

Nantes, château 1 bridge 2 Boulangerie tower
3 Pied-de-Biche tower 4 Bâtiment du Harnachement 5 Grand-Logis 6 Pavillon de la Couronne
d'Or 7 well 8 Bâtiment du Grand Gouvernement
9 Tour du fer à cheval 10 donjon

Portus Namnetum (harbour of the
Namnetes, corrupted to Nantes). In
the Middle Ages the old river port, 47
km inland, was considered impreg-
nable from the sea. As overseas trade
increased, gold and money streamed
into the town, some of it from the
slave trade, and this led to a period of
intensive building. The metropolis
naturally had a few setbacks in the
modern era, some in the Wars of
Religion, which ended in 1598 with
the famous Edict of Nantes, granting
the Huguenots freedom of religion
and political rights, at least on a temporary basis. Allied bombing caused
severe damage in the Second World
War, and at the time of the French

Revolution the town sadly became
famous for the so-called noyades (in
1793 about 15,000 people were tied
up in pairs, man and woman together,
loaded into boats with sliding bottoms
and drowned in the Loire). But
despite its chequered history, Nantes,
thanks to its situation and the shipping industry, is considered one of the
most buoyant towns in France.

Château: This massive, largely 15C
building is protected by a curtain wall
with 6 towers and the old 13C keep.
Adjacent to it is a shallow moat,
originally fed from the Loire. An 18C
stone bridge and a 15C drawbridge
lead between two defiant round
towers, the Boulangerie and Pied-de-
Biche towers, to the extensive, largely
open square, on the other side of
which is the Bâtiment du Harnachement, an undistinguished building
added in 1784. On the right of the

Nantes, Town Hall

entrance is the *Grand-Logis*, built under Duchess Anne to plans by M.Rodier; its lower sections are very plain, but the roof has unusually high dormers lavishly decorated with gables and finials. At the S. end of this building is the *Pavillon de la Couronne d'Or*, which has two parallel staircase towers and loggias in the two upper storeys. In front of the building is a fine octagonal stone well, with an elegant wrought-iron ducal crown housing 7 sets of winding gear.

Interior; the following *museums* are housed in the building:

Musée des Arts Populaires et Régionaux in the Bâtiment du Grand Gouvernement, the large 17C administrative building by the Grand-Logis; the collection includes costume, pottery, faience and other Breton folk art;

Musée des Arts Décoratifs in the Tour du fer à cheval, which exhibits furniture, ceramics and other objets d'art;

Musée des Salorges in the Bâtiment du Harnachement, which covers the town's maritime trade and the crafts which used to flourish here.

St-Pierre: It took an unusually long time to build this essentially Gothic cathedral: more than 700 years. Work started in 1143, and was concluded in 1893 with the completion of apse and chapels. The order of work was as follows: from 1334 to 1508 the façade with two 207 ft. towers, three portal arches and the fine carved figures (like the Grand-Logis to a design by M.Rodier) were built; in the 16C came the nave with its elegant triforium and two aisles; in 1628 the vault was added, in 1637 the S. transept and in the 19C (1893) the choir, which had been started in 1650, was completed. Despite all these delays the 335 ft. long, 123 ft. high church makes a surprisingly uniform impression.

Among other interesting features in the *interior* are the lavishly decorated late-16C columns at the far end of the nave and two tombs: the *Tombeau de François II*, Duke of Britanny, who

died in 1488 and also built the château in Nantes, in the right arm of the transept: a Renaissance masterpiece by M.Colombe (1430–1512), and the *Tombeau de Lamorcière* in the first transept arm, by P.Dubois 1897.

By the church, in the so-called *Psalette*, the former arch-deaconry, is the *Musée d'Art Religieux*.

Ste-Croix: This church was built in the 17C and altered in the 19C; it is a mixture of various styles and has a high tower which dominates the old town. While the portal (1685) suggests a Romanesque church the windows in the nave are Gothic, but the pulpit and an altar with paintings are 18C.

Town: The E. part of the town is medieval and the W. part is 18C.

In the *medieval town* are the château, the cathedral and the *préfecture*, which is housed in the former Chambre des comtes de Bretagne, and the 17C *Hôtel de Ville*, made up of three former town houses.

The *18C town* was founded by merchants and shipbuilders, who outgrew the medieval town; they settled near the harbour and by the gigantic sugar, tobacco, cotton and spice warehouses. Fine features of this W. area are the *Place Royale*, designed *c.* 1790 by M.Crucy, and rebuilt after being destroyed in 1943 in 18C style, the *Place Graslin* with the Grand Théâtre (1788), the *Cours Cambronne*, the *Quai de la Fosse*, the *Rue Kervegan* and the *Ile Feydau* with its palace supported by timber in the Venetian manner.

Museums: *Musée des Beaux-Arts* (Rue de Clemenceau): This is one of the most important museums of its kind in France. It has about 2,000 paintings and is housed in a 19C building. The collections include numerous works of the Italian school

Porcelain work by della Robbia in the château ▷

Nantes, portal of St-Pierre cathedral

(pictures by Tintoretto, Guardi and Canaletto among others); of the Flemish school (Bruegel, Rubens); and French painters (G. de la Tour, Le Nain, Watteau, Lancret, Greuze, Géricault, Delacroix, Ingres and Courbet). It also shows Impressionists (Monet, Sisley) and modern painters (Dufy, Vlaminck, Rouault, Kandinsky).

Musée Dobrée (Place Jean V); The collections are presented in two historical buildings and a modern one: in the Manoir de Jean (15C) are the prehistoric collection, Greek ceramics, Roman and Merovingian antiquities; in the Palais Dobrée, a 19C building, medieval art (ivory carvings, illuminated manuscripts, tapestries, sculpture), 16&17C furniture and, in a cabinet of engravings, etchings by Rembrandt and Dürer. The section built in 1975 is devoted to the Vendée war.

Musée d'Histoire Naturelle (Place de la Monnaie): This modern scientific museum was founded towards the end of the 18C; its important collections and wide-ranging library have earned it a good reputation.

Musée Compagnonnique: this 'journeyman museum', established recently in the Manoir de la Hautière, has a representative collection of old tools.

Musée Jules Verne (Rue de Hermitage): This museum is devoted to Jules Vernes, who was born in Nantes (1828–1905).

Environs: Ancenis (37 km. NE): Remains of a 15C *château* (gatehouse with round side towers), 16C (residence) and 17C (pavilions). 15&16C *church* and *statue* of the famous Renaissance poet Joachim du Bellay. 3.5 km. S. of Ancenis: **Liré**. This village became famous through a

Nantes, St-Pierre cathedral, detail of portal

sonnet by du Bellay and also erected a *memorial* to him. 2 km. SW of Ancenis: **Château de la Turmelière** (ruined). Birthplace of J. du Bellay (1522), immortalized in his volume of poetry 'L'Olive' as the place in which he met and fell in love with his cousin Olive de Sevigny.

Blain (37 km. N.): *12C Château* surrounded by a massive fortified wall with low towers and embrasures.

Champtoceaux (32 km. NE): Set on a wooded hill above the right bank of the Loire this place, violently disputed in the Middle Ages by the counts of Anjou and the dukes of Brittany and passing frequently from one side to the other, offers from the *Promenade du Champalud* one of the finest views over the valley of the Loire. Little has survived of the *old fortress*. The widow of Charles de Blois is said to have lured her husband's adversary, the Duke of Brit-

tany here and held him prisoner for several months until he was freed by his barons; the war between the Monforts and the Blois came to an end when château and town were destroyed.

Château de Clermont (27 km. NE): the château is a large brick building dating from post 1630; it was bought in 1967 by the French comedian Louis de Funès.

Château de Goulaine (14 km. SE): Late 15C *château* with moats and fortified walls; it has two fine chamfered staircase towers.

Clisson (28 km. SE): 13C medieval *fortress* (chapel, house and kitchens) extended in the 15C by Duke François II (W. side and portal).

Loroux-Bottereau, Le (20 km. E.): *Church* with fine early-13C frescos. Ruins of a 15C *château* with an extensive view over the marshes in the area.

Oudon (35 km. NE): Very fine octagonal *keep* dating from the end of the 14C (104 ft. high).

Saint-Nazaire (57 km. W.): Nantes' second harbour at the mouth of the Loire; it is an important town with 269,800 inhabitants; it was completely destroyed by allied bombing in the Second World War and rebuilt after 1945 a little further to the W. around the handsome N.–S. axis of the Avenue de la République.

Particularly fine modern features of Saint-Nazaire are *Ste-Anne* (1957), *Notre-Dame-de-l'Espérance*, the *student quarter* and the *hospital centre*.

The finest feature of all is the *port* in the E. of the town; it consists of a pre-harbour area and two large basins. The massive concrete block in the 25 acre St-Nazaire basin was an underwater submarine base with 24 pens, built by the Germans in the Second World War.

Nouans-les-Fontaines
37 Indre-et-Loire   p.138☐M 5

Church: 13C building with fine vaults, in which a surprising discovery was made in the Thirties: a monumental church picture by J.Fouquet (or his school), thought lost, was discovered under the dust of centuries. Fouquet was born in 1420, the son of a priest in Tours: even in his lifetime he was known as the greatest painter of portraits and miniatures of his century, and he is still considered as such today. The rediscovery of this picture dating from 1470 is equally important for painting at the point of transition from the Middle Ages to the modern period. The only puzzling feature is how the painting came to be in this rather ordinary village church. It depicts the Descent from the Cross in a quiet and

Nouans-les-Fontaines, Wailing over the Body of Christ

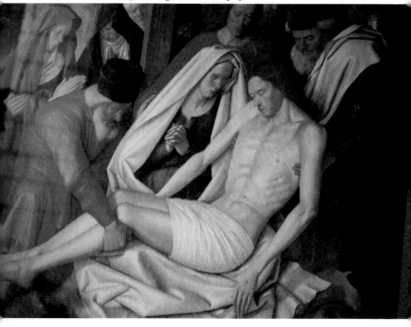

touching fashion. Christ is laid in Mary's lap by two bearded old men with fur hats, and John bends lovingly over Mary. On the right in the foreground is the founder, kneeling in a rich, bright garment. In the background are dark mourning figures, three nuns, and biblical figures behind them. At this point the picture, which was originally larger, is cut off. Even so it is still almost 8 by 5 ft. in size.

Orléans

45 Loiret   p.138☐N/O 1/2

There is good reason for the saying 'Paris is the head of France, Orléans is its heart.' In the Gallic period the town of *Genabum*, conquered by Caesar in 52 BC, stood on the site. The Romans called the place, an important base for them, *Aurelianis*, and the modern name derives from this. The Huns under Attila tried to conquer the town in 451, but they were not successful until 498, under Clovis.

Orléans, general view

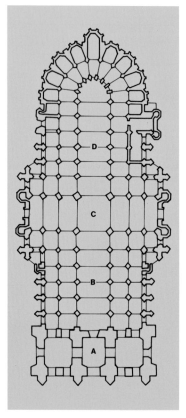

Orléans, Ste-Croix cathedral The ground plan reveals a regular design: the transept is placed precisely in the middle of the basilica with nave and four aisles **A** vestibule **B** six-bayed nave **C** three-aisled transept **D** three-bayed choir with ambulatory and 9 radiating chapels

In the early 7C the Merovingians made it the seat of their king and the capital of W. France. In the early 9C, through Bishop Theodulf, Orléans acquired an academic reputation which attracted scholars from all over Europe. In 1305 the development started by Theodulf led to the founding of the famous university under Philip the Fair.

In the early 15C this peaceful development came to an abrupt end.

Two thirds of France were in English hands, including Paris itself. It seemed that it could only be a question of time before Orléans also fell into the hands of the English. In October 1428 the English and the Burgundians, under the leadership of Sir John Talbot, marched from the left bank of the Loire against the second most important town in France and laid siege to it. At the end of April 1429 Joan of Arc reached the town, to rescue it from the enemy in accordance with the charge which she felt she had received from God. Within a few days the seventeen-year-old shepherd girl succeeded in raising the siege and putting the enemy to flight. On May 8 1429 the Maid was able to enter Orléans as its deliverer. For more than 500 years the feast of the national saint of France has been celebrated every year on the 7 and 8 of May.

The town was again plunged into confusion by war in 1562 when Prince Condé made Orléans the headquarters of the Protestant cause and billeted an army of 20,000 men there. Henry IV was not able to recapture the town until 1594. At the time of the Revolution the town was heavily involved. In the last war it suffered doubly. In 1940 it was bombed by the Germans, and then occupied, in 1943 it was bombed by the Americans, who recaptured Orléans on August 16. Despite very severe damage an astonishing amount has been restored.

Ste-Croix cathedral: This cathedral, dating from the 4C, is felt by the French to be a monument to their national history, even if Marcel Proust thought it was the ugliest cathedral in France. Its building history began c 375, when St.Evortius, then Bishop of Orléans, started to build the first church on the site. It was established in 1937 that this was a basilica with three aisles, transepts and apse. Its remains are open to the public;

Orléans, Ste-Croix cathedral ▷

Orléans, Sainte-Croix cathedral, detail of portal

they are beneath the choir. When the bishop, who was later canonized, was about to consecrate the church, the hand of God appeared to him, raised in blessing above the building. He therefore declared the church a 'temple consecrated by the hand of God,' and did not continue with the ceremony of consecration. For the same reason none of the later buildings on the site was consecrated by a bishop. Even the present cathedral was not consecrated, but the keystone of the apse is decorated with the hand of God raised in blessing.

A round building was added to the first basilica under Bishop Theodulf at the beginning of the 9C, and fragments of its mosaic floor have survived. In this building the grandson of Charlemagne, Charles the Bald, was crowned king of the West Franks in 848. The church burned down in

989 along with large parts of the town. King Robert the Pious and Bishop Arnoul I began to rebuild the church. Because the building was intended as a large pilgrimage church with ambulatory, choir chapel, nave, three aisles and a twin-towered W. façade, work went on into the 12C. It was one of the largest French churches of the period.

In the second half of the 13C it became clear that the Romanesque architects had not built solidly enough. In 1278 and then again in 1286 large parts of the church collapsed, to the extent that repairs were no longer possible. On September 11 1287 the foundation stone of the present cathedral was laid and building of the choir chapels and the apse E. of the old church was begun. Work was then interrupted by the Hundred Years War, so that when Joan of Arc entered the town she had to go through the damaged Romanesque nave to pray in the Gothic choir.

In the second half of the 15C the transept and the adjacent four bays of the nave to the W. façade of the earlier Romanesque building were added. In 1511 the crossing tower was completed, but the cathedral was not destined to to be left in peace. In 1568 the building was largely destroyed by the Calvinists in the Wars of Religion. Only the choir, some side chapels and two bays of the nave survived to some extent.

The cathedral was in ruins until 1599. Then attempts were made to convince Henry IV, who had just been reconverted to Catholicism, that rebuilding the cathedral would be the best sign of the king's real feeling for the Church. Whether for personal or political reasons, the king allowed himself to be persuaded, and in 1601 he laid the foundation stone for the rebuilding of the cathedral. In 1632 the choir, which included the two surviving 13&14C choir chapels, was completed. The high choir itself remained in the Flamboyant style. The transept was rebuilt by 1690, and

Orléans, Ste-Croix cathedral, interior

Orléans, Ste-Croix, stained glass

Louis XIV made sure that it was built in 'Gothic order'. The architect was the Jesuit Etienne Martellange, a devoted servant of his king. He was responsible not only for the neoclassical transept façades with their gabled and columned portals, but also for the sun-shaped rosettes, a direct tribute to the king. In the middle they have a symbolic head of Louis XIV as sun god, and in order to rule out any possible misunderstanding, the motto of the king as well 'NEC PLURIBUS IMPAR' (= no-one is his equal). The façades were also decorated with tracery windows, tracery arches and quatrefoils. The polygonal corner towers were intended to ensure that sufficient attention was paid to Gothic design criteria.

From 1767 the W. façade with its three-bayed vestibule and two generously proportioned W. towers was added. It was also the king's wish that this façade should be in pure Gothic style, but it is quite clear that certain elements were seen through neoclassical spectacles. The architect of the façade with its towers bluntly topped with bizarre crowns was L.F. Trouard, who managed to complete it in 1793. The cathedral was still far from complete, however; the Revolution prevented the joining of the nave to the tower façade.

It was not until 1829 that the nave was connected with the towered façade, and the church at least closed to the elements. The ridge turret at the the crossing, modelled on Amiens cathedral, was added in 1858 under E.Boeswillwald. At a height of 374 ft. it is one of the symbols of the town. But still the cathedral was not complete. Again the builders had not been careful enough, and in 1904 the choir vault collapsed and the crossing tower had to be renewed as well. Further rebuilding was also needed after the last war.

The *façade*, a good 131 ft. high and 180 feet wide, clearly consists of three sections. Over the three portals are three large rose windows separated by turrets decorated with statues. The three sections are unified by a gallery above the rose windows decorated with tracery, the two outer parts of which form the basis for the two *towers*, each 269 ft. high. They each have three storeys, and the higher they rise the smaller the plan becomes. The two lower storeys are square in plan, the uppermost one is round. The lowest storey of each tower has an open-plan staircase tower at each corner, the second storeys are decorated with rows of high columns, and the upper storeys are open circles of columns topped with stylized crowns.

Despite the lengthy building period the *interior* of the cathedral is remarkably uniform. The nave and the choir each have six bays. The outer edge of the ambulatory is formed by nine individual chapels, of which two are still 13C; the others are modelled on these two. The central chapel, the *Chapelle de Notre-Dame de la Compassion*, is considerably deeper than the others. It contains a marble Pietà made by M.Bourdin in 1623. The Reformation and the Revolution between them removed most of the original furnishings. The fine, early 18C carved wooden *choir stalls* did survive, however; they are among the finest specimens of French court art. They were made by J.-M. Degoullons from 1702–6, to designs by C.le Brun and J.Gabriel. The beautifully crafted decoration forms medallions depicting the Life of Christ. The pews were commissioned by Cardinal Pierre du Cambout de Coislin, Bishop of Orléans. There is a portrait of him by H.Rigaud in the ambulatory. The marble statue of Joan of Arc, canonized in 1920, is a work by A.C.Ver-

mare dating from 1912. The same artist was responsible for the marble statue of Cardinal Touchet (1927), kneeling before the altar of the saint; he was the bishop of Orléans who achieved Joan's canonisation. Both statues are to be found in the chapel dedicated to St.Joan (1st on the left side of the choir). The great organ came from Saint-Benoît-sur-Loire.

The *crypt* is actually an excavated chamber 91 ft. by 36 ft. showingB the remains of the earlier churches. There are finds from the Romanesque cathedral, the Carolingian mosaic floor and the Gallo-Roman basilica. Various 13&14C bishops' tombs with lavish grave goods were also discovered. The remains of crosiers, rings, altar vessels and ceremonial vestments are on show in the sacristy treasury, along with other valuable objects. The finest exhibits are a 12C enamel cross, 11C Byzantine enamelled discs and a 15C Flemish Tree of Jesse.

St-Aignan: St-Aignan dates from a church built in the 6C over the grave of the bishop and Saint Anianus (d. 453). In 451 Anianus succeeded in persuading Attila the Hun to raise the siege of the town. King Robert the Pious built a church on the site of several earlier buildings, and this was consecrated in 1029. The crypt survived, and parts of this date from the 9C. This church was destroyed in the Hundred Years War and rebuilt in the Flamboyant style after the liberation of Orléans. The Calvinists pulled down the nave in the 16C Wars of Religion, so only the choir and transept survive. The polygonal apse has an ambulatory with five large individual chapels. The great high altar retable was a gift from Louis XIII in 1619. Remarkably fine capitals were found in the crypt, discovered in 1862.

Stained glass, St.Joan burned at the stake ▷

Notre-Dame de Recouvrance: This church was built 1513–19 in early Renaissance style, but was restored in the previous century. The large window over the high altar depicting the Birth of Christ is worth seeing.

St-Paul: In 1940 only the tower and the chapel of Notre-Dame-des-Miracles remained of the church completed in 1627. This contains the 16C **Black Madonna**. The miraculous image is a copy of an older one dating from the 5C and burned by the Huguenots in 1562.

Town Hall: Built *c.* 1550 for Jacques Groslot, the governor of Orléans. His lively brick and ashlar walls are clearly late Gothic, but the flight of steps and portals are pure Renaissance. Francis II died here in 1560, after opening the provincial assembly.

Charles IX met the beautiful Marie Touchet here, and felt attracted to her for the rest of his life. In the 19C the building was restored and extended by the addition of the wings. The steps are decorated with a statue of Joan of Arc.

Salles des Thèses: This 15C hall is all that remains of the once so famous university, which had up to 5000 students even in the Middle Ages. The reformer Calvin studied law here in 1528.

Renaissance houses: Unfortunately many were destroyed in the war. Worth seeing: *Hôtel Toutin*: The arcaded gallery in the courtyard makes this the finest surviving Renaissance building in the town. The *Maison de la Coquille* with a large shell decorating the façade, and the *Maison d'Alibert* are also interesting.

Orléans, Roman aqueduct

Orléans, Town Hall

Museums: *Musée des Beaux-Arts* in the Hôtel des Crénaux, a 15&16C building. The bell tower in the courtyard was built as a town tower in the 15C. The museum is famous for its collection of 17&18C portraits and engravings. One of the most valuable exhibits is a 15C work by Matteo di Giovanni, representing the Madonna and Child with 2 angels. *Musée historique et archéologique* in the 16C Hôtel de Cabus. Gallo-Roman and medieval collections in two rooms. Particularly fine is the Gallo-Roman treasure of Neuvy-en-Sullias with impressive bronze statues. The *Maison de Jeanne d'Arc* houses numerous documents on the life and work of the Maid of Orléans. There is also a collection of weapons from the Hundred Years War.

Environs: Chécy (10 km. E): This is the point at which St.Joan crossed the Loire on April 28 1429 in order to bring help to besieged Orléans. There is an annual ceremony in memory of this event.
Church with Romanesque vestibule (13,14&15C).

Fay-aux-Loges (16 km. E.): *Notre-Dame* dates from the 11C, but was altered and extended in the 12&13C.

Olivet (4 km. S.): Old *abbey* with a fine 12C chapterhouse.

Orléans-la-Source (8 km. S.): The source of the Loiret is simply an arm of the Loire which trickles into the ground near St-Benoît and reappears in a large park here as a spring. *Château de la Source:* The château belonged to Cardinal Briçonnet in the 16C. The building in its present form dates from 1632.

Saint-Hilaire-Saint-Mesmin (6 km. SW): 13&15C *church*.

Orléans, former bishop's palace

Plessis-Bourré, Le

49 Maine-et-Loire   p.136□F 3

This château in a moorland area far away from large centres of population is one of the most remarkable in Anjou. It belonged to Jean Bourré, treasurer to Louis XI and financial secretary to Charles VIII and Louis XII. It draws its distinction firstly from being built very quickly, in five years (1468–73), which gave it remarkable unity, and from the excellent materials used in its construction, which meant that it has survived in very good condition. The second striking feature is its low elevation, which sets it apart from other châteaux. In the early days fortresses sought safety in height (siege ladders could only be a certain length) and the later châteaux aimed for a classical balance (aesthetic considerations and domestic comfort were now the prime factors); Le Plessis-Bourré stands at a transitional point, and is trying to fulfil both a defensive and a domestic function. The château is also evidence of military techniques which do not involve the use of siege ladders. Artillery was the new feature, and it was important to present as few surfaces as possible to it. Thus the buildings, with the exception of the

Le Plessis-Bourré, château ▷

Pontlevoy, former abbey church

residential section, are kept low and the moats are broad, to hold the guns at a distance.

Château: A bridge 141 ft. long, with seven arches and drawbridges, leads from the farm yard, with entrance pavilions and outbuildings, to the main portal, protected by a double drawbridge and machicolations. The château buildings form a square, with round towers as broad as they are high and with conical roofs at three of the corners, and the donjon at the fourth; this has a wall passage and a narrower top storey, and is reminiscent of Langeais, which Louis XI commissioned J.Bourré to build. The main building opposite the entrance portal, with polygonal staircase towers at either end, is three storeys high in contrast with the rest of the buildings; this makes it extremely light.

There are various interesting rooms in the *interior*, particularly the guard room with its painted wooden ceiling, the grand salon with Louis-Quinze wainscotting and the parliament room with shallow rib vaulting, large fireplace and original floor tiles.

Environs: Champigné (10 km. N.): *Manoir de Charnacé*, a 16C manor house.
Château de la Harmonière (8.5 km. N.): Elegant *manor* with two residential wings (15C).
Thorigné-d'Anjou (11 km. NW): 15&18C *church*.

Pontlevoy
41 Loir-et-Cher   p.138☐L 4

This little market town N. of the Cher has an interesting history. It started as a hermitage belonging to the monastery of St-Martin in Tours. A fortress

Pontlevoy, monastery, main façade

was built in the 9C, parts of which have survived. In 1423 the castle was extended and heavily fortified by Charles VII as a protection against the English.

In 1034 Count Gelduin de Chaumont was shipwrecked and miraculously rescued, and in his gratitude he vowed to the Virgin Mary that he would found a monastery. In fulfilment of this vow he brought Benedictine monks to Pontlevoy from St-Florent in Saumur. In 1629 Richelieu became commendatory abbot of the monastery. The cardinal extended the buildings and named Pierre de Bérulle as his successor; he brought reformed Benedictines from Saint-Maur, and they opened a school, which in 1776 attained the rank of military academy. The school was a respected national institution even at the time of the Revolution, and it continued to exist until 1940.

Former abbey church: Started in the 13C and extended in the 14&15C, but not completed. The choir with side aisles, the ambulatory and three chapels were finished. There are interesting 17C altars, including one in marble by A.Charpentier (1651). The porphyry and bronze tabernacle and the 17C choir stalls are also very fine. The Virgin on the right of the ambulatory dates from the 11C.

To the right of the church are the former *monastery buildings*. The large main façade (1701) and the monumental buildings around the courtyard are of interest.

St-Pierre: The parish church retains sections from its 11C predecessor in the transept.

Environs: Couddes (14 km. SE): Romanesque *church* (nave) with old frescos, some of which date from the

13C but are still Romanesque in their execution. In the small 15C chapel on the left the old tiles and 17C wooden candlesticks are still in evidence.

Château Gué-Péan (9 km. SE): This elegant 14&15C *hunting lodge* is unjustly neglected by visitors to the Loire valley; the pretty blue and white Renaissance château has the charm of a house which has always been lived in, and seems alive, rather than like a museum.

The château has attracted distinguished visitors in all periods. Royal guests include Louis XII, Francis I, Henri II and Henri III, and even Queen Mary of England. Fénelon, La Fayette, Rochambeau and Balzac also enjoyed staying here.

The château is built around a square with four corner towers dating from the 14&15C. The highest of the towers has a bell-shaped slate roof with lavishly decorated machicola-tions. The S. tower houses the chapel; the side sections and individual pavilions are broken up and articulated with open arcades. The differing types of roof are an integral part of the design of the building.

The large guard room, the wall passage of the large tower and a series of rooms furnished in Louis-Quinze and Louis-Seize styles and with fine tapestries and paintings by Andrea del Sarto, G.Reni, H.Rigaud, J-H.Fragonard, J-L.David and F.Gérard are open to the public. The grand salon has a massive fireplace by G.Pilon. The library houses a fine collection of autographs and numerous historical documents.

Thenay (3 km. E.): Parts of the *village church* date from the 12C. The finest feature of the furnishings is a triptych, carved in wood and painted and gilded, of the Adoration of the Magi. It dates from the late 15C.

Pontlevoy, St-Pierre

Ponts-de-Cé, Les

49 Maine-et-Loire   p.136□F 3/4

This town on the Loire, the Authion and the Louet is one of the strangest places one could imagine. It starts on a bridge, and really consists of just a street and four bridges. However, as the 'gateway from Angers to the South' it has made such a name for itself as a battlefield that tradition has transferred to Les Ponts-de-Cé the battle between the Angevin hero Dumnacus and the allies of Caesar after the fruitless siege of Poitiers in the year 51 BC, which is presumed to have been fought further S. But there have in fact been more than enough battles in this town, extended as a key fortress by the counts and dukes of Anjou; in 1369, in the course of the Hundred Years War, it was taken by the English and not reconquered by the French until 1438. In 1648–53 it was involved in the Fronde Wars (of the nobility and parliament against the absolutist régime of Cardinal Mazarin), and in 1793–6 it was drawn into the Vendée Wars (the revolt of peasants true to the king against the French Revolution). The town was especially badly hit in the Second World War, when Germans and French were involved in an artillery battle over the river.

We should also not omit to mention the essentially comic battle, the so-called 'drôlerie des Ponts-de-Cé', between the partisans of the Queen Mother, Maria de Medici and the supporters of Louis XIII, in which both sides shouted 'long live the King!' and in the evening celebrated the lack of bloodshed by the reconciliation of the two parties in the Château de Brissac.

Les Ponts-de-Cé, Loire bridge

Churches: The two *chapels* (on the right after the Authion bridge), with remains of 16C wall paintings, are more interesting than the 12&15C *St-Aubin*, badly damaged in 1944 and rebuilt in 1946 and the 19C *St-Maurille*, with fine 16C choir stalls.

Château: Only the pentagonal donjon survives of the 15C château on an island in the Loire from which King René the Good enjoyed watching the competitions of the beautiful fisherwomen (la baillée des filles).

Dumnacus memorial: Set on the bridge over the larger arm of the Loire (28 arches), it was made by René Guilleux in 1960 as a memorial to the battle between the Gallic Andecaves and the Romans, which was probably not fought in Les Ponts-de-Cé.

Environs: Beaulieu-sur-Layon (16 km. SW): A neat, beautifully-situated wine-growing village famous for its white wines, and with some elegant old houses. In the choir of the

Les Ponts-de-Cé, keep

old *church*, which has now been turned into a chapel, is a wooden figure of the Virgin dating from 1598. **Erigné** (3 km. SW): 12C *church* with finely-carved 16C beams.

Preuilly-sur-Claise
37 Indre-et-Loire   p.136☐K/L 6

This typical little Loire valley market town on a hill on the right bank of the Claise has a number of fine 16&17C houses, an old château and several old churches.

Old château: Only ruins have survived of the château built on the hill by the barons of Preuilly in the 12&15C; they include a fortified gate and parts of the 12C collegiate church of St-Mélaine. Next to this is the *new château*, which has looked majestically down over the town since the 19C.

Churches: For its size (1579 inhabitants) Preuilly has an astonishing number of churches, including the old *Notre-Dame-des-Echelles*, dating from 1217, now used as a parish room, the 12C *St-Nicolas* the 16C Calvinist *sermon hall* and the *cemetery chapel* of 1682.
St-Pierre is particularly important; it originally belonged to the abbey founded in 1001. The present building, or those parts of it which survived 'restoration' in the 19C, is no older than late 11/ early 12C. The most striking feature of the church is the combination of Touraine and Poitou styles. The lavish arcatures above the windows are very fine. The church has a nave and two aisles and is 188 ft. long and 54 ft. high, with choir and ambulatory (the apex chapel is the only radiating chapel to survive). There is a striking variety of vaults and decorated capitals.

Preuilly-sur-Claise, general view ▷

Only parts of the 12C cloister, the monks' dormitory, now the priest's house, and the chapterhouse above it have survived of the *monastery* which belonged to the church.

Environs: Bossay-sur-Claise (4 km. SE): Restored Romanesque *church*. Restored 15C *château*.
Château de Fontbaudry (11 km. NE): Ruined château.

Richelieu
37 Indre-et-Loire   p.136□I 5

Armand Jean Duplessis (1585–1642), Duke of Richelieu from 1630, was a cardinal and churchman, but in reality more a politician who paved the way for French absolutism; he not only made his mark on the French state, but also on the village in which the house of his ancestors stood. In his search for fame he wanted to leave a worthy monument for posterity and commissioned the master builder

Richelieu, Notre-Dame, façade

J.Lemercier to build a château to his design, and then a town for which he proceeded to import the population. If considered realistically the site was not suitable for a settlement of any size; the village was too far away from the centre of things, and the land too infertile. Jean de La Fontaine (1621–95) made fun of the little neoclassical town and called it 'the first village in the universe' and considered that it was 'handsomely built, but badly sited'. Even today, when the inhabitants have found other sources of income and live here from choice, the place is lacking in life and seems ostentatious and domineering.

Town: The *château* built by the almighty cardinal on the site of the home of his ancestors, which was in his view by no means splendid enough, was pulled down in the 19C

and the town, designed absolutely symmetrically around the residence, still gives the impression of being an amazingly splendid approach which has been left without a heart, or perhaps better without a head. The N.-S. axis, the *Grande Rue*, is lined with 28 imposing 'hôtels', all of which have monumental portals with round arches, and leads to a semicircular square in which Ramey's (1754–1838) marble statue of the cardinal was placed in 1932. The square gives access to the fine *château park*, which is well worth seeing; it has belonged to the University of Paris since 1930. The Grande Rue connects two equally large squares, the *Place des Religieuses* with the old Académie Royale, founded by Richelieu in 1640 and the *Place du Marché*, with the neoclassical church of Notre-Dame, a notable wooden market hall and the

Richelieu, town gate

Richelieu, Richelieu monument and town gate

Hôtel de Ville, which houses a local history and Richelieu museum. *Notre-Dame*, with its façade decorated with the four Evangelists and two towers with pyramid roofs, is the work of J.Lemercier (1625–38). The town, which occupies an area of 820 by 436 yards, is surrounded by ramparts and ditches which used to be fed by the Mable, but have now been drained and made into elegant gardens. The *town wall* is also designed symmetrically; it has six gates, some of which have survived with their old pavilions.

Château: A domed pavilion, the canals and two other pavilions beyond the flower beds, the orangery and the wine cellar, are all that has survived of the enormous château, packed with art treasures reflecting the colossal wealth of the man who built it: paintings by Titian, Rubens and van Dyck, and the slaves created by Michelangelo for the tomb of Julius II. The magnificent building itself was seized in 1792 and pulled down after the Revolution, and so the monument erected to himself by the man who, as far as lay within his power, had all the châteaux in the area destroyed so that the isolated glory of his own château would outshine all the rest, was razed to the ground.

Environs: Braye-sous-Faye (3 km. SE): *Richelieu family vault* in an old church (11C portal).
Jaulnay (11 km. SE):15C *church*. 1 km. E. of Jaulnay: ruins of the château de **Chillou** (14&15C). 5 km. N. of Jaulnay: ruins of the château de **Mondon** (late-14C).
Razines (6 km. SE): Ruined 11C *church*.

Rochecorbon
37 Indre-et-Loire   p.136□K 4

A pretty old village with 15–18C houses at the foot of a steep slope from which an old *watch tower* looks out over the surroundings; the slender, square 15C tower is known with affectionate mockery as the 'Lanterne de Rochecorbon'. Down in the valley is a fine old *church* dating in part from the 11&12C, and much altered in the 15C; there is a roofed exterior pulpit on the S. side. At the edge of the village is a *folie*, the 18C French equivalent of the English folly, a building in the country where people met to amuse themselves. It now houses the *Musée d'Espelosin* or *Musée du Vin*, which is well worth a visit. There is a collection of old wine-presses and other winemaking equipment, and in the courtyard a set of stones from Gallo-Roman times which were used then, so ancient is the industry here, as part of the winemaking process.

Environs: Saint-Georges (2 km. S.): 11&12C *church*. Old 11C *chapel*. *Ruined château*, from which over 100 steps cut into the rock lead to the top of the hill.

Romorantin-Lanthenay
41 Loir-et-Cher   p.138□N 4

This pretty old town on the Sauldre was once the capital of the Sologne. The settlement was first documented in the 12C, as *Rivus Morantini*. It was at first in the possession of the Counts of Blois, then passed to Orléans in the late 14C. In 1445 it was acquired by the house of Valois-Angoulême, and Count Jean d'Angoulême built a new château here from 1448 to 1467. Here François d'Angoulême, later Francis I, spent his turbulent youth. In 1517 he commissioned Leonardo da Vinci to design a château for his mother, Louise de Savoie, but it was never built. The château which was the home of Francis I has only survived in part, and is not open to the public, as it is used by the local authority. The only interesting exterior feature is a

Romorantin, portal of St-Etienne

Romorantin, St-Etienne, tower

round tower with its own staircase turret and high Renaissance dormers. In the 16C the town suffered greatly at the hands of the Protestants, but some fine Renaissance *half-timbered houses* have survived, particularly in the Rue de la Résistance. A very fine specimen is the Hôtel de la Chancellerie, with its protruding upper storey. The corner post is decorated on one side with a coat-of-arms, and on the other with a bagpiper. Also worth seeing: Hôtel Saint-Pol with its interesting façade, and the Maison du Carroir Doré, dating from 1480 and decorated with statues, including St.Michael slaying the dragon, and the Annunciation.

St-Etienne: The church is on the Marin island in the river, and dates from the 12C. Parts of the central tower have survived from then. The nave, choir and apse were built in the

13C. The aisles were added in the 15C, the ambulatory and its chapels are 17C.

Musée de la course automobile: A collection of Formula 1 racing cars and exhibits on the history of motor sport, complemented by a specialized library.

Environs: Château du Moulin (13 km. W): The pretty *château* in wooded terrain with many lakes was built 1480–1502 by P.du Moulin to a design by J.de Persigny. It was restored *c.* 1900 by C.Genuys. The corner towers have disappeared, with the exception of the one at the NE corner, but the old entrance with moat, bridge and 2 gatehouse towers has survived. The courtyard contains a fine 15C fountain. The interior is worth seeing for the lovingly assembled furnishings. The *Salle des*

Selles-Saint-Denis (Romorantin), 15C frescos

Gardes in the gatehouse with bell tower has a vaulted ceiling with a central octagonal column. The broad fireplace is contemporary with the building. The interior was designed by Marchéville and has some eye-catching 15–17C tapestries. The salon on the ground floor of the residential building has a Louis XIII ceiling and an outstandingly well-crafted statue of St.Catherine (school of M.Colombe).

Lassay-sur-Croisne (11 km. W.): The 15C *village church* contains the tomb of Philippe du Moulin, who died in 1506.

Mennetou-sur-Cher (16.5 km. SE): Picturesque little place, still partially enclosed by the *fortifications*, 40 to 50 ft. high, built in 1212 by the lord of Vierzon; 3 of the 5 old towers still look down on the town. The remainder of the château was removed in 1926. The *priory* and adjacent round tower have survived of the Benedictine abbey between the Porte d'En-bas (through which Joan of Arc passed on March 3 1429, as the inscription records), and the Porte Bonne-Nouvelles.

Mur-de-Sologne (12 km. NW): Old *church* with 11C nave and 15&16C choir.

Saint-Julien-sur-Cher (9 km. S.): The 11C *village church* contains 16&17C wooden statues.

Saint-Loup (15 km. SE): The little *village church* dates from the 12&13C and contains some fine frescos. The Majestas Domini and Our Lady of Sorrows in the vault of the apse have survived in particularly good condition.

Selles-Saint-Denis (15 km. E.): *St-Genoulph* dates from the 15C and has contemporary frescos.

Villefranche-sur-Cher (8 km. S.): 12C *church* with fine capitals.

Saché, château

Saché
37 Indre-et-Loire   p.136☐I 4

Château: An irregular, plain, even inartistic 17C building, which owes its fame to Balzac's visits rather than any architectural distinction. Until 1838 the creator of the 'Comédie Humaine' worked here for a certain length of time on his huge novel, an enormous portrait of French society of the period with about 2000 characters, some of whom appear in various novels at various times of their lives.

One of the novels,'The Lily in the Valley', is set around Saché and contains a portrait of Balzac's lover Laure de Berny as the Comtesse de Mortsauf, who in fact refuses her young lover in the novel. Jean de Margonne, the owner of Saché and presumed former lover of Balzac's mother, always kept a room ready for the great novelist, into which he withdrew when his Parisian creditors were pressing him too hard. Here he would work like a man possessed for nine to twelve hours from midnight onwards, sustained by countless cups of coffee, with the shutters closed and always by artificial light. Around this room, which Balzac used to call his 'monk's cell', Paul Métadier has created a *Balzac museum*. It has been preserved just as it was in Balzac's lifetime, with his bed in the alcove, desk and chair, down to a copy of the original wall paper. In the other rooms in the upper storeys there are collections of proofs corrected by Balzac and first editions of his books, caricatures of himself and contemporary authors, and numerous pictures of himself and those closest to him, his parents, Laure de Berny and Mme Hanska, with whom he for years conducted a now famous correspondence, and whom he married shortly before his death in 1850.

Church: Attractive building with nave and one aisle dating from the 12,13&16C.

Left of the choir is the tomb of Marguerite Rousselé, who lived in the château in the 17C.

Saint-Aignan
41 Loir-et-Cher   p.138☐M 4

This picturesque little town on a slope above the Cher goes back to a fortified castle built by the counts of Blois. In the 12C Thibault II built the first château, which passed through the hands of the Donzy, Châtillon, Bourbon, Bourgogne, Beauvillier and Talleyrand families. It was originally only a barony, but Francis I made it a county in 1538, and Louis XIV made it a duchy in 1663. The first duke of Saint-Aignan was François de Beauvillier. There are still some remarkable 15&16C wooden and half-timbered houses in the steep streets of

Saché, Picasso drawing of Balzac

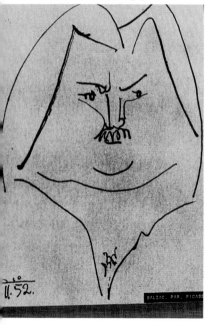

Saint-Aignan, collegiate church

the little town. The oldest house in the town dates from the 14C.

Collegiate church of St-Aignan: This dates from the late 9C, when monks from the monastery of St-Martin in Tours built a chapel in honour of the Madonna. Thanks to relics of the saint-bishop Anianus of Orléans a lively pilgrimage developed, which led to the building of a larger church in the 11C. The present church, a basilica with nave and two aisles with four bays and a transept was built from the late 11C to the early 13C. The exterior is dominated by a large W. tower, a massive crossing tower and a great ambulatory with three chapels. The church was thoroughly restored from 1845 onwards. Further restoration work was needed after the last war to make good the bomb damage.

Despite the long building period the *interior* has remarkable unity, the result of the organisation of the round arches, the patterning of the walls and the height of the vault. This harmony makes the basilica the finest Romanesque ecclesiastical building in the Loire region. Choir and transept still have the pure Romanesque tunnel vaulting, while the nave has pointed rib vaulting which foreshadows the Gothic. Astonishing treasures have survived in the church despite some clumsy restoration in the 19C. In the *chapel of Notre-Dame-des-Miracles* in the S. aisle there are 16C vault paintings, including one of the Archangel Michael as dragon-slayer and weigher of souls.

The greatest treasure in the basilica is the *crypt*. It avoided inexpert restoration in the 19C because it was being used as a wine cellar, and so escaped

Saint-Aignan, collegiate church, capital

Collegiate church, ceiling vault

attention. It is on the same ground plan as the choir, so that it has a main apse with a vaulted bay in front of it, and an ambulatory with three chapels. The vault of the main apse is decorated with three Majestas Domini and St.James and St.Peter. Both saints are seen in action: James is hearing confession and granting absolution; Peter is receiving the key from Christ and healing the lame. The Latin inscription reads CONFITEMINI ALTERUTRUM PECCATA ('we have confessed our sins one to another').

The *S. ambulatory chapel* has the Lamb of God borne by angels in the vault, and in 4 scenes on the walls the legend of St. Egidius. In the first scene the saint is giving his robe to a half-naked sick man, in the second a man bitten by a snake is being healed, in the third the saint is playing for the rescue of a ship in difficulties at sea. The fourth scene has not survived. The shape of the bodies and the linear, parallel or fan-shaped organisation of folds in fabric make the frescos clearly high Romanesque. They are thought to date from the second half of the 12C. The frescos in the middle chapel of the choir ambulatory date from the same period, but are by a different artist. The Resurrection of Lazarus can still be made out. The frescos on the side of the main apse are much later, and date from the 15C. The founder, Louis II, Lord of Chalon, with his two wives is shown twice, alongside the Majestas Domini. On the first occasion he is praying to John the Baptist, St.Anne and Mary with the Child, in the other scene he is praying to Our Lady of the Sorrows beneath the Cross. The vault in front of the apse has a last Judgement, the W. wall a Crucifixion.

Château: A majestic flight of stone steps leads from the church to the château, completely rebuilt by the Beauvillier family in the Renaissance. The château itself is not open to the public, but it is worth the climb to go into the courtyard, which is allowed, to see the wonderful view over the valley of the Cher. A 13C polygonal tower and a round tower, about a century later, remain of the medieval fortress.

Environs: Couffi (5.5 km. SE): 11, 13&15C *church*.
Noyers-sur-Cher (2 km. NE): 13C *church* with Angevin vault.
Saint-Romain: (5 km. N.): 12&16C *church* with 16C frescos. **Manoir du Bas-Morlu** (16C), built in a 12C chapel.
Thésée (9 km. NW): This was the site of the 2C Roman road station known as *Tasciaca*, on the road from Bourges to Tours. The rectangular building was 131 ft. long and 43 ft. wide. There was a smaller building next to it, of which only the foundations have been identified. In the Town Hall is a small *museum*, which displays all the finds from the Roman station, ceramics, coins, stone statues and small bronze objects from the 1–3C AD.

Saint-Aignan, château portal

Saint-Aignan, château ▷

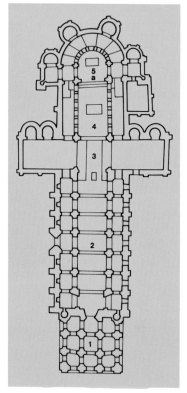

Saint-Benoît-sur-Loire, basilica 1 11C two-storey cubic vestibule **2** nave with two aisles **3** transept **4** choir **5** apse with preceding bay **(a)**

Saint-Benoît-sur-Loire
45 Loiret   p.138☐O/P 2

The Benedictine abbey has one of the best Romanesque monastery churches in France, and was one of the most important monastic centres of the early Middle Ages. There was a druidic place of worship here in the Gallic period, and abbot Léodebod of Saint-Aignan founded the Benedictine monastery of Fleury on the site in 651. When the Benedictine monastery of Monte Cassino was destroyed in 672, the monks of Fleury brought the

Saint-Benoît-sur-Loire, abbey church

bones of St.Benedict and his sister, St.Scholastica, to Fleury and dedicated the monastery to St.Benedict, the founder of the Order. The precious relics attracted pilgrims for centuries and made the monastery a bastion of Christianity.

At the time of Charlemagne Abbot Theodulf, who was also bishop of Orléans, founded the monastery school of Fleury, and its influence soon extended throughout the Christian world. It taught, as well as theology, the seven free arts (grammar, rhetoric, logic, arithmetic, geometry, music and astronomy). There were also teachers of agriculture, various crafts, medicine and art. The scriptorium produced a stream of valuable manuscripts.

In the 9&10C the monastery was repeatedly attacked and plundered by the Normans, but the monks and their costly treasures survived by with-

Saint-Benoît-sur-Loire, tomb of Philippe I

drawing inside the fortified walls of Orléans. The monastery flourished again under the famous abbots St.Abbon and Gauzlin, who later became Archbishop of Bourges. In the 15C the monastery became a benefice, and the king distributed its funds to favourites, the so-called titular abbots.

The abbey was most severely damaged at the time of the Reformation, when the abbot Odet de Châtillon-Coligny was converted to Protestantism and allowed the monastery to be plundered by the Huguenot troops of the Prince of Condé; he also had the church treasure melted down, and sold the valuable library. There was a revival under Cardinal Richelieu, but this was short-lived. The monastery was dissolved during the Revolution and the archives taken to Orléans. The estates were sold and all the buildings destroyed, with the

exception of the church. Monastery life did not start again until 1944, and the monastery has been restored to the rank of abbey since 1959.

Saint-Benoît basilica: The massive 367 ft. long building was begun in the early 11C and completed in 1218. There were three main building periods: the great portal tower was built under abbot Gauzlin (1004–1030), the choir, transept and crossing tower and also the crypt date from 1067–1108, while the nave was built 1150–1218.

Portal tower: This is the oldest part of the basilica and was built by Abbot Gauzlin, who claimed that he had 'given an example to the whole of Gaul'. The claim was proved by an almost square three-storey tower which at first stood alone, and is unparalleled in the whole of Romanesque architecture. The present cubic building lost its second upper storey in 1527 on the orders of Francis I, because the monks refused to accept Cardinal Duprat as titular abbot. The present roof with belfry and lantern was added in the 17C. The ground floor is open on three sides with three arches on half columns. In the interior the space is divided into 9 groin-vaulted bays by 4 piers, also with half columns. The capitals are a striking feature; they are decorated with stylised plant motifs and fantastic animals, and also scenes from the Apocalypse and the Life of Christ. Particularly fine scenes are the Flight to Egypt, the Last Judgement, and St.Martin being carried by angels to Heaven. One of the façade capitals bears the signature of at least one craftsman: VNBERTVS ME FECIT (Umbertus made me).

N. portal This dates from 1200 and was partially destroyed in 1562 by the soldiers of the Prince de Condé. The column figures (there are similar ones in Chartres cathedral) suffered particularly from his destructive fury. Fortunately the figures in the tympanum were spared. In the centre is God the Father with an open book, surrounded by the Evangelists. The archivolts are decorated with angels and apostles. The door jamb is decorated with three scenes depicting the journey of the relics of St.Benedict from the monastery of Monte Cassino to Fleury.

Nave: This is the latest section of the building; it was built from 1150 and consecrated in 1218. Its five bays have rib vaults which, like the pointed arches, show the transition to the Gothic style. The aisles in the nave are still groin vaulted and lead to the ambulatory around the choir and apse.

Transept: This was completed in 1108 and has two semicircular chapels on the E. side. The domes and crossing tower are supported by two squinches, one set above the other. The stalls in the crossing date from 1413, the carved rood screen (fragment) was endowed by Cardinal Richelieu in 1635. In the N. transept chapel is a 14C alabaster figure of Our Lady of Fleury.

Choir: This was begun in 1065 and consecrated in 1108; it is one of the finest Romanesque choirs in France. The apse has a small transept which itself has two little apses to the E. The apse itself has two three-quarter circular chapels to the side of its main axis. The ambulatory is an integral part of the whole and has round arches. The line of colums, blind arches and clerestory windows give a majestic impression of space. The marble floor mosaic in the long choir is particularly interesting.

Crypt: The impressive room under the choir shows late 11C architectural mastery. Stubby round pillars set in a semicircle form two walks around the massive central pier, which contains the relics of St.Benedict.

Furnishings: Little of the once magnificent furnishings survived the confusion of the Reformation. There is no trace of either the statuary, or

Saint-Benoît-sur-Loire, crypt

Saint-Benoît-sur-Loire, abbey church ▷

the paintwork which is assumed to have existed. A hint of the former glory is given by the 550 *capitals*. The finest of them are on the right flank of the choir. The oldest tomb in the church is that of the Capet King Philip I, who died in 1108. A particular treasure is the tiny *Mumma shrine*, which was found under the high altar in 1642. It is a small wooden shrine decorated with gilded embossed copper plates, named after the person who endowed it. It is a rare example of Merovingian art. The shrine dates from the second half of the 7C, the time of the foundation of the monastery. The twelve stylised figures on the roof of the shrine probably represent the 12 Apostles.

Saint-Denis-d'Anjou
72 Sarthe   p.134□F 2

This little village, known for its excellent white wines, has a fine *church*, parts of which date from the 12C with important 15&16C *wall paintings*, a fine (restored) 15C *Town Hall* and wooden *market halls* with stone façades dating from 1509.

Environs: Miré (4.5 km. SW, in the Département of Maine-et-Loire): Old church with 12C bell tower and fine wooden vaulting; the 39 panels are painted with scenes from the Old and New Testaments. **Châteaux de Vaux** (4 km. NW of Miré): Ruins of an elegant *manor house*, built by Jean Bourré before he started on his Château de Plessis-Bourré. 5 km. SE of Miré: **Chemiré-sur-Sarthe**. *Church* with 12C transept and choir. 2 16C *houses*. 1 km. E. of Chemiré: **Morannes**. Late-12C *church* in Plantagenet style with fine figures in the choir.

Sainte-Catherine-de-Fierbois
37 Indre-et-Loire   p.136□K 5

The core of this little parish is a chapel which was already in existence at the time of Charles Martel, in which the Carolingian mayor of the palace (717–41) is said to have laid down his sword in gratitude for his victory over the Arabs. Around 1400 a hostel for pilgrims was established in the village, in which Joan of Arc stayed on March 5 1429. A good month later, on April 23 of the same year, following the Maid's instructions, the people searched behind the altar and found a sword with five crosses, which they identified as Charles Martel's; it helped Joan to victory in her battles against the English. In memory of this a bronze statue of the Maid was set up in the square in front of the church in 1895.

Church: This Gothic building in the Flamboyant style, dominated by a free-standing bell tower 134 ft. high is the only church in France to possess a relic of St.Catherine; it is kept in a costly silver reliquary.

Also worth seeing: By the church is the so-called *Maison du Dauphin*, dating from 1515, and a little further on is the *priest's house*, which is in the former pilgrims' hostel, and has an inscription about St.Joan's visit and the discovery of the sword.

Environs: Château de Comacre (1 km. SE): By the old château, of which only one tower survives, is a new château, built in the mid 19C in 15C style.
Notre-Dame de Lorette (1.5 km. SW): A *chapel* cut into the limestone.

Sainte-Maure-de-Touraine
37 Indre-et-Loire   p.136□K 5

The little market town on a hill above the right bank of the Manse was known as *Ariacum* in Roman times, and was renamed after the discovery of the graves of two holy women, St.Maure and St.Bridget, in the mid 5C. In the 20C a chapel was built to the two women in a dominant position above the valley. Originally in the possession of the counts of Touraine, the village was taken in the 10C by the notorious Foulques Nerra of Anjou, who built a fortress in 990 which subsequently passed to various noble families. Freed of its lords in the French Revolution, the town was rechristened Maure-Libre, but did not keep this name for long, as freedom from saints and noblemen was not destined to last.

Château: The old 15C château, in which Louis XIV spent a night in 1661, is set on a hill, with a 14C square tower next to it. Little remains of the curtain wall but a 14C tower has survived.

Church: The church, which is inside the castle walls, has a nave and two aisles with three apses, and dates from the late 12C (W. section and bell tower 1869). The nave of the former crypt is said to date from the year 1000 and the second, later section with nave, two aisles and apse is 12C. In the *interior*, in the right aisle, are a Christ Blessing, a 16C altar panel and in the chapel in the same aisle a marble statue of the Blessed Virgin (also 16C).

Also worth seeing: It is worth strolling round the little town itself. In the Rue Auguste-Chevalier there is a fine *Renaissance building* which used to house the post office. In the *Hôtel de Ville* is a small *museum* of archaeology and natural history with some interesting fossils from the local muschelkalk. One should also not miss the 17C *market halls* and the remains of the 12C *St-Mesmin chapel*, which is unfortunately not in very good condition.

Chalonnes-sur-Loire (Saint-Florent-le-Vieil), church

Environs: **Château de Brou** (7.5 km. NW): 15C *château* restored and extended by Morandière in the 19C. **Rilly** (12.5 km. SW): 11,12&15C *church*.
Sepmes (6.5 km. SE): 12C *church*. Ruins of a 16C *château*. 2 km. N. of Sepmes in the Manse valley: *Château de la Roche-Ploquin* with a 15C tower (school of agriculture).
Verneuil-le-Château (15.5 km. SW): 11&12C *church*. 4 km. N. of Verneuil-le-Château: **Lièze** (Chézelles parish). 12C *church* with a fine Romanesque portal. In the interior part beams, part Angevin vault. 2 km. S. of Verneuil-le-Château: **Luzé** 11&12C *church*. 3 km. SE of Luzé: **Abbey of Bois-Aubry**. The abbey was founded in 1138; surviving sections are the 12,13&15C *church* with a particularly fine square 15C *tower* 130 ft. high with a stone spire, the 12C *chapterhouse* and *dormitory* and an inn with a round cellar with a 15C domical vault.

Saint-Florent-le-Vieil

49 Maine-et-Loire　　　　　　　　p.134☐E 4

This little town in a beautiful setting on the left bank of the Loire affords a splendid view of the broad river and its many islands; it went into history because of the Vendée wars in the French Revolution. It was in Saint-Florent-le-Vieil that the revolt of the strictly Catholic farmers, craftsmen and minor nobility true to the king took shape in protest against the mass executions of priests. It started here, and the Royalists returned here six months later having conquered the whole of Anjou, taking 5,000 Republican prisoners after the bloody defeat at Cholet. Their own leader, the Marquis de Bonchamps, was fatally wounded. Embittered by the cruelty of their opponents, they decided to make short work of their prisoners, but then spared their lives on the orders of the dying Bonchamps. The

story of the relics of St.Florentin is equally interesting; towards the end of the 4C he founded an abbey, in which he was later buried, on Mont-Glonne, as the hill was called at the time. During the Norman attacks of 853 and 866 his relics were taken for safety to the monks of Tournus in Burgundy, but they did not wish to part with them when the danger had passed. They were not to enjoy them for long, however. The much-coveted bones of the saint did not find rest here, but found their way mysteriously to Saumur, to Angers and to Roye in Picardy, until finally some of them ended up in the abbey of St-Florin-lès-Saumur, also known as St-Florin-le-Jeune. Saint-Florent-le-Vieil was reduced to the rank of priory, even though it is still called abbey as matter of habit.

St-Pierre: David d'Angers, the son of one of the pardoned prisoners, placed a beautiful marble memorial to the Marquis de Bonchamps, the leader of the Vendée revolt, in the old abbey church, which has largely survived in good condition; parts of it were heavily restored in the late 19C.

Also worth seeing: *Museum* on the Vendée wars in the old Chapelle du Sacré-Coeur, built in 1674. 1965 *cable bridge*, the first of its kind in France. Upstream on the quay is the little *Tour de la Gabelle*, where the salt tax used to be levied.

Environs: Chalonnes-sur-Loire: (22 km. E.): This little town is known for its fine white wines and has a beautiful old *church* directly on the river. The pendentive dome in the choir dates from the 12C and the Angevin vault with sculpted keystones in the two choirs is 13C.
Château de la Bourgonnière (6.5 km. SW): Now a spacious park with a 19C château with an Ionic peristyle. Only a cylindrical tower and a machi-

Saint-Florent-le-Vieil, crypt ▷

Sainte-Paterne-Racan, terracotta group, Adoration

colated donjon with adjacent octagonal staircase tower have survived of the 15C château, which burned down in the Vendée wars. The delightful *Renaissance chapel*, with a fine round-arched portal with two Corinthian columns, is lavishly furnished inside. There is a fat round tower on one side of it and a rectangular pavilion with an outsize fireplace on the other. In the chapel there are two fine stone *retables* with typical early Renaissance decoration.

Saint-Paterne-Racan

37 Indre-et-Loire   p.136□ 3

Church: This little place, known for growing mushrooms in disused quarries, has astonishing art treasures for a village of its size. The works kept in the church largely came from the Cistercian abbey of Clarté-Dieu, 3 km. to the W. and founded in 1239; those abbey buildings which remain are used as a farm. The finest among the art treasures are: a terracotta group left of the high altar (16C Adoration of the Kings), which includes a particularly beautiful **Mary with Child**; in the S. chapel an 18C stone retable, a finely carved 16C lectern; 16 or 17C carved figures of St.Anne and Mary in stone, and statues of St.Jerome and St.Augustine (18C).

Environs: Bueil-en-Touraine (10 km. NE): The *parish church* built between 1480 and 1512, next to the old collegiate church of 1394, has a fine font dating from 1521 with a carved lid decorated with figures of the four Apostles, and some old tombs. 16C *cross* in the cemetery.

Saint-Paterne-Racan, Adoration, detail

Saint-Paterne-Racan, St.Jerome

Château de la Roche-Rocan (1.5 km. S.): This *château*, with its light, high façade, built for Honorat de Bueil, Baron of Racan, by J.Gabriel, an ancestor of the famous architect, has an octagonal tower and a terrace with stone balustrade.

Saint - Christophe - sur - le - Nais (2.5 km. NE): This village in a picturesque setting on the slope is annually, on the last Sunday but one in July, the goal of an extremely popular pilgrimage at which cars are blessed. The patron saint of the pilgrimage is St.Christopher, and an enormous statue of him greets the pilgrims at the entrance to the *church*.

Saint-Philbert-de-Grand-Lieu
44 Loire-Atlantique   p.134☐C 5

In 836 the monks of the island of Noirmoutier were looking for sanctuary from the Normans with their treasure, the bones of St.Philbert, and built a new funerary church for their saint on the edge of the marshes, in the old Déas, the present Saint-Philbert-de-Grand-Lieu. However, they had to flee further in the same year, to Cunault, and finally as far as Tournus in Burgundy, not returning to Saint-Philbert until the 11C.

The mortal remains of the saint did not return until much later, in 1937, when they were placed in the magnificent sarcophagus which the builders of the church had made its central feature.

Abbey church: This church, built in the 9C, partially rebuilt in the 11C and restored in the 19C, is not only one of the oldest surviving churches in France, but also a predecessor of the great pilgrimage churches which were to line the pilgrimage routes in the later Middle Ages, and like these it has a walk around the upper crypt with apsidal chapels, principally intended to direct the stream of pilgrims around the sarcophagus, which incidentally is still in this position. The massive cruciform piers, alternately in brick and white stone, are an interesting example of Carolingian architecture.

Saint-Viâtre
41 Loir-et-Cher   p.138☐N/O 3

This village, set among innumerable ponds, is named after a 6C saint.

Village church: The oldest sections date from the 11C, but they were not part of the earliest building on the site. The crypt of the 11C church was built in the 11C as a funerary chapel for St.Viâtre. Most of the church dates from the 13C, the façade tower and portal are 14C and the transept 15C.

Environs: Marcilly-en-Gault (11.5 km. SW): 12&13C *church*.
Nouan-le-Fuzelier (8 km. E.): The *church* dates from the 13&16C. To the NE is the *Château de Moléon*, a 15C brick building.

Salbris
41 Loir-et-Cher   p.138☐O 3/4

St-Georges: 12,15&16C brick building with a 17C stone retable with a fine Pietà and a 17C gilded wooden chandelier.

Environs: Ferté-Imbault, La (9

Salbris, retable

Saumur, view of town

km. SW): *Collegiate church of St-Thaurin*, founded in 1164; only the old round-arched portal and a chapel have survived.

The 16&17C *château* has been heavily restored.

Souesmes (11 km. NE): *Church* with Romanesque nave and 16C choir. 18C *château* with 16C machicolated turrets. Old *half-timbered houses.*

Saumur

49 Maine-et-Loire p.136☐G 4

This handsome town with a massive yet picturesque château above it turns its most attractive face to the river, 3 km. before the confluence of the Loire and the Thouet.

The monks of Saint-Florent-le-Vieil settled here *c.* 850, after their monastery had been burned down by Nomi-noë, the king of Brittany. Charles the Bold gave them the Villa Lohannis to compensate for this loss, but they had to leave here as well with their valuable relics, in flight from the Normans. In 984 the relics returned to Saumur (as the place presumably became known just shortly afterwards) and in 950 Thibaut the Betrayer, Count of Blois, built a new monastery. The Count of Blois also built a fortress against the Counts of Anjou; this was walled (which probably led to the name *Salvus Murus*, shortened to *Saumur*). But Thibaut was not destined to enjoy his possessions for long. Foulques Nerra, known from many other Loire towns as an enthusiastic builder, showed his warlike side in Saumur. He burned down the town and left it to his successors to rebuild it. When the counts of Anjou came to the English throne as Plantagenets, Saumur became

Saumur, half-timbered house

English, but in the 12C it returned to the French crown and part of the newly-created duchy of Anjou. Around 1370 Duke Louis I of Anjou, wishing to keep up with his influential and powerful brothers, King Charles V and the Duc de Berry, built a truly breathtaking château, which is familiar to us thanks to a picture in the 'Très Riches Heures' of the Duc de Berry (*c.* 1410) and was the scene of many brilliant tournaments in the 15C, under King René the Good, who liked staying in Saumur.

The greatest period in the history of Saumur, which flourished during the Reformation, was the 17C, when a Protestant university was founded by Duplessis-Mornay, known as the 'Huguenot Pope' and made governor of the town by the former Huguenot leader and later Catholic King Henri IV. This soon acquired such a reputation in Europe that students

streamed to it from many countries, making Saumur a major centre of Protestantism. This development was brought to an abrupt end in 1685 by the repeal of the Edict of Nantes, which had granted freedom of belief and political rights to the Protestants. Thousands of citizens left the town, which has never really recovered from the blow. The foundation of the cavalry school in 1767 assisted recovery, and the town has added mushroom growing, the devotional industry and the manufacture of carnival masks (in which it is No. 1 in Europe) to its traditional sources of income, wine and champagne. And yet Saumur has never reached its former size in terms of number of inhabitants.

Château: The present château dates largely from the second half of the 14C, but it no longer looks as it did in the 'Très Riches Heures' of the Duc de Berry: it seems broader, squatter, heavier—it has lost its picturebook quality. The soaring battlements, dormers, chimneys, gables decorated with crockets and gilded weather vanes have disappeared in the course of the centuries, and so has the kitchen with its chimneys and central pyramid, reminiscent of the kitchen in Fontevraud. Also, after the deposing of governor Duplessis-Mornay in 1621 the NW building collapsed and was replaced by a terrace. The overall pattern has remained, however: the remaining three buildings, set more or less at right angles to each other around a courtyard, and with 4 outer corner towers at the points of the compass. Under the blue slate roof of each of these protruding towers, round at their lower and polygonal at their higher levels, is a wall passage with machicolations, supported on

Saumur, château 1 N. tower with staircase **2** Provisions shaft (formerly in the collapsed NW wing) **3** S. tower **4** Entrance **5** SE wing with section of the Musée des arts décoratifs **6** NE wing with Musée des Arts décoratifs and Musée du Cheval **7** SW wing with cells

Saumur, château

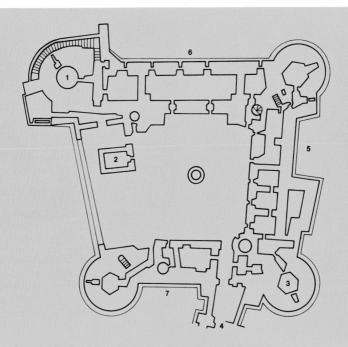

sharply profiled buttresses. In the N. tower is the *main staircase*, which has traceried loggias opening on to the courtyard in all storeys. In front of it is a *shaft*, almost 200 ft. deep, which used to supply water for the château; it is now protected by a little barrier. It is said that this shaft used to be connected to one of the wall towers on the Loire, so that the inhabitants of the château and the troops could be supplied with food and ammunition in case of emergency. The château was clearly prepared for any eventuality. Around 1600 it was also reinforced with outer walls and bastions, and as there was only one entrance, along a ramp leading into the courtyard through a protruding gatehouse covered from the S. tower, it must have been very difficult to take.

Shortly after the dismissal of the governor, who used the château as a residence, it began to fall into disrepair,

Saumur, St-Pierre

and after it had stood empty for a time, it was used as a gaol. In 1810 Napoleon made it a state prison, later it was an arsenal and a barracks, and at the beginning of our century it became a possession of the town, which restored the SE and NE buildings and made them into museums.

Musée des Arts décoratifs: This fine museum of applied art occupies the first floor of the two restored buildings. The collections include a number of fine medieval and Renaissance works: Limoges enamel, wood and alabaster sculptures, objects of worship, paintings, and a considerable quantity of baroque faience and porcelain, all exhibited with furniture and tapestries from the correct period. The 15&16C *tapestries* are particularly worth seeing, above all the Masked Ball, the Return from the Hunt, the Coronation of Vespasian and the Taking of Jerusalem.

Musée du Cheval: This museum on the second floor of the NE wing gives a view of the role of the horse in history and the development of riding as a sport, by means of old prints and collections of saddles, bits, stirrups etc.

The *dungeons* in the unrestored SW building are also open to the public; many famous men have been shut up in them over the centuries. There is also a huge vault under the courtyard, which is said to have been used as a cistern.

From the watchtower there is a fine view over the valleys of the Loire and the Thouet.

St-Pierre: This church, with its tall, solid crossing tower and steep spire, is also an emblem of Saumur; it dates from the late 12C (choir and transept) and the early 13C (nave). The side chapels in the nave were added in the 15&16C, the entrance façade burned down in 1674 and was restored in the style of the period. There is a fine Romanesque portal in the S. arm of the transept.

The different building periods show

clearly in the *interior*. The pointed-arched Angevin vault in the three-bayed nave is clearly superior to the heavier, older vaulting in the choir and transept. Fine features of the transept are two late 12C *pier figures*: in the S. arm *Christ the Victor*, in the N. *St.Peter*; the *choir stalls* and above all the *tapestries* showing the life of St.Florentin (in the first two chapels, 1524) and the life of St.Peter (in the S. arm of the transept and the adjacent side apse, 1546) are also worth seeing.

Notre-Dame-de-Nantilly: This rather severe Romanesque building, which used to be part of the abbey of St.Florentin, dates largely from the first half of the 12C. In the 14C the transept with its two apsidioles was rebuilt, and between 1470 and 1483 a S. aisle in Flamboyant style was added to the formerly single-aisled

building by order of Louis XI. The lavishly decorated king's oratory is now used as a baptismal chapel. Striking features are the severe, 13C carved wooden miraculous image of the Madonna and Child in a small side apse on the N. side of the choir, and the wonderful collection of 15&16C *tapestries* from Flanders, the Loire and Aubusson (17C), including above all the 'Tree of Jesse' (France, 1529) in the N. arm of the transept.

Notre-Dame-des-Ardilliers: This church about 1 km. upstream from the Loire bridge was built in the 17C on the site of a pilgrimage chapel (1553). In 1454 a peasant found an old statue of the Madonna in the clay (French 'argileux' or 'ardilles', hence the name); the statue proved to have miraculous powers, and attracted many pilgrims. The church, started by the Oratorians in 1655, but not

Saumur, St-Pierre, tapestry

Saumur, Town Hall

completed until 1693, with the help of a lavish donation by Louis XIV, is a fine example of neoclassical architecture; it is a large rotunda with a slate-clad dome, and a small nave with two side chapels. One of the chapels was built in 1635 by Cardinal Richelieu, the other, in the S., was added on the same pattern by A.Sevien, Seneschal of Anjou, in 1655. *Interior:* A fine portal leads to a round space lit by 8 windows and decorated with medallions of the four Evangelists and the four church fathers Gregory, Leo, Augustine and Jerome. The windows are by the 20C artist M.Ingrand (1908–69), who also designed the windows of the church in Gien; the monumental tufa and black marble retable in the choir is by the sculptors Biardeau and Charpentier (17C), with the exception of the central Crucifixion, for which Canon Choyer was responsible (1856); he also created the altarpiece for the Richelieu chapel with the miraculous image.

St-Jean chapel: (Rue Corneille): This little rectangular building in the mairie, dating from 1210–20, has an outstanding Angevin vault; its subtle lines are in remarkable tension with the simplicity of the walls.

Hôtel de Ville: The late Gothic Town Hall (early 16C) on the banks of the Loire is a massive, low cube with wall passage, corner turrets and a high pyramid roof with lantern; from the outside it looks more like a bastion than an administrative building, and it was once part of the town walls. In the 19C a second building, which also did not look very official, was added in Renaissance style by the architect Joly-Leterme, who designed it to harmonise with the inner façade of the older building. *Interior:* There are about 3 dozen 12–15C manuscripts in the considerable library (*c.* 20,000 volumes).

Ecole de Cavalerie: (1768): The cavalry school is the town's pride and joy; the riding tradition is an important one (the first riding school was founded by Henri IV in the late 16C). The buildings now house a military school for tank and cavalry regiments; the annual parades in late July have become a kind of folk festival.

Maison de la Reine de Sicile: (in the Quartier des Ponts on the island of Offard): The Queen of Sicily's house is an elegant early 15C manor house built by Yolande of Aragon, the mother of King René the Good, Duke of Anjou and titular King of Sicily. Yolande, who was influential at the court of Charles VII, received Joan of Arc, whose mission she supported in every way she could, in this house in May 1429. The house was badly damaged in 1940 and rebuilt after the war.

Saumur, St-Pierre, tapestry

'Jeanne Delanou' hospice: This 18C building has fine 17C Aubusson tapestries in the conference room of the administrative division.

Musée de la Cavalerie (Avenue Foch): The history of the French cavalry from the 18C, with special reference to the Saumur school, is presented by means of valuable ceremonial swords, chased Mameluke sabres, helmets, armour and uniforms (the latter as porcelain figures from Meissen and Sèvres).

Musée des Blindés (Place du Chardonnet): The museum shows the development of the so-called 'modern cavalry' since 1918 by means of more than 150 model tanks.

Also worth seeing: Remains of the old fortifications, the *Tour Grainetière* (15C), in the Place de l'Arche-Dorée and another tower in the Rue du Prêche. *Rue Haute-St-Pierre* with a series of old houses (Nos. 11,13,15,19,23,27). *Maison du Roi*, 16C (No. 3 Place St-Pierre). The picturesque *Rue du Fort:*, in the quarter which forms the setting for Balzac's famous novel 'Eugénie Grandet'.

Environs: Bagneux (2 km. SW): *Dolmen*, one of the finest in Anjou: a covered avenue of 15 blocks of sandstone 66 ft. long, 25 ft. wide, 11 ft. high at the beginning but only 8 ft. high at the end. 200 yards to the W. is another, smaller *dolmen* and somewhat further S. a *menhir*.

Brézé (11 km. S.): Heavily restored *Renaissance château*, surrounded by a narrow moat cut directly into the limestone tufa. The building is in three sections, with a courtyard opening over a terrace to the W.

Chacé (6 km. S.): Old 17C *château.* Numerous *caves* cut into the limestone tufa and used as wine and champagne cellars (the area is known for its white wines).

Dampierre (5 km. SE): In the direction of Souzay is the *manor house* on a hill in which the unhappy daughter of King René, Margaret of Anjou, spent the rest of her life after the murder of her husband, Henry VI of England, and her son in the Wars of the Roses.

Distré (5 km.SW): Old *church* dating from the 10C, presumably once part of the priory which was founded in the 10C by the abbey of Saint-Florent and which existed until the 18C.

Saint-Florent (2 km. NW): *Limestone tufa caves,* in which the white wines of Saumur are made into champagne. 13C Gothic *church* with two aisles fortified in 1418 and extended by one bay in 1865 (2 13C crosses). Saint-Florent is mainly known for its *abbey,* founded *c.* 1025 by monks from St-Florent-le-Vieil, and thus sometimes known as Saint-Florent-le-Jeune. In the hope that they were at last safe here, and to make a permanent resting place for their valuable relics, they built a very beautiful church in the Plantagenet style in the 12C, which was unfortunately almost entirely destroyed in 1803. Only the crypt and the fine portal porch have survived; the latter is a spacious square building, which interestingly combines Romanesque capitals decorated with fantastic plants and animals with Gothic foliate capitals.

Saint-Hilaire (3 km. NW): Part of the parish of Saint-Hilaire-Saint-Florent. 12&15C *church. Manoir de la Tour de Ménives* (15&16C). *Dolmen.*

Souzay: (6 km. SE): *Church* and turreted 15C *houses.*

Selles-sur-Cher

41 Loir-et-Cher   p.138☐M 4

This little town on the borders of Touraine, Sologne and Berry grew up around the hermitage of St.Eusicius, who had a cell here in the first half of the 6C. It later became a monastery, with which the present parish church was connected.

St-Eusice: This church was built in the 12C, then extended and rebuilt in the 15C. In 1562 it was plundered by Coligny and restored in the 17&19C. The majority of the façade, the tower, the S. aisle and the capitals have survived from the Romanesque period. The most interesting feature of the church is the two-part Romanesque frieze above and below the exterior windows of the choir. The frieze above the windows shows scenes from the life of St.Eusicius. The figures in the lower frieze are rather naive and clumsy, and so this section is probably earlier, while the Eusicius frieze has figures of finer design, and is therefore probably later. The cha-

Selles-sur-Cher, St-Eusice, frieze

pel on the N. side has a bas-relief with pictures of the months and a particularly successful Visitation of Mary. The late 13C *portal* in the N. wall has decorated capitals joined by a garland of wild roses.

The nave and aisles were rebuilt in 1300, with the exception of the S. wall and the row of columns with fine Romanesque *capitals*. There nave and transept are striking for their extraordinary height, the choir has an ambulatory and three apsidal chapels. The *crypt* contains the empty sarcophagus of St.Eusicius, dating from the 6C. The relics of the saint are walled up in the piers of the choir. The finest item in the church treasure is a 14C ivory *triptych*. Parts of the monastery buildings were rebuilt in the 17C, and now accommodate a *local history museum*.

Château: These buildings on the banks of the Cher are completely surrounded by moats. They were built in the 13C on the site of a fortress which had been pulled down. The fortress was partially rebuilt and extended under Henri IV by Pierre-Philippe de Béthune, the brother of minister Sully. The E. section was almost entirely new. It has a bridge with a handsome Renaissance tower on either side of it; these are joined by a broad gallery with arches and round windows. In the W. section the *Intendants' hall* is open to the public; it contains a collection of halberds and mail shirts. Pierre-Philippe's chambers are in the two towers. There is a particularly fine coffered ciling, and a fireplace with carvings dating from 1604. The NE pavilion contains the chambers of the Queen of Poland, the wife of Johann Sibieski. A fine stone fireplace and an early-17C canopied bed have survived. The

Selles-sur-Cher, St.Eusice, frieze, detail

games and music room is furnished with Spanish and Italian furniture. The old guardroom contains a massive fireplace with an asymmetrical basket arch. Furniture also early 17C.

Environs:Billy (5 km. N.): Old *church* with 11C nave and three bas-reliefs from the same period on the gable side. 15C frescos. *Château,* parts of which date from the 16C.

Chabris (8 km. SE): The *church* dates from the 10C and was rebuilt and extended in the 12&15C. Its oldest masonry includes carvings which could be Carolingian. There are clearly recognisable zodiac scenes and a scene showing the Visitation of Mary. The crypt under the choir contains a wooden statue of St.Phalier.

Meusnes (7 km.SW): The only *flint museum* in France was established here in 1962. For three centuries the area produced flints for the armies of Europe. Napoleon's armies alone took delivery of more than 30 million flints per year. The museum documents the history of flint manufacture from prehistoric times until the present day.

Serrant
49 Maine-et-Loire   p.136☐E/F 4

One and a half kilometres from Saint-Georges-sur-Loire, the village to which it belongs for administrative purposes, this château is more like a royal residence then a simple nobleman's house. It has a large and beautiful park, a broad circular moat, a spacious courtyard and majestic buildings on a large scale. Its builder, Charles de Brie, so overreached himself with the project that building was stopped immediately after his death in

Selles-sur-Cher, St-Eusice

1593, and the half-completed château was sold as soon as a buyer, the Duke of Montbazon, could be found. But even he was unable to complete the château, and sold it in 1636 to ambassador Guillaume Bautrus, a founder member of the Académie Française, who finally restarted building work about 50 years later; the present building was largely completed under his son. Only the balustrade which runs along the upper storey and the large top-floor windows protruding into the roof are later (19C). All in all building continued for over 200 years, which makes the uniformity of the building all the more astonishing; it was only achieved by strictly following the plans available.

Château: This is a long main building with two massive round, domed corner towers and with two shorter wings set at right angles on the inside. On the side opposite the main section 2 pavilions mark the corners of the square site, with an unusually high gate forming an axis opposite the entrance to the central building. The strictly geometrical layout is emphasised by the moat surrounding the whole building; this makes a very precise impression because of the organisation of its walls and bridges. The individual parts of the building also seem very strictly designed, partly because of the horizontal articulation, softened by pilaster articulation typical of the time of Francis I, and partly by the use of light and dark stone on the façade, which reproduces the geometrical figures on a smaller scale. An outstanding feature is the *staircase* in the main block opposite the gate; it has parallel flights of stairs separated by walls and fine coffered vaults and ceilings.

In the *interior* is the fine *marble tomb* of Nicolas Bautrus, the nephew of the man who completed the château. It is in the early-18C chapel, attributed by many commentators to J.Hardouin-Mansart. The melodramatic tomb was commissioned from A.Coysevox, the most important sculptor at the court of Louis XIV, by the widow, and it was probably completed in 1705 to a design by Le Brun; it shows Bautrus, who fell at the battle of Altenheim, in the pose of victor, in a frame of Corinthian columns before a background of black marble. Above him hovers the goddess of victory, at his feet is the mourning widow. She, according to contemporary reports, not only gave her husband a princely funeral, but also expressed her mourning in a curious fashion. She is said to have spent the rest of her days in contemplation of her husband's heart, which she set up on a little altar, lit by two candles.

Environs: Champtocé-sur-Loire (9.5 km. W.): Just outside the little town, which has several 15&17C houses, are the ruins of a 13&15C *château*, whose owner, Gilles de Retz (1404–40), notorious for his cruelty, provided the writer and collector of fairy-tales Perrault (1628–1703) with the model for his Bluebeard.

Ingrandes (13.5 km. W.): Pretty place on the right bank of the Loire with a suspension bridge marking the border between Anjou and Brittany, and an old salt tax office. As it had a large salt store, Ingrande used to have a garrison of customs officers and a salt court, which in the 17&18C dealt mainly with Breton salt smugglers.

Saint-Georges-sur-Loire (1.5 km. SW): A little place with about 2,000 inhabitants which grew up around an abbey founded in the 12C. Nothing has survived of the original buildings. The present *abbey church*, a neoclassical building with a Doric peristyle, is 17C, like the rest of the buildings. 3 km. NW of Saint-Georges-sur-Loire: **Prieuré d'Epinay**, a priory built in the 15C and altered in the 17&18C.

Sully-sur-Loire
45 Loiret   p.138☐P 2

This little town on the edge of the Sologne grew up around an old Loire crossing. The first holder of bridge rights was Maurice de Sully, bishop of Paris and builder of Notre-Dame. Charles VII was in residence here while Joan of Arc defeated the English at Patay and captured their leader Talbot. Shortly afterwards she was here to try to persuade the reluctant king to be crowned. In 1602 Maximilien de Béthune, Baron of Rosny, bought the château and the barony attached to it. Henri IV's minister was raised to the rank of Duke here in 1606, and called himself

Serrant, château

Duke of Sully from then on. He modernised and extended the town and made the fortress into the present château. On the Loire side he built a dam to keep out the annual floods, made new moats around the buildings and diverted a nearby stream to fill them. The park was also redesigned under his direction. The 22-year-old Voltaire, then still known as François-Marie Arouet, took refuge in the château when he was banned from Paris because of his biting satire. In 1940 château and town were damaged by bombing, and the château became the residence of a major-general.

Collegiate church of St-Ythier: This dates from a chapel built in 1529 and was built in its present form in 1605. There are two striking stained-glass windows dating from the second half of the 16C. The one in the S. aisle shows the legend of St.James, and the

one on the central apse has a Tree of Jesse with Mary and the Child enthroned in an open lily. The Pietà above the altar in the transept is also 16C.

Château: The oldest section is the *keep* on the Loire side. It was built before 1360, and is built on a square plan with three fat round corner towers. Even though two of the towers have lost their wall passages and pepperpot roofs, this part of the château still looks authentically medieval.

The courtyard adjacent to the donjon was originally surrounded on all sides by buildings built or rebuilt by the Duke of Sully. Now only the E. building remains; its lower part was rebuilt after a fire in 1918, and the higher part is called the 'little château' and is directly connected with the Duke of Sully. He had his study on the ground floor, where he wrote his famous

memoirs, and his bedroom is preserved in the upper storey.
The old castle has the great guard-room, the kitchen and the chapel with a copy of the Duke of Sully's tomb. The first floor includes the great hall in which Voltaire's first plays were performed. The second floor contains an open medieval *roof* dating from 1363; it is considered to be one of the finest specimens of medieval artistry and craftsmanship. The square beams were cut from fifty- to hundred-year-old chestnut trees with an axe, and not sawn. The finished beams were treated with water for years, to draw out the sap. Then the beams were so skilfully fitted together that they always have air circulating around them, and have survived the 600 years without deterioration. The interior of the roof is in the form of an inverted ship, and outside it covers a wall passage.

Environs: Cerdon-du-Loiret (15 km. SE): Typical Sologne village with a 13C *church*.

Talcy
41 Loir-et-Cher   p.138□M 2

Château: The little village of Talcy on the Route de la Rose is typical of the Beauce, the granary of France, but is not an obvious site for a château. The château came into being thanks to a Florentine financier in the service of Francis I. Bernard Salviati, a cousin of Catherine de Medici, bought the 13C country seat in 1517, and turned it into a château. He was given permission to extend the building with 'walls, towers, battlements, embrasures, drawbridges, outworks, ramparts and other provisions for its defence'. But because he only ranked

◁ *Sully, château*

as a tradesman, he was not allowed to call himself lord of the château, nor to administer justice, nor to mount guards. As all he wished to do was build an impressive château he was little troubled by these restrictions.
Cassandra, the daughter, and Diane, the granddaughter of the rich Florentine, became famous. Pierre de Ronsard fell in love with the daughter, and Théodore Agrippa d'Aubigné with the granddaughter. Both celebrated the women they loved in numerous poems, mainly sonnets. Although the château had various owners over the centuries it retained its original character. When it was sold to the French state in 1933 the seller had the contract worded in such a way as to prevent the alteration of the original interior.
Buildings: The oldest section is the 15C rectangular *keep* with two polygonal corner towers and two entrances (a vehicular entrance and a smaller gate). The decorative wall passage was added by Bernard Salviati after 1520. The building adjacent to the keep has flat arches with a gallery; the arches themselves are made to look like pairs by the use of gables. In the courtyard is the famous *well* with a slate dome supported by three columns. The well and the rose which grew in front of it became the symbol of the love between Cassandra and Ronsard. The W. side of the

Talcy, château, dovecote

Talcy, château, well

courtyard was originally closed, but the section was not rebuilt after the fire in the 16C which destroyed the W. wing and a corner tower of the keep. The second courtyard was used as a farmyard and still has some interesting features. The dovecote dates from the 16C; it is cylindrical, and almost all of its 1,500 nesting boxes are intact. The individual nesting boxes were reached by means of a ladder on a turntable. There used to be dovecotes of this kind in every stately home, but most of them disappeared in the Revolution, because they were seen as symbols of the nobility, and thus destroyed. There is also a *wine press*, which is almost a century later in date, and which is still in complete working order.

Interior: The room in the best condition on the ground floor is the *kitchen*. It is still as it originally was, with a flat-arched fireplace with oven

and an apparatus for turning a spit. The adjacent *guardroom* has a fine beamed ceiling and a fireplace from the time of the Florentine. The *bedrooms*, in which Charles IX and Catherine de Medici slept, are furnished with 16&17C items. The great *dining room* was not furnished until the 18C; it has a floor made up of octagonal white tiles decorated with small square black tiles.The white beamed ceiling and the entirely white furniture harmonize well with the floor, and the blue-green wall coverings painted with flower ornaments form an agreeable contrast. The *grand salon* on the upper floor of the keep also has a tiled floor, with a large Savonnerie carpet. There are also Aubusson tapestries showing mythological scenes like the death of Eurydice or the birth of Bacchus.

Environs: Marchenoir (8.5 km.

NW): Old fortress village on the S. edge of the Forêt de Marchenoir, formerly Silva Longinqua, the long wood; because it is so large (5,400 hectares) it is a natural barrier, and played an important part in the Hundred Years War (1339–1453) and in the Franco-Prussian War (1870–1). Little remains of the village *fortifications* except the ruins of a keep. The *church* dates from the 12&15C.

Villiers (7 km. SW): *St-Vincent* dates from the late 11C. Late-12C frescos were discovered here in 1948. They represent God the Father, surrounded by the symbols of the Evangelists, and underneath six Apostles can be made out.

Tavant

37 Indre-et-Loire   p.136☐I 5

The little village of Tavant, on the road to Loches to Chinon, was founded by monks from Marmoutier, who built a priory here in the late 10C; it attracted the attention of art historians in 1945, when Romanesque frescos were discovered under the whitewash of the village church. They are so unusual, and have such 'élan sauvage', expressive force unrefined by culture, that they have defied classification; the possibility of German influence was considered for a time.

St-Nicolas: This plain, appealingly simple little village church was built *c.* 1120. It was originally a basilica with nave, two aisles, transept, crossing tower, choir and transept side apses; over the centuries it has become a single-aisled church with an entrance portal which occupies the whole breadth of the façade. It appears that the interior round arches and tunnel vaulting were once entirely decorated with wall paintings. The choir gives an impression of what this must have been like, with the Christ in Mandorla in the apse and the most

Tavant, St-Nicolas, capital

important events associated with the Birth of Christ (Annunciation, Visitation, Birth, Flight to Egypt etc) in the two painted areas in the tunnel vaulting of the choir bay. The fine capitals on the half columns are a harmonious part of the overall picture.

The **crypt** has a surprise in store for the visitor: the little room, divided into three aisles by 2 rows of round columns, is (with the exception of a few areas in the vault) entirely covered with painted figures and scenes, a loose and unorthodox ensemble of biblical, cosmological, hagiographic and allegorical scenes juxtaposed in a completely uninhibited fashion and arousing considerable curiosity about the artist and his patron. Unfortunately absolutely nothing is known about either. It is assumed that the scenes in the crypt are by the same artist, or at least from the same studio, as those in the choir.

Environs: Anché (6 km. NW): 12&15C *church.*
Brétignolles (5 km. NW): 15C *château* with 16C chapel.
Rivière (9 km. NW): Old *church* with a very old crypt and a fine raised choir (11C) reached by 15 steps.
Sazilly (3.5 km. NW): 13C *church* in Plantagenet style.

Tours
37 Indre-et-Loire   p.136☐K 4

Tours is now the capital of the département of Indre-et-Loire; in the Middle Ages it was fought over by its neighbours to the W. and E., the counts of Anjou and the counts of Blois, in the Roman period it was the camp of the third Roman division and in the Celtic period the home of the Turon tribe, from which the name Tours is derived. The town has had a chequered history: it was involved in the Gallic revolts under Vercinge-torix, defeated by the Romans, rechristened *Caesarodunum*, surrounded by ramparts (of which many have survived, along with a round corner tower in the Rue du Petit-Cupido) and provided with an aqueduct, an arena seating *c.* 12,000 spectators and one of the largest round temples built in Gaul; in the 5C it was the scene of clashes between the Visigoths and the Franks, in the 9C it was the victim of the plundering Normans, who sailed up the Loire from Nantes as far as St-Benoît-sur Loire in their fast ships, and under the Plantagenets, who built new walls to protect their expensively-bought possession, part of the Angevin-English Empire. In 1204 Tours was finally united with the French crown, and the town's fortunes fluctuated. It gained a great deal from St.Martin, the patron of the

Tavant, St-Nicolas, portal

Frankish kings, the Capets, whose name derives from capa, the cape which the saint shared with Jesus in the shape of a beggar. Shortly after his death (397) the grave of this merciful man became the most famous place of pilgrimage in Gaul; the account of the life of the saint and reports of the miracles which he achieved after his death spread throughout the known world: copies of this Vita have been found in Rome, in North Africa (Carthage and Alexandria), Asia Minor (Syria) and in S. Egypt. The kings and great ones of the time were generous in their gifts, and the monastery founded by St.Martin was soon one of the richest in the West. It acquired estates in every province of France, and most of the countries of Europe, and had about 20,000 vassals. Pilgrims streamed to Tours in their thousands. And because they all had to be accommodated and cared for, a

second town *Martinopole* (later called *Châteauneuf*) came into being outside the gates of the Roman town, where the mortal remains of the saint had been buried according to Roman custom. This pilgrim town was walled in the 10C to protect it against attack from the Normans, and it was not until the Hundred Years War (1339–1453) that it came within the walls of the Gallo-Roman old town; these walls were renewed when the town grew rapidly in the 16&17C. Tours was at the height of its development, like all the towns of the Loire, in the 15&16C, when Louis XI (1461–83) took up permanent residence here and introduced the manufacture of silk and brocade. Being a royal residence always meant economic growth for a town; the court was an important employer, and the new industries attracted workers and craftsmen. As a town of scholars,

Tours, Roman aqueduct

Tours, St-Gatien cathedral

artists and craftsmen Tours was very receptive to new ideas. The town adopted the Reformation and flourished as a bastion of the Protestant faith just as it had as a bastion of the cult of St.Martin. But the Catholics were not slow to retaliate. 10 years before Paris Tours had its own 'St.Bartholomew's Eve' which, as in Saumur, was the beginning of the town's decline. The upturn in its fortunes did not come until the 19C, when the introduction of the railway opened up new trading and transport opportunities, and made the town interesting to industrialists. In the 19C chocolate factories, foundries, ceramic workshops and printing works were among the firms established, in the 20C manufacturing concerns such as the metal, chemical, plastics, electronics and textile industries. Tours is also the centre in mid-Western France for wine and agricul-

ture, and an important town for trade fairs, not forgetting the less important but extremely colourful garlic fair in July. As well as all this the town is an important tourist centre; it was badly damaged in the Second World War, but has been beautifully rebuilt, and has many graceful buildings and important art treasures.

St.Martin also played an important role in cultural development, within the town and also well beyond its boundaries. His successors on the episcopal throne were all worthy men. They included Gregory of Tours (d. 595), the author of the first history of France, and the town soon acquired a reputation for scholarship as a result of: this. This reputation was consolidated by Alcuin, the scholar-monk from York, summoned by Charlemagne in 796 to lead the abbey founded by St.Martin. Alcuin established the first French school of theo-

Tours, St-Gatien, cloister

Tours, cathedral, portal

logy and philosophy in Tours and also made the monastery one of the most famous schools of calligraphy in the West, and it soon became one of the most important centres of medieval manuscript illumination. In the Carolingian Renaissance large numbers of Bibles and other manuscripts, decorated with magnificent miniatures which are still admired today, were created in Tours, and so enhanced the reputation of the town that Luitgard, the wife of Charlemagne, chose to be buried before the doors of the basilica of St-Martin.

But throughout the centuries the town which produced such famous sons as the painters Jean Fouquet and François Clouet, the novelist Honoré de Balzac and the playwright Georges Courteline made itself so attractive that a number of famous authors born elsewhere, including François Rabelais, Pierre de Ronsard, Anatole

France and Jules Romains, chose to make it their home.

St-Gatien cathedral: The cathedral was started *c.* 1220–30 on the site of earlier 4,6 and early 12C buildings (remains of the Romanesque church, which had burned down and collapsed, were included in the transept) and lasted for 3 centuries: *c.* 1280 the choir and apse were completed under the direction of E. de Mortagne, the building was vaulted in 1465 (the transept and the first two bays of the nave had been built by S.de Mans, the remaining bays by J.de Dammartin); the N. tower was completed in 1509 and the S. tower in 1547. As a result of this protracted building period the cathedral embraces the full Gothic range, from the early Gothic (apse) via high Gothic (nave and choir) to late Gothic (façade).

The façade was built from 1426–1547 by J.de Dammartin, J.Papin and J.Durand. It has magnificent late Gothic decoration, broken tympanums, foliate designs on gables and archivolts, and with all its niches and finials it is one of the finest examples of the Flamboyant style at its richest, but it harks back to the Romanesque in its massive buttresses and points forward to the Renaissance in the interruption of its soaring verticals, and the by no means identical cupolas on the towers are completely of the latter period.

Interior: The nave looks astonishingly high from the outside, and this is confirmed in the interior by the overwhelming spaciousness of the massive, six-bayed choir with five aisles and polygonal apse with three storeys, which for all its monumental qualities seems light and elegant, above all because of the triforium and the high windows in the upper walls of the

apse, which admit floods of light, broken only by the beauty of the colours.

Compared with this the eight-bayed nave seems narrower, partly because its layout is a little more confined, as it was necessary to incorporate parts of earlier buildings, and partly because the double aisles are separated by massive piers, which seem to form a kind of hall in their own right.

The greatest treasure in the cathedral is its *stained-glass windows*. The façade rose dates from the 15C, the transept rose from the 14C, and 15 unbelievably beautiful tall windows in the apse were added between 1265 and 1270, at the same time as the triforium windows below them representing the Virgin and the 12 Apostles; they represent lives of the saints, the creation of the world, the bishops of Tours, the Passion of Christ and the tree of Jesse.

Another magnificent feature is the *marble tomb of the children of Anne of Brittany and Charles VIII*, probably the work of a pupil of M.Colombe, the best-known Renaissance sculptor produced by the town.

Tours, St-Gatien cathedral The irregularities of the ground plan (particularly in the transept) are explained by the incorporation of older sections 1 Creation of the World 2 Christ's Passion 3 Martin legend

Tours, St-Gatien, cloister ▷

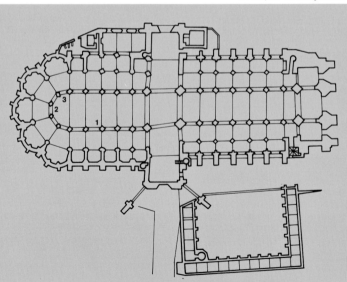

N. of the cathedral is the *cloître de la Psallette*, locally known as the 'choir school' as this is where the choirboys have their rehearsals. The openwork staircase in the NE corner was built 1508–1524.

St-Martin: The first church in honour of the saint, a modest wooden oratory built by his successor bishop, was replaced by a larger basilica in the 5C, or rather by what Gregory of Tours called the most important building in the West from the decline of the Roman empire to the Frankish empire of Charlemagne: a building 160 ft. long, 60 ft. wide and 40 ft. high, which burned down in a major fire in 997. The building which replaced it, consecrated in 1014, was an architectural innovation, as it was the first church with an ambulatory and radiating chapels, and these and the tunnel vault, which replaced the open roof, served as a model for many pilgrimage churches on the route to Santiago de Compostella. After much alteration and extension in the Gothic period (in the 13C St-Martin was considered to be the largest church in the West) the church was used as stabling by the army at the time of the French Revolution, its lead roof was stolen, leading to a partial collapse of the building, which fell into disrepair, thus signalling the end of the cult of St.Martin. Only the N. transept tower (Tour Charlemagne) and the S. façade tower (Tour de l'Horloge) survived. But the rediscovery of the tomb of the saint in 1860 led to a revival of the cult. From 1887 to 1924 a cruciform basilica in Romanesque-Byzantine style with crossing dome crowned with a bronze statue of the saint was built to plans by Laloux. On the column capitals in the new nave the heads of bishops, kings and saints who visited the old churches of St-Martin, or who were involved in the building of them, remind us of the famous past of this house of God, in which Clovis, the founder of the Frankish empire, vowed on St.Mar-

tin's day 498 that he and his family would be baptized.

St-Julien: This former abbey church, founded by Clovis, suffered greatly under attacks from the Normans and the pillaging of Geoffroi Martel, Count of Anjou, in the 10&11C. It was destroyed by a storm in 1225, and all that survived of the 10&11C Romanesque church was the vestibule with tower, rebuilt in 1080 and dating from 996. The present building, a basilica with five bays, nave, two aisles, a transept which protrudes unusually far and a three-bayed choir with a straight conclusion, dates from the 13C, though the stained glass is modern.

The following sections of the associated *monastery* have survived: the cloister courtyard with a 16C wine press, the medieval wine cellar, which houses the *Touraine wine museum*, and the nine-bayed 12C chapterhouse with its fine Gothic vault, in which Henri III summoned Parliament in 1589, when he had been driven from Paris by the Catholic league of the Guise.

Notre-Dame-la-Riche (for a long time known as Notre-Dame-la-Pauvre): One of the first churches to be founded in Tours, built in the early 4C by St.Lidoire in a Christian cemetery, it was often destroyed in the course of the centuries, for example by the Protestants in 1562,C and rebuilt. The present building, with the exception of later alterations, dates from the 15 (choir) and 16C.

Old Town: As has already been mentioned, this is in two parts, divided by the Rue Nationale: the Roman town with its quiet, straight streets and the cathedral at its centre, and the pilgrim town of Martinopolis, known as Châteauneuf since the 12C, with the St-Martin basilica at its heart. The first was ruled by the bishops, and the second by the monastery chapter, until spiritual leadership gave way in

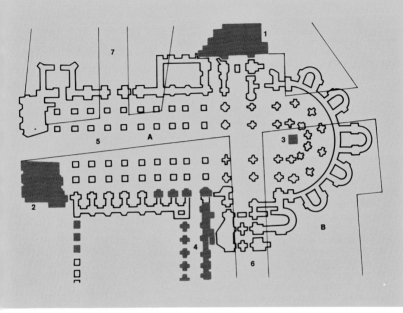

Tours, former basilica of St.Martin (A) and new basilica of St.Martin (B) Surviving sections of the old basilica: **1** Tour Charlemagne **2** Tour de l'Horloge **3** Grave of the Saint **4** E. walk of the cloister. Newly aligned streets: **5** Rue des Halles **6** Rue Descartes **7** Rue du Change

both cases to secular, that of two counts, and the two towns were united in 1354. Today they are connected by two charming medieval shopping streets: the Rue de la Scellerie/Rue des Halles and the Rue Colbert/Rue du Commerce, along which the traffic from Chinon to Amboise used to pass in Roman times, while in the 16C the residences of the nobility were built around its axis.

The old *Roman town*, in the NE of modern Tours, still the administrative quarter today, has many 15&16C houses. In the *Rue Colbert* or in the narrow *Place Foire-le-Roi* (named after the free market estab-lished here by Francis I in 1545) with their gabled houses and the *Hôtel Babou de la Bourdaisière*, the town palace of François Premier's superintendent of finance, built by the architects M. and G.François, who were also involved in the building of the cathedral. At that time there was also a keep. Nothing remains of the royal castle built in 1160 by Henry II Plantaganet to defend the Loire bridge and fortified with walls and bridges in the 13C but the round *Guise Tower* (12C, 15C machicolations), named after the young Duke of Guise who was imprisoned here after the murder of his father from 1588–91. From here remains of the 4C *Gallo-Roman town wall* run to the *Palais de l'ancien archevêché*; this dates from the 11&14C, but is essentially 17&18C. This was also the area in which the enormous *amphitheatre* used to stand, 469 ft. by 440 ft.; the Rue du Général-

Meusnier still follows its lines to some extent today.

W. of the Roman quarter is the *centre*, the *Rue Nationale*, an elegant shopping street laid out after 1763 to a coherent plan, badly damaged in the Second World War but largely rebuilt, with the enormously excessively decorated *Hôtel de Ville*, built by Laloux in 1904&5, the fine *Palais du Commerce* built by Pierre Meusnier of Tours and the *Hôtel de Semblançay*: an early Renaissance gallery and an elegant façade, all that remains of the town palace of the superintendent of finance under Louis XII and Francis I, Jacques de Beaune de Semblançay, who was hanged in 1527 after being accused of misappropriation of taxes. The so-called *Beaune fountain* outside this building, with a black stone basin and dominated by an elegant pyramid, is the work of M. and G.François (1511).

The old *pilgrim town* in the NW of modern Tours has twisty narrow streets and a number of old buildings. The *Rue Paul-Louis-Courier* is lined almost entirely with old buildings, including the late-16C Hôtel-Quantin (No. 15), in which Joan of Arc stayed during her visit to Jean Dupuy in Tours, the adviser of Yolande of Aragon, Queen of Sicily, and the late-15C No. 10. The *Place Plumereau* is the centre of old Tours, and has picturesque gabled houses and a group of very fine 15C *wooden houses*. The *Rue Briçonnet* is one of the most interesting streets in the old town, with Romanesque (No. 35) and Gothic (No. 31) façades and the charming Hôtel Pierre du Puy, late 15C. The *Place du Grand-Marché* has 15C houses (Nos. 1,11,13,and 15), and many attractive and welcoming streets leading off it. The most magnificent secular building of the old Martinopolis is the *Hôtel Gouin* (Rue du Commerce); this was built on Roman foundations and was constantly altered by its various owners; it now has an elaborate 16C Renaissance façade, and is used as a museum

of the development of fine art in Tours.

All these differing old buildings with their half-timbering, their curved gables, their staircase towers, oak stairways and galleries decorated with masks are witness to the lively activity of the once flourishing trade and merchant settlement around which the old town grew and which reached the height of its development and wealth in the 15&16C. In the 19C the siting of the station meant that the economic centre of the town moved further S. and the older part became increasingly less important. To avoid the decline which might have been caused by this, the town introduced a plan for rehabilitation of the area which set an example to the whole of Europe; the interiors of the buildings were modernised, but the exteriors preserved in the architectural forms of the 15–17C, with their mixture of timber-frame and stone houses.

Musée archéologique: This museum in the Hôtel Gouin has prehistoric, Gallo-Roman and Merovingian collections in the basement, medieval and Renaissance collections on the ground floor (including a particularly fine keystone from St-Clement), and on the first floor old engravings of Tours and coins struck there, etc.

Musée des Beaux-Arts: This museum has been housed in the former archbishop's palace at the SW corner of the old walls since 1910. It has a fine collection, consisting largely of paintings and furniture confiscated during the Revolution from the châteaux of Amboise, Chanteloup and Richelieu, and the abbeys of Marmoutier, Beaumont and Liget. The exhibits range from the Middle Ages to the Renaissance, the 17&18C and on into the 19&20C and are arranged in period groups, with local panelling

Tours, cathedral, rose window ▷

and silks, from the time of Louis XIII to that of Louis XVI. As well as work by local artists, such as the head of a monk by J.Fouquet, the famous 15C son of the town, there are numerous works from other countries. The particular pride of the museum are two panels by Mantegna ('Christ in the Garden of Gethsemane' and 'Resurrection', 1456–9) and a 'Flight into Egypt' painted on wood by Rembrandt and also pictures by Rubens, Boucher, Delacroix, Degas etc.

Musée du Compagnonnage (Rue Nationale 8): This museum in the monks' dormitory of the former abbey of St-Julien is unique in Europe, and is devoted to extinct crafts and to the life and doings of the compagnons, the wandering medieval craftsmen who formed professional groups (to some extent forerunners of the guilds), but also had connections with groups of rogues and vagabonds. In the abbey cellar is the **Musée des vins de Touraine**.

Musée du Gemmail: This museum in the Hôtel Raimbault (Rue du Mûrier) a fine Restauration building (1825) shows works by Picasso, Braque, Rouault and Cocteau in the Gemmail technique developed by the decorative artist R.Malherbe-Navarre in co-operation with the painter J.Crotti: pieces of coloured glass are mounted in layers and illuminated from behind.

Also worth seeing: The *botanical gardens*, laid out in 1843 and the *Jardin des Prébendes-d'Oé* (1872), a well-planted landscape garden.

Greater Tours

Marmoutier abbey (4 km. E.): founded in 372 by St.Martin, destroyed by the Normans in 853 and taken over by the Benedictines from Cluny; it had over 200 priories and domains at home and abroad, and was one of the most powerful monasteries in the whole of France. Pope Urban II called for a Crusade here in 1095. In 1818 however, the abbey and church, built 1214–1312 to plans by E. de Mortagnes (d.1294), were destroyed; the church was 367 ft. long, and said to be one of the finest of the Middle Ages. All that has survived are the *Portail de la Crosse* (1220), with wall passage and a small watchtower withembrasures, the 12C *prior's house*, a square 12C bell tower and the *Chapelle-des-Sept-Dormants*, built into the side of the hill and with graves cut deeply into the rock. St.Gatien is said to have celebrated the first mass in this grotto, and introduced the cult of Mary to France. The 'seven sleepers' were disciples of St.Martin, who are said to have died at a time appointed by him, and whose undecomposed bodies are therefore able to work miracles.

Tours, St-Martin

Adjacent to this chapel are hermits' cells, including that of St.Léobard or Liber (6C), who dug his own grave in the course of the 22 years which he spent here, and an old chapel dug out of the rock, the 'Repos de St.Martin', so-called because the saint is said to have liked to withdraw here for meditation. In the damp cell behind it St.Martin's successor, St.Brice, is said to have expiated his errors. In another cave there is a well dug by St.Martin himself, the water of which is said to have miraculous powers.

In 1847 the domain, sold as state property, was acquired by the Sisters of the Sacred Heart, who built a new abbey on the site.

Mettray dolmen (*c.* 10 km. N.): One of the most important stone monuments in France, consisting of twelve stones, 36 ft. long and 12 ft. high.

Grange-de-Meslay (*c.* 10 km. NE): Old 13C *tithe barn* of a farm run by the monks of Marmoutier; the remains of a curtain wall and the fine entrance gateway have survived.

Parçay-Meslay (approx. 8 km. NE) 12C *church* with Romanesque frescos in the choir.

Plessis-lès-Tours, Le (3 km. SW): The favourite residence of Louis XI, in which his daughter, canonised in 1950 as Joan of France, was born in 1464 and where he died in 1482. Only the S. section of the main building, but without the arches on the courtyard side, still exists of the Gothic château, plain even when it was built in 1463, and consisting of a royal wing with two storeys and two adjacent wings at right angles.

Saint-Avertin (SE): Popular fishing and rowing centre for the Tourangeaux, as the inhabitants of Tours are called. Formerly known as *Vençay* (from *Ventiacum*) the place took the name of a Scottish hermit, St.Avertin,

Tours, cathedral, stained glass

Tours, cathedral, interior

Tours, tomb, Charles VIII's children

who died here in 1180. In the 15C a fellow-countryman of the saint, Jean de Coningham, M. de Cangé, built the château of Cangé here, which was restored in the 19C, and added a choir to the 11C *church*.

Saint-Cosme (1.5 km. NW): Originally an island in the Loire, to which the heretic Bérenger (d. 1088) fled. In 1092 canons from the abbey of St-Martin in Tours founded a priory here, to which the famous Renaissance poet P.de Ronsard (1524–85) withdrew at the height of his fame to complete his 'Franciade', a kind of national epic, in which he traced the origins of the French nation—flatteringly at the time of the Renaissance—back to antiquity. The Romanesque choir of the church, the 12C monks' refectory, the 15C prior's house, altered in the 17C, in which Ronsard died, are the only old buildings to have survived.

Saint-Cyr-sur-Loire (NW): Late-15C *church* with fine early-16C porch. *La Gaudinière:* Farm, on which the philosopher of 'l'élan vital', Bergson (1859–1941), lived. *La Grenadière:* House in which Honoré de Balzac, who was born in Tours, spent some time in 1830; his birthplace was unfortunately destroyed in the Second World War. 1 km. N. of Saint-Cyr: **La Béchellerie:** Pretty *house*, in which Anatole France spent the last ten years of his life.

Saint-Radegonde (N., part of Tours since 1964): Heavily restored *parish church*, with a little square 12C bell tower and a crypt cut into the rock, which is said to have been used as an oratory by St.Gatien (3C).

Saint-Symphorien (N.): 15&16C *church* dating in part from the second half of the 12C (crossing, polygonal apse and small bell tower gable). The main portal with sculpted figures is

Trèves, St-Aubin, detail of tabernacle

Trèves, St-Aubin, font

Renaissance (1531). In the interior 'Adoration of the Magi', painting by Bassano, and a wooden figure of Christ by Lecreux.

Environs: Azay-sur-Cher (15 km. SE): Square *tower* with a small staircase turret, only surviving part of an old house. 3 km. from Azay-sur-Cher: Remains of the **St-Jean-du-Grais priory** (12C): Romanesque *bell tower*, fine *chapterhouse* with Gothic vault, 2 15C *houses*.
Bléré (27 km. SE): *Church* with 12C parallel nave and two aisles (left aisle with choir and Romanesque apse and right aisle with Plantagenet vault) and nave with a 15C Pietà. In the Place de la République (formerly a cemetery) Renaissance *funerary chapel*.
Larçay (9.5 km. E.): 5C Gallo-Roman *citadel* 246 ft. long.
Veretz (11.5 km. SE): *Renaissance church*. 15C *château* with a tower from

an earlier building from the time of Charles VIII (1483–98).
Vouvray (12 km. NE): Small wine-growing town known beyond the frontiers of France for its white wines.

Trèves
49 Maine-et-Loire   p.136☐G 4

This charming little village on the bank of the Loire with its church among the cypresses and massive defensive tower was apparently once a fortified bastion. That well-known enthusiast for building and fighting Foulques Nerra, Count of Anjou, built a fortress at the end of the limestone massif as early as the 11C. In 1435 the Chancellor of France, Robert le Maçon, built a château on the same site, of which only the impressive cylindrical *keep*, almost 100 ft. high, has survived. 500 yards

S. of this are the ruins of the *St-Macé priory*, founded in 1106.

St-Aubin: The little Romanesque church was started under the walls of the castle in 1106, and built higher, with large arches, just a little later. Much later, presumably not until the 15C, the side walls of the nave were pierced with small arches to connect it to the aisles; they have disappeared again over the years.

In the *interior* the massive columns with their carved foliate capitals are an impressive feature.

Environs: Chênehutte-les-Tuf-faux (3.5 km. SE): 12C *church* with 2 Romanesque portals. At the top of the hill are an old château on wide terraces with a fine view of the Loire, the remains of a priory and the ruins of a small 10C church.

La Mimerolle (5 km. SE): 18C house, in which Honoré de Balzac worked for a time.

Ussé

37 Indre-et-Loire   p.136☐I 4

Château: A building which has come straight from a picture book—towers and turrets, big ones and little ones, round ones and square ones and so many angles and corners that it is almost impossible to count them, and the onlooker only has one thought in mind: what secret can these walls conceal? The great French Renaissance collector of fairy tales Charles Perrault (1628–1703) is said to have been

Ussé, château, King's Room   *Ussé, château* ▷

Ussé, triptych in château chapel

inspired by this château to write his French version of the story of the Sleeping Beauty. The interior is much easier to assimilate, but even in the courtyard one can spend a long time looking, because there is such a mixture of styles: the façade of the E. wing was altered and restored in the 19C, but still gives glimpses of the original Flamboyant style, the W. section dates from the time of Francis I and was altered in the 17C and the S. wing, an arcade dating from *c.* 1500 with an added storey above it also dates from the 17C in its present form.

The château was started in the second half of the 15C; it changed hands in 1485, while it was still incomplete, and was not finished until 1535. In the 17C the N. wing of the building, which had been closed around a courtyard, was pulled down to open up the view over the Indre. A terraced garden was established on the slope where the N. wing had stood, and at the same time the W. wing was extended by a neoclassical building with a flat roof. Alterations to the E. wing were carried out in the mid 19C. Because of all these alterations the **interior** of the château lacks unity. Most building periods are represented: there is even part of the building's medieval predecessor: the octagonal room on the ground floor of the defensive tower, with an anachronistic tunnel vault; in the adjacent staircase tower there are Gothic spiral staircases and the main steps are splendid Renaissance work. When you open the door of the King's chamber, you step into the 18C. The room was originally made for Louis XIV, and is still furnished as it was in the 18C: canopied bed, pompous Corinthian columns dividing the alcoves from the room, furniture and earlier

Ussé, chapel, entrance

wall coverings in red silk with Chinese designs.

The *chapel*, on the other hand, built 1523–35, is a uniform and very beautiful late Gothic/early Renaissance building, combining the two periods impressively. This is most striking in the façade, flanked with 2 buttresses with canopied niches and with a low door with a conchiform tympanum and a high clerestory, surrounded by a jamb decorated with arabesques. Particularly striking are the medallions with three-dimensional heads, unknown in France until that time, and the candelabra ornaments which replace the earlier Gothic finials.

Particularly worth seeing are the 17C Aubusson tapestries, an L.della Robbia terracotta Madonna (15C), a 15C Tuscan triptych and the finely carved choir stalls dating from the foundation of the chapter.

Valençay
36 Indre   p.138☐M 5

Château: This extremely spacious building was built on the site of a 13C castle of the Valençay family. It was acquired by Jacques d'Estampes *c.*

1540, after his marriage to Jeanne Bernard d'Estiau, the daughter of the chamberlain of Anjou. He decided that he would use her money to build a residence 'suited to his station' and had the present château built on the model of Chambord and Chenonceau. The château was brought to life, however, by one of the most extraordinary personalities in France, Charles-Maurice de Talleyrand-Périgord. This master of imaginative intrigue had become Bishop of Autun at the age of 34 and a year later was made a member of the National Assembly. After only three years as a bishop he broke with the church and became Napoleon Bonaparte's foreign minister in 1799. In 1803 Napoleon gave him this commission: 'I wish you to purchase a fine country seat, and to receive the corps diplomatique and foreigners of high rank there, so that one may come with friends to you and that an invitation thither be considered a reward to the ambassadors of those rulers, with whom I am well pleased.'

Talleyrand would not have been Talleyrand if he had not used this opportunity to acquire 'one of the largest feudal estates in France'. As well as the château it consisted of 23 parishes with the village of Valençay at the centre. The château alone possessed 9,000 hectares of land. Because he was intended to entertain at the château, Talleyrand had Napoleon pay a large proportion of the purchase price, but this apparently skilful move was to rebound on him in 1807. The foreign minister fell into disfavour, had to resign, and in 1808 the Spanish King Ferdinand VII, exiled by Napoleon, was billeted on him at Valençay. Talleyrand had to put up with this imposition until 1814, as Napoleon had paid for part of the château. In 1829

Valençay, château, dome

Valençay, château

the statesman left the château to his nephew, Napoléon-Louis de Talleyrand, who was created Duke of Valençay by King Charles X, and the château is still in the possession of his family.

The *buildings* show once again how it was possible for the man commissioning the work to overestimate the possibilities. Jacques d'Estampes planned a courtyard surrounded by four wings. There were to be massive round towers at the corners, and N. wing was to have a donjon-like entrance pavilion on the model of Chenonceaux. What was actually built was the NW tower with dome and the first half of the N. wing with an arcade on the courtyard side. The entrance pavilion was just completed, but the second half of the N. wing remained only one storey high. The corner tower was correspondingly inadequate.

The details of the ornamentation of the walls give a clear idea of the way in which Estampes had overestimated both himself and his means. He acted as though he had inexhaustible funds, and planned pilaster articulation with Doric capitals on the ground floor, Ionic capitals on the first floor and Corinthian capitals on the third floor. The three storey entrance pavilion has little corner turrets on its outer side and a wall passage with lavishly carved corbels.

It was not until the mid 17C that Dominique d'Estampes, a descendant of the original owner, found the means to build the present park wing and an E. wing which has disappeared in the meantime. The S. round tower was added in the 18C by Legendre Villemorien-Luçay, who was also responsible for the new pilastered façade on the E. side of the park wing with an open gallery on the ground

Valençay, peacock in château park

Vendôme, l. bell tower, r. abbey tower

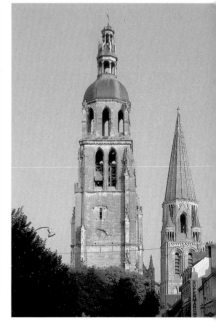

floor. The first thing which Talleyrand did was to close this up again, as he wished to accommodate his guests there and so had the interior completely redesigned in Empire style. It was in this wing that the Spanish King Ferdinand VII spent his six years of exile.

In the *interior* only the park wing is open to the public, as descendants of Talleyrand live in the rest of the château. Busts and portraits are the dominant feature of the parts of the building which may be visited. The very first room, the lower gallery, is almost exclusively furnished with mementoes of this kind. The grand salon contains striking Empire furniture. There is a mahogany writing table said to have been used by Talleyrand at the Congress of Vienna. The finest portrait is of Talleyrand by P-P.Prud'hon. There are more portraits in the blue drawing room, and also Louis-Quatorze and Régence

furniture. The duchess's room occupies the ground floor of the new tower, and is decorated in delicate green, grey and white. This was once the home of Dorothee de Dino, Talleyrand's niece and lover. The finest feature of the furnishings is a collection of plates in Sèvres porcelain, which is part of a service given to Talleyrand by Napoleon. On the upper floor in the king's room, still largely decorated as it was when Ferdinand lived in it from 1804–14. The finest features after the somewhat excessive canopied bed are the grisaille painted wallpaper telling the story of Psyche, and Italian gouache paintings.

The beautifully kept park is inhabited by llamas, fallow deer, cranes, peacocks, flamingos and parrots.

The *Talleyrand museum* is housed in a late 18C building, and contains memorabilia of the statesman, including his orders, various items of clothing and his orthopaedic shoes (he had a limp from childhood).

Vendôme, former Trinity abbey 1 Abbey church **2** Cloister **3** Chapterhouse **4** Monks' house **5** Museum **6** Abbot's lodging **7** Abbot's chapel **8** Guest house **9** Bell tower

Environs: Varennes-sur-Fouzon (8 km. N.): Late 12C *church* with a fine portal.

Vendôme, abbey church, portal ▷

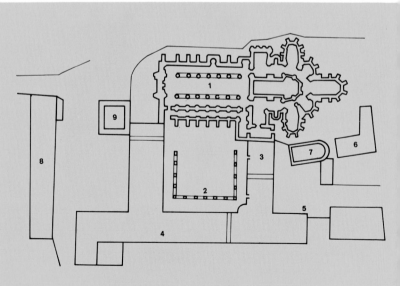

Vendôme
41 Loir-et-Cher   p.138□L 2

This site on the Loir was settled even in Neolithic times. It became of more than local importance through the counts of the house of Bouchard, the faithful vassals of the Capet kings. The town flourished in the 11C because of Fulques Nerra, Count of Anjou and his son Geoffroy Martel, who founded Holy Trinity abbey. When the whole of Anjou was inherited by Henry Plantagenet Vendôme was on the boundary between French and English territory, and was thus constantly in the firing line and changed hands on a number of occasions. In 1371 the town came to the Bourbons, in 1515 Francis I made it a duchy and in 1589 it was punished for taking the part of the Catholic league by extensive destruction by its liege lord Henry IV. Only the church of the Holy Trinity survived. It was badly damaged again by air raids in 1940.

Former abbey of the Holy Tri-

Museum, terracotta head of Christ

nity: The abbey was founded by Geoffroy Martel, Count of Anjou, and was dedicated to the Holy Trinity in 1040. The Benedictine monastery was so successful that its abbot became a cardinal. The first cardinal abbot was Geoffroy de Vendôme (1093–1129), a confidant of Pope Urban II. The monastery was a popular place of pilgrimage until the Reformation, as Geoffroy Martel had brought back from a crusade the Holy Tear shed by Christ at the grave of Lazarus.

The *abbey church* is an outstanding example of Gothic art in France, and almost all the phases of Gothic are represented in it. Building started in 1040, but only fragments of the walls of this first monastery church have survived; they became part of the transept. The present church was built from 1306 (choir and E. bays of the nave). The W. bays and the façade were completed in 1506. Building ceased altogether during the Hundred Years War, hence the long delay.

The splendid free-standing *bell tower* dates from the 12C in its entirety and was the model for the Old Tower of Chartres cathedral. To understand its dominant design one has to see its double function: it was the keep of the abbey and the bell tower of the church. For this reason the windows increase in size the higher they are set, and their arches become more heavily splayed. The transition from square to octagonal plan is handled by the use of corner turrets. The cornice on the first floor is decorated with carved masks and animals. The iron cross on the top of the tower is over 13 ft. high. The masterly late Gothic façade is the work of Jéhan de Beauce, the architect of the New Tower of Chartres cathedral. The beautifully decorated open-work façade has a fine chased canopy. The *nave* has a large triforium and massive clerestory windows. Although it took almost two centuries to build and clearly bears the mark of

Abbey church, 12C stained glass ▷

Vendôme, town gate

more than one architectural style, the interior still has remarkable unity, which makes it all the more interesting to use the differently designed capitals, friezes, triforium and vaulting to date the individual bays. In the crossing the columns and capitals are still Romanesque, and date from the 13C. The capitals are decorated with painted statues of St.Peter, Mary with the Angel of the Annunciation and St.Eutrope.

Parts of the *transept* walls come from the 11C church. The vault was rebuilt in the 14C in the Angevin style. The well-decorated keystones also date from this period. The Gothic windows in the N. aisle are 13C, while those in the S. aisle were added in the 16C. The N. transept contains fine 14C statues of John the Baptist, and a 16C statue of Mary. The fine 16C choir stalls extend into the crossing. They have misericords with grotes-

ques, animal figures and little scenes showing work in the various seasons.

Work on the *choir* started in 1306 and was completed before 1357. The ambulatory has five chapels; the first two practically form a second transept, the central one is also unusually deep. The chapels contain splendid 16C stained glass windows. The central chapel has a valuable 12C window showing the Virgin and Child; it is the oldest known stained glass Madonna and Child. N. of the high altar is the base, decorated with tears, of the 'stone shrine' which once held the relic.

The *monastery buildings* have suffered considerably from the fact that a regiment of cavalry was once billeted in them. All of the 14C cloister was destroyed, with the exception of the S. walk. There is a *museum* in part of the former monastery showing wall paintings from the Loir valley and religious

Vendôme, local history museum

art of the Middle Ages and Renaissance. There are also vault keystones from the destroyed cloister, the old aquamanile from the abbey and parts of the tombs of François de Bourbon-Vendôme and Marie de Luxembourg. Another section is devoted to prehistory and antiquity, 16–18C painting and faience.

Ruined castle: The castle is set on a ridge above the Loir and dates from the 13C. Ramparts, remains of walls and a machicolated round tower have survived. The larger tower, also known as the 'Tour de Poitiers', was rebuilt in the 15C and used as a keep. The early 17C Porte de Beauce leads to a garden laid out on a large scale, in which the outline of the walls of the collegiate church of St-Georges can be seen. It was also founded by Geoffroy Martel and served as the funerary church of the lords of Vendôme.

Antoine de Bourbon and Jeanne d'Albret, the parents of Henry IV, were buried here. The Promenade de la Montagne affords a splendid view of the Loir valley and Vendôme.

Also worth seeing: The *old town* on the island between the two arms of the Loir still has some interesting features, despite the destruction it has undergone. *Ste-Madeleine* was completed in 1474 and is recognisable from a distance by its slender bell tower with a crocketed stone spire. The nave has a wooden tunnel vault. The former *Oratorian college* is a neoclassical brick building now used as a grammar school. The 8-year-old Honoré de Balzac was educated here from 1807. The *St-Jacques chapel* to the E. of the grammar school, was once part of a pilgrims' hospice in which pilgrims stayed on their way to Santiago de Compostella. The chapel has a fine Renaissance turret. On its N. side there are Romanesque elements in pillars, capitals, and a portal which is half buried in the ground. The entrance to the hospice was formerly on the E. side, and for this reason the late Gothic façade is richly decorated.

Environs: Areines (3 km. E.): It is no longer possible to tell that the village once contained a Roman amphitheatre for 3,000–4,000 spectators. The little *church* dates from the 11&12C. In 1931 frescos thought to date from the time of building were discovered under various later accretions in the choir and apse vaults. In the apse is God the Father, surrounded by the symbols of the Evangelists, and underneath are the Apostles. The choir vault contains the Lamb of God in a halo borne by 4 angels. Next to this are the Annunciation and the birth of Christ. The Virgin and Child in the portal are 14C, and the terracotta statues of St.Anne and the Virgin are 16C.

Azé (9.5 km. NW): The old *church* (the nave is 11C and the choir = built over a stone crypt 15C) has a Carolingian bas-relief, 17C wood carvings and 18C gilded wooden candelabra and crucifix.

Château de Rochambeau 9 km. W.): The château dates from the 16C and was extended in the 18C. There are numerous caves in the vicinity, one of which was used as a hiding-place by the Duke of Beaufort in 1648 in his flight from Vincennes. The château contains memorabilia of the Marshall of Rochambeau, the commander of the French forces in the American War of Independence. The château and its surroundings became

Vendôme, museum, Gregogna patchwork

Villandry, château, corner towers 14C

well-known through Balzac's novel 'Louis Lambert'.

Danzé (13 km. N.): 12&15C *church* with 17C wooden figures. 16C moated *house*.

Epiais (16 km. E.): 11&15C *church* (17C altarpiece).

Mozangé (11 km. NW): Parts of *St-Lubin* date from the 11C. The church was extended and partially rebuilt in the 16C. The wooden vaulting in the nave was added in 1563. The lower part of the tower dates from the 12C, the octagonal upper part was built in the 16C.

Naveil (1 km. W.): Remains of a Gallo-Roman or Merovingian settlement, the so-called *Villa Tourteline* or *Condita of Naveil* have been excavated near the village.

Pezou (11 km. NE): 11&16C *church* with a Romanesque portal.

Selommes (13 km. SE): 11C *church* with 16C wooden vault. *Ruined château* (15C) in a marshy part of the valley.

Villeromain (9 km. SE): 11C *church*.

Villetrun (8.5 km. E.): Old *church*, parts of which are 12C. Only a 16C pavilion and a 17C gate have survived of the *château*.

Villandry
37 Indre-et-Loire   p.136☐I 4

Château: Villandry was built in 1532 on the foundations of a medieval castle, pulled down except for a corner tower, and is one of the last Renaissance châteaux, indeed one of the last major building projects in the Loire valley. It owes its recognition as such to a 20C private individual, the Spanish doctor Dr. Carvallo, who bought the property from a pharma-

Villandry, château garden

Villandry, château, cour d'honneur

cist in 1906. At that time the château and park had been so altered in the baroque and Romantic periods, that its original appearance was almost completely concealed. The château seemed to consist entirely of windows, balconies and blind openings, and the park, with flowers and shrubs approaching the château and half covering it up, had been laid out as an English garden. Only by dint of a great deal of effort and much removal of plaster was the keen new owner able to distinguish false from real windows and rediscover the original architecture of the Renaissance château. What had happened was that not only had false windows been put in, but existing windows had been turned into doors, and the first floor had been surrounded by balconies with balustrades and the ground floor with a balustraded terrace, in order to make it possible to get out of

the building at as many points as possible. On the other hand the arcades of the courtyard had been walled up to provide kitchens on one side and corridors on the other. In short, the restorers were faced with an almost impossible task.

However, château and garden were gradually restored to their original, or at least to what was probably their original form; in the case of the garden Carvallo had to work from old engravings by Jacques Androuet de Cerceau, as there were no comparable gardens. And so the château now looks much as it did when it was built: a typical Renaissance building arranged symmetrically around a central axis. The central section has mullioned windows framed by two rows of pilasters and dormers of equal height; it is divided into two by the entrance and framed on each side by an identical wing. Both wings have arcades and concluding pavilions. The entire façade is geometrically articulated with a heavily emphasised double cornice and pilasters, and high dormers on the window axes.

The *gardens* became very famous, as they had been so much harder to restore because of the lack of models. They are laid out as three gardens on three different levels: at the highest level is a *water garden* with a large central pool which occupies the central space and is surrounded by lawns and avenues of lime trees; this pool feeds the garden moat and the château moat. The central level is a *decorative garden* in two sections. By shapes (topiary box and yew trees) and by colours (flowers) it represents four types of love: tender love by hearts, masks, flames and the colour pink, tragic love by swords, daggers and the colour red, love run wild by a labyrinth of mis-shapen hearts and mixed colours, and idle flirtation by fans, butterflies' wings, love letters and the colour yellow. Most interesting of all, however, is the *vegetable garden* on the lowest level, which is not easily recognisable as such even if

Villandry, château

Villesavin, château

Villesavin, ceiling painting in chapel

one looks very closely, as it too is divided into geometrical patterns by flower beds and the vegetables (only varieties known in France in the 16C) are arranged in graded shades of green.

Villesavin

41 Loir-et-Cher   p.138☐M 3

Château: This building on the border of Sologne and Blésois was built in 1537 by Jean Le Breton, lord of the château of Villandry, secretary of state and finance minister to Francis I, administrator of the county of Blois, chairman of the audit office and responsible to the king for the building of the château of Chambord. The king must have appreciated the services of Le Breton, because after his death his wife Anne Gédouin continued to work in Chambord, and

his daughter remained administrator of the royal château. Given this background it is interesting to see what such a man built for himself. It is also possible to differentiate what he did because he liked it himself (and so realised it in Villesavin) and what pleased the king (and therefore was realised in Chambord). Chambord is a hopeless design muddle with no sense of proportion, whereas in Villesavin sense of proportion might itself have been the architect. And so this elegant Renaissance building came into being, with some admirably suitable neoclassical features.

It is essentially a central building with four axes and a high hipped roof and with two square pavilions at the sides. The central axis is emphasised with a protruding section crowned with a lantern. On the ground floor it forms a round-arched niche containing a bust of Francis I, in the upper storey it forms a rectangular niche containing a statue of the hunt goddess Diana. The courtyard has a side wing at right angles on one side and a wall on the other. At the front the eye is caught by two pavilions with lavishly decorated dormers. They are the only part of the château modelled directly on Chambord. Like many Loire châteaux Villesavin was once moated, to reflect the building, but the moats have long been filled in.

A feature which has survived, however, is the marble *fountain basin* in the middle of the courtyard. Its ornate design makes it a fine example of Renaissance sculpture, but it also tells us a great deal about the sensibilities and life style of the man who built the château. The fountain was not made by the sculptors who worked at Chambord, but by Italian artists specially sought out by Le Breton. Although the château has not yet been fully restored it is still worth visiting the interior, in which there is a fine collection of pewter, among other things. The kitchen has survived in almost its original condition. An interesting feature of the *chapel* in the left front pavilion, in which some original painting has survived. It is said to be the work of N.dell'Abbate. In the former farm buildings there is a collection of coaches, and an original 16C dovecote with revolving ladder.

Environs: Bracieux (3 km. E.): Old *granary* above a hall with wooden columns.

Château Herbault (6 km. E.): This château is built in stone and brick, and surrounded by water on three sides. It has a high slate roof over the living quarters and wings with large round and small polygonal staircase towers. The whole design, but particularly the large, lavishly decorated dormers with highly ornamented gables, make it a typical Renaissance building of the time of Francis I (1515–47); the administrative buildings are Louis-Treize. The whole building was restored in the 19C, unfortunately not always with a due sense of style.

Fontaines-en-Sologne (8 km. SE.): *Church* in Planatagenet style (12&13C) with an early-16C painted wooden Virgin. 16C *château*.

Mont-près-Chambord (5 km. W.): 15C *Descent from the Cross*.

Glossary

Acanthus: Decorative element found especially on → Corinthian capitals; it developed from the stylized representation of a sharply serrated, thistle-like leaf.

Aedicule: Wall niche housing a bust or statue; usually with a → gable, → pillars or → columns.

Aisle: Longitudinal section of a church or other building, usually divided from other such sections by an → arcade.

Altar: Sacrificial table of Greeks and Romans. The Lord's table in the Christian faith. Catholic churches often have several side altars as well as the high altar.

Ambo: Stand or lectern by the choir screen in early Christian and medieval churches; predecessor of the → pulpit.

Ambulatory: A corridor created by continuing the side aisles around the choir; often used for processions.

Antependium: Covering for the front of the altar.

Apse: Large recess at end of the → choir, usually semicircular or polygonal. As a rule it contains the → altar.

Apsidiole: A small apsidal chapel.

Aquamanile: Pouring-vessel or bowl for ritual washing in the Catholic liturgy.

Aqueduct: Water pipe or channel across an arched bridge; frequently built as monumental structures by the Romans.

Arabesque: Stylized foliage used as a decorative motif.

Arcade: A series of arches borne by columns or pillars. When the arcade is attached to a wall (and is purely decorative), it is called a blind arcade.

Arch: A curved structure of support employed in spanning a space.

Architrave: Main stone member on top of the columns; lowest part of the → entablature.

Archivolt: The face of an arch in Romanesque and Gothic portals; often more than one.

Ashlar: Hewn block of stone (as opposed to that straight from the quarry).

Atrium: In Roman houses a central hall with an opening in the roof. In Christian architecture, a forecourt usually surrounded by columns; also known as a → paradise.

Attic: A (usually richly decorated) storey above the main → entablature; intended to conceal the roof.

Baldacchino: Canopy above altars, tombs, statues, portals, etc.

Baluster: Short squat or shaped column.

Balustrade: Rail formed of → balusters.

Baptistery: Place of baptism; may be a separate building.

Baroque: Architectural style from *c* .1600–*c* .1750. Distinguished by powerfully agitated, interlocking forms.

Bartizan: A small corner turret projecting from the top of a building.

Base: Foot of a column or pillar.

Basket arch: A flattened round arch.

Basilica: Greek hall of kings. In church architecture, a type of church with nave and two or more aisles, the roof of the nave being higher than the roofs above the aisles.

Bay: Vertical division of a building between pillars, columns, windows, wall arches, etc.

Blind arcade: → Arcade.

Blind tracery: → Tracery.

Bosquet: Clumps of trees and bushes, particularly common in French gardens and parks.

Bracket: A projection from the wall used as a support—for a bust, statue, arch, etc.

Calotte: Half dome with no drum.

Calvary: Sculpture of the Crucifixion and Mount Calvary.

Campanile: Bell tower; usually free standing.

Capital: Topmost part of a column. The shape of

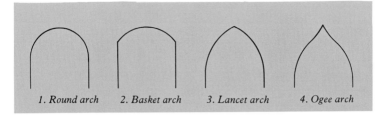

1. *Round arch*   2. *Basket arch*   3. *Lancet arch*   4. *Ogee arch*

the capital determines the style or → order.

Cartouche: Decorative frame or panel imitating a scrolled piece of paper, usually with an inscription, coat-of-arms, etc.

Caryatid: A carved figure supporting the entablature.

Cella: Main room of ancient temple containing divine image.

Cenotaph: Monument to dead buried elsewhere.

Chapterhouse: Assembly room in which monks or nuns discuss the community's business.

Charnel house: House or vault in which bones are placed.

Choir: That part of the church in which divine service is sung. Shorter and often narrower than the nave, it is usually raised and at the E. end. In the Middle Ages the choir was often separated from the rest of the church by a screen.

Ciborium: Canopy over high altar; usually in the form of a dome supported on columns.

Classicism: Revival of Greek and Roman architectural principles.

Clerestory: Upper part of the main walls of the nave, above the roofs of

the aisles and pierced by windows.

Cloister: Four sided covered walk (often vaulted) and opening inwards by arcades.

Coffered ceiling: A ceiling divided into square or polygonal panels, which are painted or otherwise decorated.

Column: Support with circular cross-section, narrowing somewhat towards the top; the type of column is determined by the → order. → Pillar.

Compound pillar: Often found in Gothic buildings. A central shaft has attached or detached shafts or half-shafts clustered around it.

Conch: Semicircular recess with a half-dome.

Confessio: Chamber or recess for a relic near the altar.

Corinthian order: → Order with richly decorated → capitals; the base has two or more tiers and is similar to that of the → Ionic order.

Cornice: Projecting upper limit of a wall; topmost member of the → entablature of an → order.

Cosmati work: Decorative technique involving the use of marble inlay,

mosaics etc.; many Roman marble workers had the family name Cosma.

Crocket: Gothic leaf-like decoration projecting from the sides of pinnacles, gables etc.

Crossing: The intersection of the nave and transept.

Crypt: Burial place, usually under the → choir. Churches were often built above an old crypt.

Curtain wall: Outer wall of castle.

Cyclops wall: Ancient wall made of large rough bocks of stone of irregular shape.

Dipteros: Temple in which porticoes are connected by a double row of lateral columns.

Diptych: A painted hinged double (altar) panel.

Directoire style: French style under the Directoire (1795–9), influenced by Antiquity.

Dolmen: Chamber tomb lined and roofed with megaliths.

Doric order: → Order in which the columns lack a base and bear flat, pad-shaped → capitals.

Dormer window:

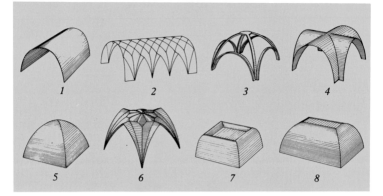

1. Barrel vault 2. Tunnel vault split into bays by transverse arches 3. Sail vault
4. Groin vault 5. Domical vault 6. Stellar vault 7. Coffered vault 8. Mirror vault

Window in sloping roof which projects and has its own gabled roof.

Drum: Substructure of a dome; as a rule either cylindrical or polygonal.

Dwarf Gallery: Romanesque feature; wall passage of small arches on the outside of a building.

Empire style: Classical style in France at the beginning of the 19C, with Graeco-Roman and Egyptian models.

Enclos Paroissal: Enclosed churchyard in France, often with a → Calvary.

Entablature: Upper part of an → order; made up of → architrave, → frieze and → cornice.

Exedra: Apse, vaulted with a half-dome; may have raised seats.

Façade: Main front of a building, often decoratively treated.

Facing: Panelling in front of structural components not intended to be visible.

Faience: Glazed pottery named after the Italian town of Faenza.

Fan vault: Looks like a highly decorated rib vault; Concave-sided cone-like sections meet or nearly meet at the apex of the vault.

Filigree work: Originally goldsmith's work in which gold and silver wire were ornamentally soldered on to a metal base. Also used in a more general sense for intricately perforated carvings and stucco.

Final: Small decorative pinnacle.

Flying buttress: Very large Gothic windows made it necessary to buttress or strengthen the outer walls by half-arches and arches. This support transmitted the thrust of the vault to the buttress.

Foliate capital: Gothic capital in which the basic form is covered with delicate leaf ornaments.

Fosse: Artificially created ditch; often separated castles from the surrounding land with access by a drawbridge.

Fresco: Pigments dispersed in water are applied without a bonding agent to the still-damp lime plaster. While the mortar dries, the pigments become adsorbed into the plaster.

Frieze: Decorative strips for the borders of a wall. The frieze can be two- or three-dimensional and can consist of figures or ornaments.

Gable: The triangular upper section of a wall. Normally at one end of a pitched roof but it may be purely decorative.

Gallery: Intermediate storey; in a church it is usually for singers and the organ.

1. Doric capital 2. Cushion capital 3. Corinthian capital 4. Ionic capital 5. Crocket capital 6. Foliate capital

Gobelin: Pictorial tapestry woven in the Gobelins factory in Paris.

Gothic: Period in European art and architecture stretching from the mid 12C to the 16C.

Grisaille: Painting in various shades of grey.

Groin vault: Vault in which two → barrel vaults intersect at right angles. The simple groin vault is to be distinguished from the rib vault, in which the intersecting edges are reinforced by ribs.

Half-timbering: Beams are used as supporting parts with an infill of loam or brick.

Hall church: In contrast to the → basilica, nave and aisles are of equal height; no → transept.

Hermitage: Pavilion in parks and gardens; originally the residence of a hermit.

Holy Sepulchre: Structure representing Christ's tomb as discovered by Constantine, who later encased it in a miniature temple.

Iconostasis: In the Eastern church, a screen of paintings between the sanctuary and the nave.

Intarsia: Inlaid work in wood, plaster, stone etc.

Ionic order: → Order in which the columns stand on a base of two or more tiers; the → capital has two lateral → volutes.

Jamb: Vertical part of arch, doorway or window.

Keep: Main tower of a castle; last refuge in time of siege.

Lantern: Small windowed turret on top of roof or dome.

Loggia: Pillared gallery, open on one or more sides; often on an upper storey.

Lunette : Semicircular panel above doors and windows, often with paintings or sculptures.

Mandorla: Almond shaped niche containing a figure of Christ enthroned.

Mannerism: Artistic style between → Renaissance and → baroque (*c.* 1530–1630). Mannerism neglects natural and classical forms in favour of an intended artificiality of manner.

Mansard: An angled roof in which the lower slope is steeper than the upper. The area gained is also called a mansard and can be used to live in. Named after the French architect F.Mansart.

Mausoleum: A splendid tomb, usually in the form of a small house or temple; from the tomb of Mausolus at Halicarnassus.

Menhir: Rough-hewn prehistoric standing stone.

Mensa: Flat surface of the altar.

Mezzanine: Intermediate storey.

Miniature: Small picture, hand illumination in old manuscripts.

Monks' choir: That section of the choir reserved for the monks, frequently closed off.

Monstrance: Ornamented receptacle in which the consecrated Host is shown (usually behind glass).

Mosaic: Decoration for wall, floor or vault, assembled from small coloured stones, pieces of glass or fragments of other materials.

Mullion: Vertical division of a window into two or more lights.

Narthex: Vestibule of basilica or church.

Nave: Central aisle of church, intended for the congregation; excludes choir and apse.

Neo-baroque: Reaction to the cool restraint of → classicism. Re-uses baroque forms; developed in the last part of the 19C as a historicizing, sumptuous style with exaggerated three-dimensional ornamentation and conspicuous colours.

Neo-Gothic: Historicizing 19C style, which was intended to revive Gothic structural forms and decorative elements.

Net vault: Vault in which the ribs cross one another repeatedly. C

Nuns' choir: Gallery from which nuns attended divine service.

Nymphaeum: Roman pleasure house, often with statues and fountains.

Obelisk: Free-standing pillar with square ground plan and pyramidal peak.

Odeum: Building, usually round, in which musical or other artistic performances were given.

Onion dome: Bulbous dome with a point, common in Russia and E.Europe; not a true dome, i.e. without a vault.

Opisthodomos: Rear section of Greek temple.

Orangery: Part of baroque castles and parks originally intended to shelter orange trees and other southern plants in winter. However, orangeries often had halls for large court assemblies.

Oratory: Small private chapel.

Order: Classical architectural system prescribing decorations and proportions according to one of the accepted forms: → Corinthian, → Doric, → Ionic, etc. An order consists of a column, which usually has a base, shaft and capital, and the entablature, which itself consists of architrave, frieze and cornice.

Oriel: Projecting window on an upper floor; it is often a decorative feature.

Pallium: A cloak worn by the Romans; in the Middle Ages, a coronation cloak for kings and emperors, later also for archbishops.

Pantheon: Temple dedicated to all gods; often modelled on that in Rome, which is a rotunda. Building in which distinguished people are buried or have memorials.

Paradise: → Atrium.

Pavilion: Polygonal or round building in parks or pleasure grounds. The main structure of baroque castles is very often linked by corner pavilions to the galleries branching off from the castle.

Pedestal: Base of a column or the base for a statue.

Pendentive: The means by which a circular dome is supported on a square base; concave area or spandrel between two walls and the base of a dome.

Peripteros: Greek temple in which the porticoes are connected laterally by single rows of columns.

Peristyle: Continuous colonnade surrounding a temple or open court.

Pilaster: Pier projecting from a wall; conforms to one of the → orders.

Pilaster strip: Pilaster without base and capital; feature of Anglo-Saxon and early Romanesque buildings.

Pillar: Supporting member, like a → column but with a square or polygonal cross section; does not conform to any order.

Plinth: Projecting lower part of wall or column.

Polyptych: An (altar) painting composed of several panels or wings.

Porch: Covered entrance to a building.

Portico: Porch supported by columns and often with a pediment; may be the centre-piece of façade.

Predella: Substructure of the altar. Paintings along lower edge of large altarpiece.

Pronaos: Area in front of ancient ' temple (also of churches); sides enclosed and columns in front.

Propylaeum: Entrance gateway, usually to temple precincts. The Propylaeum on the Acropolis at Athens was the model for later buildings.

Prothyra: Railing before door of Roman house.

Pseudoperipteros: Temple in which porticoes are connected laterally by → pilasters and not → columns.

Pulpit: Raised place in church from which the sermon is preached. May be covered by a → baldacchino or → sounding board.

Putto: Figure of naked angelic child in → Renaissance, → baroque and → rococo art and architecture.

Pylon: Entrance gate of Egyptian temple; more generally used as isolated structure to mark a boundary.

Quadriga: Chariot drawn by four horses harnessed abreast.

Refectory: Dining hall of a monastery.

Régence style: French style transitional between the → baroque and the → rococo.

Relief: Carved or moulded work in which the design stands out. The different depths of relief are, in ascending order, rilievo stiacciato, bas-relief and high relief or alto-rilievo.

Reliquary: Receptacle in which a saint's relics are preserved.

Renaissance: Italian art and architecture from the early 15C to the mid 16C. It marks the end of the medieval conception of the world and the beginning of a new view based on classical antiquity (Ital. rinascimento = rebirth).

Retable: Shrine-like structure above and behind the altar.

Rib vault: → Groin vault.

Rocaille: Decorative ornaments adapted from the shell motif; chiefly late → Renaissance and → Rococo.

Rococo: Style towards the end of the → baroque (1720–70); elegant, often dainty, tendency to oval forms.

Romanesque: Comprehensive name for architecture from 1000–c. 1300. Buildings are distinguished by round arches, calm ornament and a heavy general appearance.

Rood screen: Screen between → choir and → nave, which bears a rood or crucifix.

Rose-window: A much divided round window with rich → tracery; found especially in Gothic buildings, often above the portal.

Rotunda: Round building.

Rustication: Massive blocks of stone separated by deep joints.

Sanctuary: Area around the high altar in a church.

Sarcophagus: Stone coffin, usually richly decorated.

Scroll: Spiral-shaped ornament.

Secularization: Transfer of ecclesiastical possessions to secular use, especially in the Napoleonic period (1803).

Sedilia: Seats for clergy; usually in the wall of the S. side of the choir.

Sgraffito: Scratched-on decoration.

Sounding board: → Pulpit.

Spandrel: The triangular space between the curve of an arch, the horizontal drawn from its apex, and the vertical drawn from the point of its springing; also the area between two arches in an arcade, and that part of a vault between two adjacent ribs.

Springer: The first stone in which the curve of an arch or vault begins.

Squinch: An arch or system of arches at the internal angles of towers to form the base of a round drum or dome above a square structure. → Pendentive.

Stela: Standing block.

Strapwork: Renaissance carved work modelled on fretwork or cut leather.

Stucco: Plasterwork, made of gypsum, lime, sand and water. Used chiefly in the 17&18C for three-dimensional interior decoration.

Synagogue: Jewish place of worship.

Tabernacle: Receptacle for the consecrated host.

Telamon: Support in the form of a male figure (male caryatid).

Terracotta: Fired, unglazed clay.

Thermal baths: Roman hot-water baths.

Tracery: Geometrically conceived decorative stonework, particularly used to decorate windows, screens, etc. If it embellishes a wall, it is known as blind tracery.

Transenna: Screen or lattice in openwork found in early Christian churches.

Transept: That part of a church at right angles to the nave; → basilica.

Triforium: Arcaded wall passage looking on to the nave; between the arcade and the clerestory.

Triptych: Tripartite altar painting.

Triumphal arch: Free-standing gateway based on a Roman original.

Trompe l'oeil: Special kind of image which the eye is deceived into viewing as three dimensional.

Tunnel vault: Simplest vault; continuous structure with semicircular or pointed cross section uninterrupted by cross vaults.

Tympanum: The often semicircular panel contained within the lintel of a doorway and the arch above it.

Volute: Spiral scroll on an Ionic capital; smaller volutes on Composite and Corinthian capitals.

Winged altar: Triptych or polyptych with hinged, usually richly carved or painted, wings.

List of places mentioned in the text. Those which have a separate entry are marked △, while those which are mentioned in the environs sections are indicated by the → symbol.